Market vs Medicine:

America's Epic Fight for Better, Affordable Healthcare

DAVID W JOHNSON

ISBN: 1523903678
ISBN 13: 9781523903672

ACCLAIM FOR *MARKET VS. MEDICINE*

"Dave Johnson is a student of American healthcare. He not only has insatiable curiosity, but also has deep and broad connections to those who are actually engaged in transforming healthcare. He brings a practical reality to a discussion that often times can become academic or impractical. He outlines a compelling diagnosis for the problems bedeviling American healthcare and then highlights several high leverage areas that can be transformative to those problems. There are many things that are uncertain regarding the future of American healthcare, his premise that value will drive transformation is not one of those uncertainties."

— John Koster, M.D.
Former CEO, Providence Health & Services

"Dave Johnson has offered incisive commentary on the organization, financing and delivery of healthcare throughout his years as a finance executive and more recently as Author-in-Residence at The Health Management Academy. *Market vs. Medicine* is a must read for those who want to deepen their understanding of the forces driving today's healthcare transformation."

— Gerald E. Bisbee, Jr., Ph.D.
Chairman and CEO, The Academy

"Dave Johnson is among the most thought-provoking writers about healthcare issues in today's evolving reinvention of the industry. His *Market Corner Commentaries* are a must read every time it's published and his *Market vs. Medicine* book will expand your horizons about where the provision of healthcare services is going."

— **Peter Fine**
President and CEO, Banner Health

"For 30 years, Dave Johnson has been a trusted advisor to senior healthcare executives, Boards, and innovators on the challenges and opportunities facing U.S. healthcare providers and payers. I know of very few who can match his industry knowledge and knowhow, but it's the combination of compassion, optimism, good humor and clarity of thinking that makes him truly unique. You'll not only gain valuable insights from Dave's book, you'll also enjoy being in his company while you read it."

— **Robert J. Fraiman**
President and CEO, Cain Brothers

"Dave Johnson is like a master pathologist looking through a microscope. He identifies one of the key drivers of inefficiency in US healthcare— a healthcare system, revolving around hospitals, that has exploited the generosity of public payments to become bloated and inefficient; large hospitals are cost-centers in search of revenue streams. This sophisticated diagnosis motivates a range of solutions that emphasize competition and payment reform to disrupt the status-quo. In the process we may be able to save money and save lives."

— **Amitabh Chandra**
Malcolm Wiener Professor, Harvard University

"A fascinating perspective on the transformation of the American health system now underway from a free-market enthusiast who has seen it all and yet still believes! David Johnson's book will inform, entertain, and educate the health experts, the politicians, and the American public on the best path forward for America's health."

— **Nancy M. Kane, DBA**
Associate Dean, Harvard T. H. Chan School of Public Health

DEDICATION

For Terri

In Memory of Coleman Brown, Barb Bunnell and Jeff Shields

TABLE OF CONTENTS

INTRODUCTION

MARKET VS. MEDICINE: AN EPIC TALE

> *We should resolve now that the health of this Nation is a national concern; that financial barriers in the way of attaining health shall be removed; that the health of all its citizens deserves the help of all the Nation.*
> HARRY S. TRUMAN, 1945 SPECIAL MESSAGE TO CONGRESS

> *America's health care system is neither healthy, caring, nor a system.*
> WALTER CRONKITE

> *There are more than 9,000 billing codes for individual procedures and units of care. But there is not a single billing code for patient adherence or improvement, or for helping patients stay well.*
> CLAYTON M. CHRISTENSEN

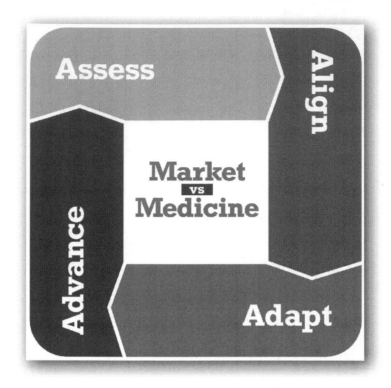

A s I began writing *Market vs. Medicine,* I kept having this recurring dream:

My great friend Tom Weeks commits to box Floyd Mayweather in Madison Square Garden to advance healthcare reform. Tom is in his mid-50s and just had hip replacement surgery. Even though he loves paddleball and golf, no one would mistake Tom for an athlete. By contrast, undefeated Mayweather holds 10 world titles in four different weight classes. He is the world's highest-paid athlete (his nickname is "Money") and many consider him history's best boxer.

Weeks has no business fighting Mayweather. He doesn't even know how to box. What does any of this have to do with health reform? The entire concept is ridiculous, so why did I keep having this dream? What was my brain trying to tell me? The dream with Boxer Tom continues.

Boxer Tom's title fight is the brainchild of boxing commissioner, Charles "Big Charlie" McSherry. Worried about boxing's declining popularity and long-term sustainability, Big Charlie dubs Boxer Tom "The People's Champion" and gives him a shot at the champ. Despite his gargantuan size, Big Charlie is meek and unassuming. Many believe he is a pushover. He plods from meal to meal promoting the match. Trying to increase attendance and viewership, Big Charlie introduces a new ticket-exchange program. It initially stumbles but is working better now. Big Charlie is center stage, but his audience isn't happy.

Fighting Mayweather becomes a quest for Boxer Tom. He adopts the theme of "Better Healthcare at Lower Prices for Everyone." He nicknames his right fist "QUALITY" and his left fist "SERVICE." This gets Boxer Tom some media attention but little sponsorship. By contrast, Mayweather's weighty sponsors include Big Medicine, Big Insurance and Big Pharma. They roll out a glitzy, high-tech multimedia campaign highlighting the champ's speed, strength and invincibility. Behind the scenes, Money keeps bragging about earning nine figures for 36 minutes of work. The sponsors are trying to get Mayweather to take the fight seriously and control his more outlandish behavior.

About six weeks before the fight, a mysterious grizzled trainer named Dutch Smith finds Boxer Tom. They become inseparable. Dutch understands Boxer Tom's quest, offers encouragement and oversees a rigorous training program. For fun, Boxer Tom calls Dutch "Adam," his actual first name. Dutch hates this. Together Boxer Tom and Dutch devise an audacious plan to defeat Mayweather.

I've concluded the Weeks-Mayweather dream was my subconscious pushing me to dig deeper into the market-based conflicts at the core of healthcare reform. The result is this book, *Market vs. Medicine: America's Epic Battle for Better, Affordable Healthcare.* It narrates how market-driven reform, much more than regulatory change (think Obamacare), will transform and improve America's broken healthcare system. At one level, it's surprising that an English literature major turned Peace Corps volunteer turned public policy professional turned investment banker is chronicling the market's attack on U.S. healthcare's inefficiency. On another level, it may require literary sensibility, cultural sensitivity, public policy acumen and economic expertise to unravel healthcare's complexity and articulate the market's superior ability to deliver better, more affordable and more convenient healthcare services.

Tom Weeks and I met in 1981 during math review. We were incoming members of Harvard University's Master in Public Policy class. Like me, Weeks had just returned from serving two years in the Peace Corps. Weeks' Peace Corps service was in Micronesia and mine was in Liberia, West Africa. I taught language arts and math at an understaffed regional high school. With more than 100 students per class, I was woefully unprepared and made numerous mistakes. On the positive side, I coached the school soccer team to their first county championship. The town held a victory parade and carried me through the streets.

Boxer Tom is a composite character incorporating Weeks' savvy political instincts; Dr. Deb Oyer's (Weeks' wife) unbending determination to practice preventive care; John Weeks' (Tom's brother) 30-year odyssey to make integrative medicine mainstream and my own hard-earned knowledge of market dynamics.

My dream continues. Fight day arrives. The bell rings. Boxer Tom approaches Mayweather, his fists raised in defiant determination. There's little he can do to avoid Mayweather's onslaught. Somehow Boxer Tom survives the first round and collapses in his corner. Dutch wipes Boxer Tom's brow with a cold compress, whispers encouragement and urges him to keep delivering value.

Nothing came easily for me in Liberia. The culture was alien and my instincts were often wrong. Peace Corps really is "the toughest job you'll ever love," but I enjoyed the people and embraced the opportunity. It became my morning habit to detail the day's goals and tactics, adjusting for what had and hadn't worked. My teaching improved. I learned that small changes have big impact and poor execution destroys good programs. My life settled into a productive routine and then revolution struck. In April 1980, Master Sergeant Samuel Doe assassinated Liberia's President William R. Tolbert. Overnight, Liberia shifted from civilian to military government. Still teaching, I witnessed civil strife that would lead to devastating civil war.

After Peace Corps, I enrolled at Harvard intent on pursing a career in international development. Investment banking, my future career, was nonexistent in my mind. I didn't even understand discounted cash-flow analytics, the core principle underlying debt structuring and capital formation. On the plus side, my future wife, Terri, was a classmate. She also earned a degree from Columbia Law School and now is a senior leadership coach at the University of Chicago's Booth School of Business.

Back to the fight. It's Round 2. Mayweather attacks Boxer Tom with force and precision. The crowd leans in, sensing blood. They feel Mayweather's frustration as Boxer Tom avoids multiple knockout punches. By Round 5, Boxer Tom feels refreshed and has Mayweather's full attention.

While Weeks pursued his PhD in Public Policy, Oyer enrolled at Harvard Medical School. They earned their respective degrees and returned home to Seattle. Weeks chose public service. He became the youngest candidate to win a Seattle City Council seat and led a campaign to create Seattle Commons (think Central Park on the waterfront) that local business owners opposed. Despite widespread support, the initiative lost narrowly. A focused few defeated the well-intentioned many. After two terms, Weeks surprised the political establishment by resigning his City Council seat to tackle education reform at the Seattle Public Schools. No small challenges for him. Later, he led the effort to revolutionize Seattle's ineffective mass transit system through monorails. Seattle voters approved the Seattle Monorail Project four times before entrenched interests derailed the project.

Oyer practiced family medicine and eventually opened her own practice. Over time, she increased preventive care, which reduced the number of procedures her clients required. Great healthcare. Wonderful for patients. Bad for business. American healthcare pays for activity, not outcomes, and nothing pays better than surgery. While performing surgeries, the system compensated Oyer well. Once she shifted her practice toward preventive care, her practice revenues decreased in lockstep with declining surgeries.

In the mid-1980s, John Weeks pioneered the integration of Eastern medical practices into Western medicine. His energy, enthusiasm and unquenchable commitment have won him a nationwide following. John Weeks received a living testimonial in 2014 for his three decades as an "integrative health connector, crusader and chronicler."

Boxer Tom battles Mayweather into the late rounds. With each bell, Boxer Tom's energy, agility and ingenuity increase. Momentum shifts. There's worry in the champ's corner. The crowd is chanting for Boxer Tom and better healthcare. His quality-and-service punch combinations stun Mayweather. Desperate to maintain dominance, Mayweather's team scrambles for new strategies. Dutch likes what he sees. He keeps yelling, "Lead with QUALITY! Win with SERVICE!" This match is going the distance.

The Good Fight

In my dream, Boxer Tom personifies a people's champion with the skills, knowledge and courage necessary to defeat institutionalized medicine at its own game. Of course, the fragmented U.S. healthcare system isn't a dream and improving it isn't a game. The United State's long-term quality of life, standard of living and social mobility depend on converting America's "sickcare" system into a true healthcare system.

Boxer Tom's everyman role fighting Floyd Mayweather (a.k.a. the medical- industrial complex) reflects my deep-seated belief that America can only fix its broken healthcare system by forcing incumbents to meet consumer demands for better, more convenient and more affordable healthcare services. Every hero needs a Yoda-like mentor, so Adam "Dutch" Smith embodies the disruptive strategies coalescing to overcome medicine's entrenched interests. If his initials (CMS) don't give him away, Big Charlie represents government—well-intentioned but subject to manipulation and too often adding unnecessary cost and complexity. Together Boxer Tom and Dutch stun Mayweather/Big Healthcare with relentless, bottom-up transformational tactics. Each fight round generates more intensity as resourceful companies deliver increased value to customers. Each time the bell rings, it signals advancing consumerism.

My Healthcare Journey

Like my dream's metaphorical boxer, I've gone several rounds against entrenched beliefs during my long investment-banking career. My post-Harvard career began in finance, transportation and economic development as a U.S. Presidential Management Intern for the Port Authority of New York and New Jersey. After serving as the first CFO for the Port Authority's nascent Hudson River ferry program, I shifted into healthcare investment banking in 1986, rotated into a healthcare coverage group and stayed in healthcare investment banking until 2014. No one would be more surprised by my career path than my 25-year-old self.

While I love finance and working with health systems, investment banking was not an ideal match for my professional orientation and temperament. The best investment bankers are skilled strategic advisors with long-term perspectives who place their clients' interests first. Relationships trump transactions. These types of investment bankers are increasingly rare. In today's super-sized banks, transactions and short-term profits trump relationships. It's impossible to overstate the narrowness of investment banks' focus on transactions and revenues. Uber-banker Gordon Gekko caught the sentiment in the movie *Wall Street*, remarking to his protégé, "If you want a friend, get a dog."

Ultimately, Wall Street and I accommodated each other. As long as I generated adequate revenue, my managers let me practice in accordance with my values and pursue broader interests. These interests included healthcare policy, economics, behavioral science, board governance, writing and teaching. In 2002, I left Merrill Lynch with several colleagues to join Citigroup. I could have stayed and run Merrill's healthcare practice, but Citigroup's business model emphasizing cross-fertilization and specialized expertise appealed to me. I believed our combined teams could build an unparalleled investment banking practice encompassing capital formation, strategic advice and risk stratification. This vision became reality. Citigroup became Wall Street's dominant health system practice with 25 percent market share. Competitors called us "the Yankees."

Orchestrating capital formation programs for large American health systems gave me a front-row view into healthcare's inner-workings. The industry operates within an artificial economic model that rewards activity (not outcomes), obscures prices, regulates through process compliance and invites manipulation. Healthcare's economic model is artificial because the supply of healthcare services drives their demand independent of service levels and prices. In normal markets, demand for services at specific prices drives their supply.

Bigger hasn't always meant better. During my career, healthcare has doubled its share of the U.S. economy without delivering a commensurate increase in value. Through growth and consolidation, strong incumbents dominate the healthcare industry. They're fighting with everything they've got to maintain the status quo.

> *In my dream, the fight continues round after round, bell after bell. Boxer Tom is relentless. Dutch is insatiable. The champ knows he's in the fight of his life. He battles on. Big Charlie is conflicted. He senses Boxer Tom's potential but is wary of alienating Mayweather's sponsors. It's all so exhausting. The crowd loves the action. Many now wear neck chains with QUALITY-and-SERVICE boxing gloves. Their engagement makes Boxer Tom push even harder to win for them. It is clear that Boxer Tom's fight is America's fight.*

Speak Now

Throughout my investment-banking career, I've worked closely with large health systems and managed over $30 billion in healthcare financings. In this sense, I have participated in the overbuilding of America's acute-care delivery system. At the same time, helping large health systems raise capital sparked my keen interest in market-driven healthcare reform. I've observed how markets respond to targeted capital investments. As a cancer survivor and too-frequent visitor to operating rooms, I also am able to evaluate how American healthcare delivers for its patients/customers. Too often, U.S. healthcare fails to put patients' needs first.

While working for BMO Capital Markets from 2010 to 2014, I wrote a widely read series on market-based healthcare reform. My writing highlighted the system's current flaws and spotlighted innovative companies providing better, more convenient healthcare services at lower prices. Writing *Market vs. Medicine* provides the opportunity

U.S. healthcare has the ability to leapfrog these centralized health systems through innovation, value creation and customer-focused service delivery. As companies deliver higher value, American healthcare will become both better and more affordable.

I'm indebted to Eric Beinhocker's *The Origins of Wealth*, which applies evolutionary science and complexity theory to market behavior. In the same way nature employs natural selection to determine a species' biological "fitness", markets use consumer selection to delineate economic winners and losers. Results are nonlinear. Small differences can stimulate competitive leaps. Luck plays a role. Today's winners are often tomorrow's losers.

I am also indebted to Robert Wright's *Non-Zero*, which chronicles human progress as a series of increasingly complex win-win arrangements. The integration of competitive and cooperative forces defines success and failure in all human endeavors. Healthcare is no exception.

The Good News

The public's patience with healthcare institutions is wavering. Consumers want doctors, nurses and hospitals that treat illness and injury efficiently and practice with compassion. Dr. Clive Fields—a second-generation primary-care physician and CEO of Village Family Practice (VFP) in Houston—offers this reality check: "Hospitals are buildings, walls and floors. Hospitals don't treat people. Doctors do."

Value is driving financial performance in post-reform healthcare. America's unique ability to promote and fund innovation is turbocharging healthcare transformation. Promising companies attract investment capital. As consumers and employers demand greater value, more investment capital is flowing into companies delivering better, more affordable and more convenient healthcare services.

For decades, America has tried unsuccessfully to fix its broken healthcare system through government-led regulatory change. Here's the good news: This time is different. Purchasers, not providers, of healthcare are driving reform. The same American business ethos that has transformed manufacturing, warehousing, communications and technology is taking aim at healthcare.

Authenticity

John Powers was among America's first marketing wizards. Author Jonah Sachs brings Powers to life in his book *Winning the Story Wars.* Powers had the following three commandments for successful marketing campaigns: Be Interesting; Tell the Truth; and Live the Truth. Powers' last commandment is the most difficult. Powers' advice, "If you can't live the truth, change what you're doing so you can." Marketing truth works. Here's a typical John Powers advertisement: "These neckties are not as good as they look, but they're good enough: 25 cents." Customers flocked to Wanamaker's Department Stores in droves and doubled annual sales in a few short years. Customers trusted Wanamaker's (the first store to use price tags) and responded by purchasing goods and services there.

Power's three commandments provide effective criteria for evaluating healthcare companies:

1. Are they interesting—do they have a unique product or service and/or competitive advantage?

2. Do they speak the truth—regarding capabilities, limitations and market potential?

3. Do they live the truth—do their operating profiles align with their marketing rhetoric?

Human beings are hard-wired to identify and punish hypocrisy. Far too many incumbent health companies do not live their truths. They proclaim to put patients first, but their services are inconsistent, inconvenient, uncompassionate, disconnected and overpriced. Recent polling indicates that consumers dislike the healthcare industry more than the banking industry (that's saying something) but still hold hospitals, doctors and nurses in high regard. While the good karma lasts, health companies have the opportunity to "live their truths" by aligning operations with rhetoric. In this era of market-based reform, health companies that speak and live the truth will earn customers' confidence and win market share. Health companies that say one thing and do another will disappear.

Healthcare reform is an epic tale with legacies, upstarts, plot twists, compelling characters and fierce rivalries. Combatants elbow one another to win customers. In epic tales, good ultimately triumphs over evil. Cinderella gets her slipper. Society uses epic stories to instill morals and guide behavior. In the same way, healthcare's epic battle is refocusing a fragmented industry on delivering better healthcare at lower prices for everyone. Like all epic tales, *Market vs. Medicine* has a moral. It is "Value Rules."

SECTION I: Assess

TRENDS THAT CANNOT CONTINUE WON'T

If something cannot go on forever, it will stop.
HERBERT STEIN

- Chapter 1: Motherhood, Apple Pie and Perverse Incentives

- Chapter 2: Overbuild It and They Still Come

- Chapter 3: Healthcare's Productivity Paradox

- Chapter 4: It's A Drag

Economist Herbert Stein's 1980s maxim captures the economic truth embedded in current U.S. health spending: American healthcare misallocates resources, fails to address core issues and is economically unsustainable. To illustrate these inherent flaws, I ask audiences the following three questions about American healthcare:

1. Healthcare expenditure accounted for 17.9 percent of the U.S. economy in 2011. Do we need to spend more than 18 percent of our economy to provide adequate or even superior healthcare services to everyone in the country?

2. Chronic disease accounts for 80 percent of U.S. healthcare spending. Are we winning the battle against chronic disease?

3. On a relative basis, should we shift resources away from acute and specialty care and into primary care, chronic disease management, behavioral health and health promotion?

Not one person has ever said America should spend more than 18 percent of U.S. GNP on healthcare; yet, the Centers for Medicare and Medicaid Services (CMS) projects that healthcare spending will consume 19.3 percent of GNP by 2023.[1] The U.S. spends significantly more on healthcare per capita than other advanced economies—a whopping six percentage points more than the next highest spender (the Netherlands).[2] In 2015, the U.S. GNP was roughly $18 trillion. Relative to the Netherlands, this translates into an additional $1 trillion in U.S. health expenditure. This is more than the U.S. government spent in 2015 for defense ($736 billion)[3] and Social Security ($888 billion).[4]

Despite spending significantly more per capita on healthcare, America has inferior health status relative to the Netherlands and

1 http://www.cms.gov/Research-Statistics-Data-and-Systems/Statistics-Trends-and-Reports/NationalHealthExpendData/index.html

2 http://www.theatlantic.com/business/archive/2014/07/why-do-other-rich-nations-spend-so-much-less-on-healthcare/374576/

3 http://useconomy.about.com/od/usfederalbudget/p/military_budget.htm

4 http://www.usgovernmentspending.com/social_security_spending_by_year

other advanced economies. A devastating 2013 Institute of Medicine (IOM) report, *U.S. Health in International Perspective: Shorter Lives, Poorer Health,* finds the U.S. lags behind 16 peer countries in life expectancy, infant mortality, obesity, sexually transmitted diseases, homicides and drug-related deaths. Even worse, America's health-status gap is widening. The report identifies these four principal causes: an inaccessible and unaffordable health system; unhealthy behaviors; social and economic inequality and automobile-centric physical environments.[5]

America spends enough money on healthcare. The nation's healthcare challenges relate to distribution, not funding. More of the same is neither acceptable nor financially sustainable. It is impossible to solve problems without first defining them. It is essential to understand how U.S. healthcare has arrived at this dangerous juncture.

Section I, *Assess,* explores how the U.S. healthcare system became so expensive, fragmented and acute-care centric:

- Chapter 1, ***Motherhood, Apple Pie and Perverse Incentives,*** explores American exceptionalism in healthcare: how America's unique values, history and experience are interwoven into healthcare's supply-driven economic model to create a healthcare delivery system with mediocre outcomes, crippling expenditures and poor customer service.

- Chapter 2, ***Overbuild It and They Still Come,*** examines the causes and consequences of America's massive over-investment in acute care facilities and practitioners.

- Chapter 3, ***Healthcare's Productivity Paradox,*** digs into the lethal consequences of private market exploitation of healthcare's centralized payment policies.

- Chapter 4, ***It's A Drag,*** explains the macroeconomic consequences of America's spending too much on healthcare while receiving too little value in return.

---

5 http://www.iom.edu/~/media/Files/Report%20Files/2013/US-Health-International-Perspective/USHealth_Intl_PerspectiveRB.pdf

Gloria Steinem observed, "The truth will set you free, but first it will piss you off." The economics of U.S. healthcare infuriate those who understand the system's perverse incentives and the damage they cause. Holding onto that anger is a prerequisite for tackling the enormous challenges embedded in transforming U.S. healthcare.

CHAPTER 1

MOTHERHOOD, APPLE PIE AND PERVERSE INCENTIVES

If change is to be for the better, it should be based on an understanding of why things are the way they are.[6]
VICTOR FUCHS

Hypocrisy is the tribute that vice pays to virtue.[7]
FRANÇOIS DE LA ROUCHEFOUCAULD

---

6 V. R. Fuchs, *Who Shall Live?* (2002)
7 F. de La Rouchefoucauld, *Reflections or Sentences and Moral Maxims* (1665)

I n 1990, a New Jersey policy organization asked me to address them on the unique character of American healthcare. Great Britain, Canada, Germany, Japan and all other advanced economies provide and pay for healthcare services for all citizens through national systems. By contrast, U.S. healthcare is fundamentally different. It blends private and public funding for healthcare services in multiple delivery models. It spends more per capita but and doesn't provide universal coverage. It relies on philanthropy and promotes free-market participation. The N.J. group wanted to know why American healthcare is the way it is.

I accepted their speaking invitation without having any idea what I was going to say. I'd never thought about the topic. I hadn't been in healthcare long, was eager for the exposure and had a couple of months to figure it out. Plenty of time or so I thought. A month before the speech, I had nothing. A week before the speech, I still had nothing and was nervous. Clearing away cobwebs, I reread college notes on American intellectual history and American religion. An answer to their question emerged.

American Exceptionalism

I attended Colgate University in the late 1970s. At the time, Colgate required all first-year students to study philosophy and religion. That experience changed my academic orientation. In addition to history and English literature, I studied philosophy and religion. During my junior year, Professor Coleman Brown taught a mind-expanding course titled "Religion in America." Historians credit John Locke's *Second Treatise of Government* (1689) and Jean-Jacques Rousseau's *Du contrat social* (1762) for shaping the Founding Father's vision for the U.S. Constitution, but Protestant theology also played a dominant role. Brown had numerous examples. The separation of powers doctrine emanates from an innate distrust of human motivation. Better not to give too much power to individuals and/or institutions because of the human tendency to abuse power. The U.S. Senate's insistence on "unfettered dialogue" arises from the belief that no individual or group can fully comprehend God's intent. Insistence on individual rights and religious pluralism stem from the Protestant belief that no institution should stand between a person and his or her God.

Professor Brown's course also explored "American exceptionalism"—the collection of beliefs and attitudes that define America's national character. Puritan John Winthrop's famous "City Upon a Hill" sermon from 1630 captures this belief in the unique American "experiment":

> *For we must consider that we shall be as a city upon a hill. The eyes of all people are upon us.*

American exceptionalism encompasses reverence for the individual, suspicion of authority and belief in national destiny.

It is impossible to understand and appreciate U.S. healthcare without understanding how deeply American exceptionalism is woven into U.S. identity and culture. This became the theme of my 1990 presentation and inspired the first iteration of the "values chart." This chart (below) has become my vehicle for illustrating how U.S. healthcare incorporates and reflects American values and experience. It explains why U.S. healthcare is and always will be unique.

AMERICAN EXCEPTIONALISM SHAPES U.S. HEALTHCARE

Individualism • Desire to be the Best • Strong Charitable Tradition • Trust in Competitive Markets • Faith in Technology • Distrust of Big Government • Pragmatic and Innovative • Aversion to Central Planning • Belief in Miracles • Good in a Crisis • Instant Gratification • Community Orientation

- The best health care money can buy
- Remarkable technological innovation
- Very responsive to incentives
- Sizable for-profit component
- Consumer-orientated
- Unmatched philanthropic support
- Strong volunteer support

- Consumes 18% of GDP
- Uneven distribution of facilities and practitioners
- Individual benefit trumps "group good"
- Assigns blame for personal failure
- Significant/service variation
- Over/Under treatment plans

U.S. healthcare reflects the American people's collective values and experience. To an extent, this is a truism. Any enterprise so expansive that it consumes 18 percent of GNP, employs millions and touches all citizens will reflect national identity and values. At the same time, the system's size and complexity combined with its structural anomalies (the independence of physicians, the predominance of nonprofit hospitals, a third-party payment system) make broad generalizations about U.S. healthcare impossible. We have to dig deeper. It is American values and exceptionalism that shape modern U.S. healthcare. It is ironic that these core American values create U.S. healthcare's contradictory and often perverse characteristics.

The relationships between these values are complex, interrelated and deeply held. They shape our national character, identity and politics. They also complicate attempts to reform healthcare payment and service delivery. For example, Americans support their local hospitals through philanthropy and volunteerism. Americans also expect hospitals to maintain financial viability and raise capital in the private capital markets. Mission collides with profits. Hospitals struggle to navigate between the competing currents. Exploring core American values illuminates the contours of the healthcare policy debate.

Values, Irony, Fragmentation and U.S. Healthcare
I first met Nancy Kane in the late 1980s, when she was a very popular but under-appreciated professor at the Harvard School of Public Health. Today she is a highly-respected and still popular Associate Dean for Case-Based Teaching and Learning and Professor of Management. I had an idea for a hospital-turnaround case study that I shopped to my former professors at the Harvard Kennedy School of Government. At that time, the Kennedy School had no healthcare faculty (hard to believe) and they directed me to Kane. We wrote the case study together and became friends and collaborators. Over the years, we've engaged in a vigorous and ongoing debate regarding healthcare reform. Kane and I agree on the system's structural deficiencies but disagree on policy remedies. She thinks I place too much trust in market-based solutions. I know she places too much faith in governmental regulation.

Kane has always liked the values chart. In 2009, she asked me to co-write a paper with her on American values for a Harvard Law School symposium on fragmentation in U.S. healthcare. Oxford Press subsequently published our paper as part of the symposium's anthology. After much deliberation, we decided to illustrate values and irony within American healthcare by exploring how conflicting values contribute to the system's fragmentation in numerous areas, including the following four:

1. Individual vs. collective responsibility for health;
2. Health crisis management vs. managing health;
3. Faith in markets vs. distrust of government; and
4. Winning vs. collaboration.

Much of the following discussion comes from our joint effort in writing *The U.S. Healthcare System: A Product of American History and Values.*[8]

Individual vs. Collective Responsibility for Health

American self-reliance has generated great wealth and created "individualistic" cultural icons from Horatio Alger to Wyatt Earp to Rambo. Americans are more comfortable discussing how to expand the economic pie than how to distribute it more equitably. A by-product of rampant individualism in the new millennium is greater disparities in income and health status. A recent study indicates that life expectancy is decreasing for low-income and less-educated Americans.[9] This disparity in health status is not seen in advanced economies with universal health coverage and a great sense of collective identity.

Americans view health as an individual rather than a collective responsibility. They generally believe obese people are a product of overeating and under-exercising. Being overweight is their fault and their responsibility to address. Ubiquitous marketing by the diet

---

8 Johnson and Kane.
9 K. Sack, *The Short End of the Longer Life*, N.Y. Times, April 27, 2008, at 4.

industry encourages the overweight to "invest" (and they spend billions) in diets and exercise programs. The truth, of course, is more nuanced. Genetics, community norms and deeply seated habitual behaviors compromise the ability of many, perhaps most, individuals to make better lifestyle choices.

Meanwhile our laws and social norms allow the food industry to inundate Americans with persuasive advertising for unhealthy foods. Food advertising to children is particularly alarming. Saturday morning children's television shows broadcast 40,000 ads each year for sugary cereals, soft drinks and candy. These ads target children at ages too young to know the difference between advertising and education.[10] Opponents to public health laws that would curtail such advertising object to "paternalistic interventions into lifestyle choices," which "enfeeble the notion of personal responsibility" and constrain free speech.[11] Instead, they urge public health policymakers to exercise their right of free speech by giving consumers the information they need (e.g. through counter-advertising and food labeling) to make better food purchasing decisions. As one observer concludes, "The law is slow to realize that choices in the market may not be totally free."[12]

The undertone of individual responsibility colors political debate over universal health insurance. Health insurance is a voluntary benefit that tens of millions of Americans choose not to purchase. Policymakers advocate using economic incentives, such as tax credits and high-deductible health plans funded by tax-favored savings accounts, to convince individuals to buy health insurance. This is the new norm in America. The financial success of the Affordable Care Act (a.k.a. Obamacare) requires abundant younger, healthier enrollees to offset costs for treating older, less healthy participants. In reality, however, it is difficult to convince young "invincibles" to spend money on something they feel they don't need.

Insurance works effectively when the healthy pay for the sick, not when sick individuals have to fend for themselves. Health insurance

---

10   M.M. Mello et al., *Obesity—The New Frontier of Public Health Law*, 354 New England Journal of Medicine, 2601–10 (2006).

11   *Id.* at 2610.

12   *Id.* at 2602.

works best as a mandated, collective good. Obamacare bridges the individual-collective gap through individual mandates, Medicaid expansion, elimination of coverage denials for pre-existing conditions and generous subsidies. Obamacare is a policy solution that acknowledges and incorporates American reverence for individualism and market-based solutions.

It is Americans' deeply held commitment to individualism that enables American society to tolerate national coverage gaps and disconnections across the healthcare continuum. Americans prioritize healthcare on an individual basis rather than on a population level. The U.S. healthcare delivery system has evolved to respond to individual treatment needs rather than advance broader community wellness. The challenge for American healthcare is reforming the system in ways that respect individual preference while improving overall health status.

Health Crisis Management vs. Managing Health

Americans respond generously in a crisis but become miserly when paying for routine care or chronic disease management. High-profile children's hospitals fly conjoined twins from Bangladesh to the United States for advanced separation surgery, but the U.S. system underfunds basic prenatal care. Elderly citizens living with several chronic conditions see multiple specialists who rarely, if ever, communicate with one another. This requires patients to integrate their own care and evaluate conflicting advice. U.S. healthcare ignores the wishes of dying patients regarding end-of-life treatment. Too many elderly die in hospital intensive care units (ICUs) surrounded by high-tech equipment rather than comfortably at home surrounded by family.

To better understand why American healthcare favors the acute, dramatic and highly technical care over preventive, primary, chronic and even palliative care, it is instructive to review the origins of the Blue Cross and Blue Shield plans. Blues plans played a dominant role in the structure and design of today's healthcare financing system. As Sylvia Law pointed out in her 1974 book, *Blue Cross—What Went Wrong*, "Blue Cross is most accurately characterized today as the financing arm of American hospitals."[13] As the "child of the Depression and the American Hospital Association,"[14] Blues plans came into existence to give hospitals financial stability as the Depression reduced both patients' out-of-pocket payments and philanthropic contributions from benefactors. Born in crisis, Blues plans committed American healthcare's original sin, creating a payment system that incentivizes treatment activity rather than health outcomes.

Throughout the 1930s, medical breakthroughs reduced mortality and extended life. American communities wanted modern hospitals. Hospitals transformed from almshouses caring for the poor to high-tech treatment centers requiring substantial new capital investment. Twenty-seven of the 39 new Blues plans received all or part of their initial financing from hospitals. For decades, hospital representatives dominated Blues boards; by 1970, 42 percent of the members of local plan boards were hospital representatives and 14 percent were doctors.

Blues plans collected subscriber premiums and guaranteed payment to hospitals for the full cost of services provided to these subscribers. Full-cost reimbursement from insured patients enabled hospitals to grow and adopt new technologies at explosive rates. These spending habits continue today, despite shifts to more independent Blues plans and more restrictive prospective payment systems.

From their inception through the 1970s, Blue Cross plans' responsibility to offer subscribers affordable healthcare benefits was subservient to, and at times undermined by, their determination to keep American hospitals financially healthy and technologically advanced. Consequentially, hospitals emphasized (and billed for) their highest-cost activities—acute care services rather than low-cost preventive treatments. Given this generous payment system, healthcare costs skyrocketed. Frustration with the high-cost system mounted. In response to a 33 percent rate hike by Blue Cross in 1964, a New York judge criticized the superintendent of insurance for failing to exercise adequate control over rate increase requests, commenting:

13 SA. Law, Blue Cross: *What Went Wrong?* 2 (1974)
14 *Id.* at 6.

> *Both Blue Cross and the Superintendent seem intent on adopting the notion that no matter how costly operations become, for whatever reasons, eventually and inevitably, Blue Cross subscribers will shoulder the load. Small wonder that subscriber rates have increased 124% in the past five years.*[15]

During the debate to establish Medicare in the early 1960s, the American Hospital Association dropped its early opposition to a federal hospital insurance program on the condition that only Blue Cross plans could administer it. Simultaneously, Blue Cross and the American Hospital Association were instrumental in designing the Medicare payment system, particularly the concept of paying hospitals for their reasonable costs. This "fee-for-service" payment model has driven technology-heavy hospital expansion for decades. Concentrating power for resource allocation in the hands of the providers and their captive insurers created a hospital-dominated healthcare system that stresses and delivers high-cost acute treatments irrespective of broader community health needs.

Physicians took much longer than hospitals to accept health insurance coverage for their services. Reflecting the sentiment of his colleagues, the editor of the *Journal of the American Medical Association (JAMA)* demonized health insurance in a 1933 editorial, saying it encouraged such "evil practices" as "solicitation of patients, destructive competition among professional groups, inferior medical service, loss of the personal relationship of patient and physician, and demoralization of the professions."[16]

Patient demand for physician services rose as more of those services occurred in hospitals, where Blue Cross plans covered patients' hospital costs but did not pay for physician services. Finding private insurance coverage for physician services became a priority. Repeated state and federal proposals for compulsory health insurance in the 1930s finally led the American Medical Association (AMA) to encourage state medical societies to sponsor medical plans, particularly for payment

15 *Id.* at 15.
16 R. Cunningham & R.M. Cunningham, *The Blues: A History of the Blue Cross and Blue Shield System* 38 (1997).

of professional bills incurred during a prolonged or emergency illness. Thus, in 1939, the first prepayment plan for medical services, the California Physician's Service (now Blue Shield of California), came into existence. Its primary purpose was to stave off compulsory public insurance, rather than to enhance the health of the populations served. Primary and preventive care were not featured in early plans; the concept of preventive care did not take root in American health insurance coverage until the spread of health *maintenance* organizations in the 1980s.

Emphasizing crisis care over care management is a perpetual, negative feature of U.S. healthcare delivery. Inadequate primary-care access creates more crisis care when people go to emergency rooms for routine (and very expensive) treatments. Meanwhile, the supply of primary care physicians continues to dwindle, despite growing demand for their services.

It is ironic that the Depression-era need to guarantee physician payment has ballooned into today's expensive, activity-based delivery system that neglects basic health needs. As a consequence, powerful provider and insurance organizations have strong financial incentives to maintain the current crisis-oriented delivery system.

Faith in Markets vs. Distrust of Government

Americans have had a tortured relationship with their government since the country's origin. Thomas Paine, the author of the influential 1776 pamphlet "Common Sense," captures this ambivalence in the following two quotations: "Government even in its best state is but a necessary evil; in its worst state, an intolerable one," and "The government is best which governs least."

The colonists' struggle to overthrow British rule bred a natural distrust of authority that found sustenance in a vast land populated by rugged individualists. American citizens have never easily accepted the benefits of centralization. Thomas Jefferson decommissioned the national army and navy. Andrew Jackson dismantled the national bank. The South seceded from the United States in 1861 based on its belief in the supremacy of states' rights. The existence of term limits and recall petitions reveal that distrust of government continues unabated. Echoes of this sentiment carried into President Bill Clinton's 1996 State of the Union Address when he declared the end of the era of big government.

The same cannot be said of markets and business. Though unusually taciturn for a politician, President Calvin Coolidge made himself clear on the importance of business in 1925 when he proclaimed, "The chief business of the American people is business."[17]

And why not? Markets have proven effective at allocating resources, generating wealth, funding innovation, improving life quality and separating winners from losers. Markets seem robust while government appears ineffective. Business leaders seem decisive while government leaders appear out-of-touch, incompetent or corrupt. The country hailed the arrival of Ford CEO Robert McNamara and his whiz kids in 1961 when they brought professional management science to the Department of Defense. In 1982, President Ronald Reagan created the private sector Grace Commission to eliminate waste in the Federal Government. He instructed them to do the following:

> *Be bold. We want your team to work like tireless bloodhounds. Don't leave any stone unturned in your search to root out inefficiency.*[18]

Leave it to muck-raking journalist H.L. Mencken to describe the relationship between business and government in words with which most Americans would agree:

> *Capitalism undoubtedly has certain boils and blotches upon it, but has it as many as government? Has it as many as religion? Has it as many as marriage? I doubt it. It is the only basic institution of modern man that shows any genuine health and vigor.*[19]

---

17 https://coolidgefoundation.org/resources/essays-papers-addresses-35/

18 Remarks at a White House luncheon on March 10, 1982, with Chairman and Executive Committee of the Private Sector Survey on Cost Control *available at* http://en. wikipedia.org/ wiki/The_Grace_Commission#References (last visited May 23, 2008).

19 H.L. Mencken, from *The Library*, The American Mercury, September 28, 1924.

This dynamic between business and government also leads American policymakers to incorporate and protect the private sector's role in government-financed healthcare services. Proposals to create Medicare and Medicaid in the early 1960s appeared defeated until House Ways and Means Chairman Wilbur Mills embedded Blue Cross' cost-plus reimbursement approach into the hospital payment formula and awarded the administrative contract to the Blues plan. Legislators also wrote into the legislation a promise that Medicare would never interfere with the private practice of medicine.[20] More recent examples of the U.S. government incentivizing private sector involvement in healthcare delivery include Medicare's preferential payment structure for beneficiaries who enroll in privately-run managed care plans (e.g., through Medicare Advantage plans) and Medicare Part D, a program in which beneficiaries purchase private insurance coverage to help pay for prescription medications.

Given Americans preference for private-market policy solutions, it is not surprising the President Barack Obama incorporated significant market-oriented features into 2010's Affordable Care Act. These include the creation of public health insurance exchanges, mandates for purchasing health insurance and risk corridors (i.e. maximum profit and loss levels) for private health insurance plans.

American's reverence for private markets has had a defining role in shaping our complicated and fragmented model for providing healthcare services. Healthcare economics, however, often defy conventional economic wisdom. Other industries invest in technology to increase efficiency and reduce cost. Investment in medical technology typically increases costs. It enables providers to justify higher reimbursement payments. In normal markets, demand for products and services drives supply. In healthcare, the supply of facilities and practitioners drives demand for their services. More cardiac surgeons generate more cardiac procedures, irrespective of patient need. This latter phenomenon is termed "Roemer's Law" in reference to the work of Milton Roemer, a former professor at the UCLA School of Public

---

20   E. Patashnik & J. Zelizer, *Paying for Medicare: Benefits, Budgets, and Wilbur Mill's Policy Legacy*, 26 (1) Journal of Health Politics, Policy and Law 7–36 (2001).

Health. He concluded in the early 1960s that, "supply may induce its own demand in the presence of third-party payment."[21]

Third-party payment for services operates throughout American healthcare, undermining effective market functions. It causes economic dislocation in the following ways:

- It compensates "reimbursable care" whether or not it is appropriate;

- It discourages "appropriate care" when it is not reimbursable;

- It complicates the determination of what constitutes proper care, which in turn increases administrative costs; and

- It separates the recipient of healthcare services from the payment for those services.

This blending of public and private activity without the constraints present in efficient markets has created a high-cost system with significant coverage gaps. Hospitals and payers maximize revenues within a closed-payment system. Each sector is consolidating to improve its negotiating leverage. The result is that higher payments go to hospitals with the most negotiating leverage, not those that deliver the highest healthcare value. Payers use their leverage and enrollment systems to maximize revenue, shift coverage risk to others and/or minimize payment for care services (the medical loss ratio). This pattern of payment and service provision generates confusion and uncertainty for patients within the system. The lack of pricing transparency and the limited availability of outcomes data frustrate the ability of consumers to make informed decisions regarding healthcare purchases.

Americans believe in markets and their ability to operate within them to purchase goods and services at fair prices. With few exceptions, however, Americans are unable to make market-based decisions regarding healthcare services. Given their historic distrust

---

21   M.I. Roemer, *Bed Supply and Hospital Utilization: A Natural Experiment*, Hospitals, November 1, 1961, 36–42.

of government, reform without private sector involvement will be difficult for Americans to accept. Reform that relies on private sector involvement without pricing and outcomes transparency will continue a legacy of high-cost, low-value service provision.

Winning vs. Collaborating

America's obsession with winning is legendary. Vince Lombardi, the iconic Green Bay Packers football coach from the 1960s, famously observed "Winning isn't everything; it's the only thing," and "Show me a good loser and I'll show you a loser."[22] Being "the best" or being "number one" is a constant theme across industry, entertainment, education, and healthcare. Americans rank everything from schools to restaurants to doctors to employers. This focus on winning feeds a national identity.

Competition works. It motivates our corporations, fuels growth and allocates resources efficiently. The American economic model generates unmatched productivity, innovation and wealth creation. It's so effective that it delivers one of the world's highest living standards, despite an inefficient, high-cost healthcare system.

America's healthcare innovations have been impressive. Americans have pioneered the breakthrough science that has revolutionized diagnostics, cured disease and improved life quality. America's absolute and per capita investment in healthcare facilities, research, and treatment dwarfs that of all other nations. While impressive, healthcare innovations have not delivered benefits commensurate with the high levels of national investment. Unlike other industries, competition in healthcare delivery doesn't always create value through more efficient resource allocation. Instead American healthcare is fragmented and characterized by uneven access; overtreatment and undertreatment; inadequate care coordination and uneven information flow.

Ironically, organizations that emphasize collaboration have better outcomes and more efficient care. These include the Veterans Administration; integrated health systems; and medical foundations (e.g., the Mayo Clinic) that employ physicians, share information, and follow protocols. These organizations also are more likely to

22 http://www.vincelombardi.com/quotes.html

practice preventive care (e.g., behavioral health, and chronic disease management).

Americans want their treatment without delay and they want to receive it from the best institutions. Consequently, hospitals go to enormous effort to differentiate their services through advertising and by competing for recognition awards. They display banners highlighting awards for superior care. Here's a partial list of organizations that recognize or rank hospitals:

- *U.S. News & World Report* rankings of the best hospitals by specialty

- Healthgrades

- HealthLeaders Media

- Truven Health Analytics 100 Top Hospitals

- J.D. Power and Associates

- Magnet Designation for Nursing Excellence

- Cleverly and Associates' Community-Value Five-Star Hospitals

- Leapfrog Group

- Baldrige Award

Americans want "the best" healthcare for their families and they rely upon well-developed consumer instincts to evaluate care alternatives. Hospitals employ sophisticated marketing strategies to attract patients. The trouble is that there is too much extraneous information, too many awards and limited reliable data. True measures related to cost and outcomes are difficult to find and interpret. Consequently, consumers cannot make true value judgments for healthcare services. Instead, consumers rely upon anecdotal information including awards, advertisements and personal referrals to make healthcare decisions.

In 2008, the Dartmouth Atlas of Health Care examined spending by Medicare for chronic illnesses in the last two years of life.[23] Over one-third of Americans have chronic illnesses and approximately 70 percent die from them. Most Medicare spending relating to chronic illness in the last two years of life occurs in hospitals. In an interesting research twist, the report focused on the five academic medical centers ranked highest (the winners) by the *U.S. News & World Report* survey. The results presented below are striking for their variation:

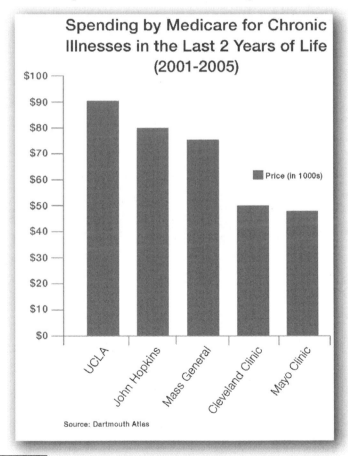

23 Dartmouth Atlas of Healthcare, *Tracking the Care of Patients with Severe Chronic Illness* (2008), ttp://www.dartmouthatlas.org/atlases/2008_Chronic_Care_Atlas.pdf.

Of the five, UCLA had the highest cost at $93,842 per patient and Mayo Clinic had the lowest at $53,432 per patient. Other academic centers, including NYU and Cedars-Sinai, had costs exceeding $105,000 per patient. The cost differential resulted from higher-cost institutions performing more tests and procedures. Defenders of these organizations highlight their aggressiveness in "going the extra mile" for patients and also say that patients at these institutions tend to be sicker than their counterparts at community hospitals. More likely, the higher costs result from uncoordinated care and a system that rewards activity over outcomes. Two quotations from a *New York Times* article describing the study are illuminating. The first comes from Dr. Denis A Cortese, the president of the Mayo Clinic, explaining their less aggressive approach to medical care management:

> *Our physicians are salaried. They have no financial incentive to do more than is necessary for the patient. In each case, multiple doctors and nurses make decisions collaboratively with the patient and family members. We really try to understand the patient's wishes for end-of-life care.*

At the other end of the cost spectrum, the Chief Medical Officer for NYU, Dr. Robert A. Press, acknowledged the findings but noted:

> *It's not an easy fix. We are dealing with a culture of physicians who have been very aggressive in their care and a patient population that has desired this type of care.*[24]

To a remarkable extent, a typical patient's values (wanting the best and wanting it now) coalesce with the values of prestigious delivery centers (wanting to "win" by doing whatever it takes for their patients). Unfortunately, this values alignment leads to high-cost, inefficient care absent a strong organizational culture that enforces care coordination based on shared information.

---

24 R. Pear, *Researchers Find Huge Variation in End-of-Life Treatment,* N.Y. Times, April 7, 2008 at A17.

Since we won't change our national fixation on winning, we need to redefine winning to mean care that produces the best outcomes consistent with patient wishes in the most efficient manner. This will require greater emphasis on care coordination through collaboration and meaningful data sharing. There can still be (and should be) competition, but it must center on delivering true cost and outcome value to patients.

Rampant Irony: "The Enemy is Us"

From the outside, the world admires, emulates and often seeks U.S. healthcare. For complex conditions, American healthcare is the best money can buy. From the inside, where it counts, American healthcare is defective. It is unwieldy, unfair and ineffective against chronic disease. It leaves too many citizens unprotected, unduly rewards vested interests and causes too much physical, emotional and financial harm to patients. Sadly, it is easier to blame some evil other guy (bad government, greedy insurers, arrogant administrators, rich doctors) than acknowledge that

America's fragmented healthcare system reflects strongly ingrained American beliefs, contradictions and mythology.

Nothing captures the irony and contradictions of American healthcare more than Obamacare politics. There's visceral disagreement between Republicans and Democrats regarding the Affordable Care Act (the "ACA" or "Obamacare"). Political positioning, however, has less to do with the Act's actual provisions than with philosophical beliefs about government. Republicans want less. Democrats want more.

Obamacare is a rallying cry for Republicans. They've won governing majorities in Congress by castigating it. Ironically, Obamacare adopted its core features from Republican policy proposals. These include the individual mandate, health insurance exchanges and insurance risk corridors. As former Department of Health and Human Services Secretary Mike Leavitt, who served under President George W. Bush, has noted, eliminating these market-based provisions, by necessity, will force America into a single-payer system. That is the last thing Republicans want; yet, many red states reject Obamacare subsidies that expand access through private-market channels.

By contrast, Democrats have embraced the ACA's market-oriented provisions. Their love has not always been so profound. Many (notably U.S. Rep. Nancy Pelosi) have fought to curtail and/or eliminate Medicare Advantage—a program that incentivizes private companies to manage the health of distinct populations. Long term, Obamacare cannot succeed without better balance between health promotion and treatment. To the extent private companies improve the health of large populations, they reduce the need for governmental assumption of health risk, a prerequisite for single-payer health systems. A single-payer Medicare-for-all health system is what most Democrats truly want. U.S. Sen. Bernie Sanders' surprising presidential campaign highlights the Democrats' internal conflict between public and private healthcare provision.

No one is really telling the truth. Since the ACA grants principal implementation responsibility to private companies, Republicans should like Obamacare more and Democrats should like it less. Even so, the bipartisan bickering and demagoguery continue.

As Obamacare's white-hot politics illustrate, policies to integrate U.S. healthcare's broken connections must accommodate rather than confront American values. This does not mean rejecting fundamental American beliefs in competitive markets, individualism or strong communities. It implores a deeper understanding of these values, born of a mature appreciation for the benefits of collaboration, collective action and accountability can deliver. Effective government programs and regulation are imperative. So are efficient resource allocation and value creation. Market and medicine must work together to align economic incentives and put patients first.

Throughout history, Americans have responded to crisis with determination, creativity and bold action. Failure to address the U.S. healthcare's structural flaws weakens global competitiveness, reduces the standard of living and contributes to widening socio-economic disparities. This unfortunate result represents an ironic manifestation of American exceptionalism. As the famous Pogo cartoon observes, "We have met the enemy and he is us." American values created the U.S. healthcare system and American values must guide its reform.

CHAPTER 2

OVERBUILD IT AND THEY STILL COME

A hospital bed is a parked taxi with the meter running.
GROUCHO MARX

Bubbles arise if the price far exceeds the asset's fundamental value, to the point that no plausible future income scenario can justify the price.[25]
JUSTIN FOX

---

25 https://hbr.org/2014/01/whats-that-youre-calling-a-bubble/

E ach year the healthcare world gathers in San Francisco the third week in January for J.P. Morgan's healthcare conference. Twenty-five thousand "suits" engage in five days of nonstop networking and deal-making. Amid the throngs, one can sense the energy pulsing through the healthcare sector as companies make their plays to capture segments of the vast healthcare marketplace. Opportunity and transformation are in the air. Often, the unexpected happens.

On the Sunday before the 2014 conference, I toured Stanford Hospital with a group of Chinese pharmaceutical representatives. My friend and former colleague, Dr. Sam Thong, manages Morgan Stanley's corporate healthcare practice in China. Thong arranged the tour in Palo Alto along with a shopping expedition and a massive seafood dinner. Welcome to America.

Since it was Sunday, the hospital was operating with minimal staffing. It appeared closed. This perplexed our Chinese guests. They peppered our volunteer guide with questions, wanting to know why there were no doctors, nurses or patients in sight. The tour culminated before an elaborate model of the new Stanford Hospital, the $2 billion, 400-bed centerpiece of the university's $5 billion comprehensive renewal project of all of its medical facilities.[26] Talk about sticker shock. This hospital prices out at just over $5 million per bed. That's a lot of appendectomies. Above the model was this wonderful, if somewhat overstated, mission statement describing Stanford Medicine's vision:

Healing humanity through science and compassion, one patient at a time. We live in a time of unprecedented possibilities for human health. Bioinformatics, genomics, and other emerging disciplines promise to transform the very concept of medicine—from treating disease after it has struck, to predicting it, preventing it, and promoting lifelong health. The new Stanford Hospital will make this bold vision of personalized medicine a reality. It will empower us to deliver compassionate, coordinated, leading edge care, tailored to the unique needs of every patient. It will capture the promises of the biomedical revolution, translating the

---

26 http://www.sumcrenewal.org/projects/project-overview/stanford-hospital/#sthash.
fw5eDiyw.dpuf

innovations of Stanford University and Silicon Valley into better health outcomes. A model of what health care can and should be in the 21st century, it will serve our community and the world for many decades to come.

I wanted to add the phrase "at exceptionally high cost" to the end of the last sentence. This vision statement encapsulates the high-tech, reductionist mindset of advanced American medicine, where progress comes through breakthrough research, genetic discovery and bioinformatics. Better health is just a pill or a procedure away. Society funds this vision through vast overpayment for routine care (i.e. cost shifting), government subsidies and philanthropy.

This conclusion is not an indictment of Stanford Medicine. America requires so-called "solution-shop" institutions where the brightest medical minds address the most complex cases; where medical researchers pursue breakthrough bio-medical discovery. Stanford aspires to be among these select few national and international referral centers. However, America does not need destination care centers in every community. Moreover, the country cannot afford to pay these advanced centers premium prices for routine care.

As payment for healthcare services becomes more transparent and customers insist on better value, it is unclear how expensive new acute-care facilities can generate adequate revenues to cover their expansive costs.[27] From coast to coast, hospital boards approve new, costly hospitals even at the expense of existing facilities and personnel.

In 2013, hospitals in Bangor, Augusta and Portland, Maine, negotiated capital and loans for major construction projects even though the state of Maine owed them a combined $484 million in overdue Medicaid payments.[28] Ironically, the Maine construction boom coincided with warnings from existing hospitals that they would have to phase out services or lay off workers to offset the Medicaid underpayment.

---

27 Stanford University cites necessary seismic upgrades as a significant cost factor. The finished facility is designed to function in an 8.0 earthquake.

28 *Medicaid debt isn't stopping Maine hospital construction*, Julie Bird, FierceHealthcare, April 2, 2013; http://www.fiercehealthcare.com/story/medicaid-debt-isnt-stopping-maine-hospital-construction/2013-04-02

Even community hospitals spend in excess of $1 million per new hospital bed. It sometimes seems that guaranteeing Americans private hospital rooms is the U.S. Constitution's 11th amendment to the Bill of Rights. New hospital construction in metropolitan Chicago has exceeded $8 billion in recent years despite a stable population. I can throw a rock from my house in Chicago's Lakeview neighborhood and hit two new ambulatory centers under construction. There are so many new facilities in metropolitan Chicago that hospitals find it difficult to distinguish their services. Elmhurst Memorial Hospital in suburban Chicago advertises private bathrooms in its emergency room; not exactly the top-of-mind concern for ambulance patients.

This overbuilding of healthcare facilities happens because the prices and payments for healthcare services have separated from logical value relationships. Negotiating leverage, not service quality and/or clinical outcomes, determines a procedure's pricing. Hospitals and doctors chase reimbursement irrespective of intrinsic market demand for their services. They particularly want patients with high-paying commercial insurance coverage. Hospitals seek to attract these patients with ever-higher levels of amenities (in-room entertainment, concierge parking, gourmet meals).

As the Chinese pharmaceutical reps discovered, our super-expensive American hospitals are frequently idle. As healthcare reform unfolds, the prices of healthcare services will reconnect with their actual cost. Acute care facilities will run much harder (e.g. surgeries on nights and weekends) to achieve greater operating efficiency. Still, the "build-it-and-patients-will-come" strategic mentality reigns within most health companies. As such, it is important to understand how and why the nation creates so much excess acute care capacity.

America's Concentrated Health Expenditure: "Follow the Money"

Construction costs comprise only one slice of healthcare costs. Since the emergence of private health insurance in the 1930s, doctors and hospitals have operated within an artificial fee-for-service economic model that pays for treatment activity rather than outcomes. This perverse payment methodology has enabled overtreatment of patients and overbuilding of healthcare infrastructure. Broadly speaking, U.S. healthcare expenditure concentrates on the sickest few, goes primarily to treating (as opposed to managing or preventing) chronic disease, overspends on end-of-life care and contains wide pricing variability. Combined, these factors explain why America spends more for healthcare services but receives less value for its healthcare spending than other advanced economies. Serving the few intensely hurts the many.

Serving the Few I: Per Capita Health Expenditure by Age

America routinely rings up the highest per capita healthcare expenditure ($9,982 in 2014[29] or 17.8 percent of the GNP) among developed nations despite lower life expectancy. America's per capita health spending is more than two-and-a-half times the average per capita health expenditure for the 34 advanced economies participating in the Organisation of Economic Co-operation and Development (OECD).[30]

Relative to other OECD countries, U.S. healthcare spending becomes even more distorted when measuring healthcare expenditures for the elderly. The healthcare consulting firm Kaufman Hall and Associates released an analysis in 2011 revealing that beyond the age of 80, the U.S. spends almost *five times more per capita* than Austria, German, Norway, Sweden and the United Kingdom. Despite the higher spending, life expectancy in the U.S. was lower than the OECD average.[31] The OECD's *Health at a Glance 2013* reports the following:

---

29 Altarum Institute Report, February 12, 2015

30 http://www.oecd.org/els/health-systems/oecd-health-statistics-2014-frequently-requested-data.htm

31 *Id.*

...life expectancy in the United States stood at 78.7 years in 2011: an increase of almost eight years since 1970, but significantly less than the ten-year gain registered across OECD countries. The gap between the United States and leading countries also widened.

The conclusions from these comparative payment and longevity statistics are evident and painful. The U.S. is in the unenviable position of spending significantly more on acute care services, particularly in the last two years of life, without achieving equivalent life expectancy. As we will discuss later in this chapter, intense end-of-life treatments are inconsistent with most terminal patients' wishes. Moreover, excessive acute-care spending crowds out logical preventive, behavioral health and chronic-disease management spending that would improve Americans' health, wellness, longevity and life quality.

Serving the Few II: Distribution of U.S. Health Spending by Intensity of Use

The National Institute for Health Care Management (NIHCM) Foundation tracks another key element of U.S. healthcare dollars— expenditure by intensity of use. The chart below, from its 2009 study, demonstrates the pattern. Five percent of the U.S. population consumes over half of the nation's total healthcare spending. Conversely, the 50 percent of the population who spend the least on healthcare consume just 3 percent of the nation's total health expenditure. This under-spending by the bottom 50 percent is as troubling as the over-spending by the top 5 percent. It illustrates how under-investment in primary and preventive care results in the excessive and expensive crisis care discussed in Chapter 1.

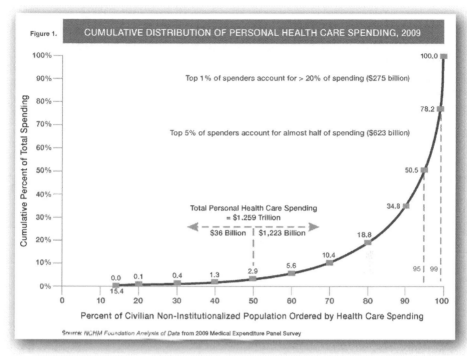

Figure 1. CUMULATIVE DISTRIBUTION OF PERSONAL HEALTH CARE SPENDING, 2009

Source: NCHM Foundation Analysis of Data from 2009 Medical Expenditure Panel Survey

It's common sense that the highest spending group includes the oldest and sickest. Health issues increase with age. Naturally, the heavy users of healthcare services are largely elderly patients. Beginning in 2011 and continuing through 2029, 8,000 baby boomers a day began turning age 65.[32] Absent health delivery reform, these aging baby boomers will consume increasing levels of healthcare services.

Sources of Excessive U.S. Health Expenditure

With an understanding of the magnitude and concentration of U.S. healthcare spending, it is important to examine the three principal sources of excessive health expenditure: explosive chronic disease; excessive end-of-life care and exploitive healthcare pricing:

---

32 http://www.aarp.org/personal-growth/transitions/boomers_65/

Explosive Chronic Disease

According to the Centers for Disease Control and Prevention ("CDC"), chronic disease consumes over 80 percent of U.S. healthcare expenditure. Chronic disease is largely self-inflicted. Tobacco and obesity are the principal culprits. More than a third of U.S adults are obese.[33] In 2012, 29 million Americans, representing over 9 percent of the population, suffered with diabetes (diagnosed and undiagnosed).[34] The disease is particularly prevalent—at 26 percent—in seniors.[35] The Dartmouth Atlas of Health Care reports that,

> *More than ninety million Americans live with at least one chronic illness, and seven out of ten Americans die from chronic disease. Like rates of diabetes, among the Medicare population, the chronic disease toll is even greater: about nine out of ten deaths are associated with nine chronic illnesses, including congestive heart failure, chronic lung disease, cancer, coronary artery disease, renal failure, peripheral vascular disease, diabetes, chronic liver disease, and dementia.*[36]

Failure to manage chronic disease leads to excessive high-cost acute episodes that compromise health status. It also leads to hidden healthcare costs as hospitals renovate to accommodate heavier patients. The University of Alabama at Birmingham's hospital "widened doors, replaced wall-mounted toilets with floor models able to hold 250 pounds or more, and bought plus-size wheelchairs (twice the price of regulars) as well as mini-cranes to hoist obese patients out of bed."[37]

---

33 http://www.cdc.gov/obesity/data/adult.html
34 http://www.diabetes.org/diabetes-basics/statistics/
35 *Id.*
36 http://www.dartmouthatlas.org/keyissues/issue.aspx?con=2944
37 http://www.reuters.com/article/2012/04/30/us-obesity-idUSBRE83T0C820120430

America's Death Spiral: Excessive End-of-Life Care

End-of-life care is the third rail of U.S. healthcare policy.[38] End-of-life care, by definition, occurs during the last six months of life,[39] is deeply personal and politically charged. Neither voters nor politicians face it realistically. My friend Nancy Kane, the Harvard Associate Dean, often quips, "Americans believe death is optional." American culture keeps death at arm's-length. Americans avoid difficult conversations about death. Too often, individuals and their families confront a death spiral under duress with no preparation. They make bad decisions that cause catastrophic emotional, medical and financial consequences. Consider these realities:

- Medicare spends 26 percent of its funding on beneficiaries in the last year of their life.[40]

- In 2011, the average American consumed $54,017 in healthcare services during their last year of life, a 58 percent increase from $34,257 in 2002.[41]

- Out-of-pocket expenses during the last five years of life averaged $39,000 for individuals, $51,000 for couples and up to $66,000 for people with long-term illnesses.[42]

- The percentage of Medicare patients seeing 10 or more doctors in the last 6 months of their lives increased from 30.8 percent in 2003 to 36.1 percent in 2007.[43]

---

38 *End of Life Care Constitutes Third Rail of U.S. Health Care Policy*, Susan Pasternak, The Medicare NewsGroup, June 3, 2013; http://www.medicarenewsgroup.com/context/understanding-medicare-blog/understanding-medicare-blog/2013/06/03/end-of-life-care-constitutes-third-rail-of-u.s.-health-care-policy-debate

39 http://www.apa.org/pi/aids/programs/eol/end-of-life-factsheet.aspx?item=1

40 MedPAC, *Spending in the Last Year of Life and the Impact of Hospice on Medicare Outlays*, June 2015, p. 9

41 *Ibid.*

42 Money Magazine, *Cutting the High Cost of End-of-Life Care*, Penelope Wang, December 12, 2012

43 The Dartmouth Atlas, *Trends and Variations in End-of-Life Care*, April 12, 2011

- Medical expenses account for 62 percent of personal bank-ruptcies in the U.S. In 72 percent of these bankruptcies, indi-viduals had health insurance."[44]

- Seventy percent of Americans would prefer to die at home.[45] Instead, 70 percent die in hospitals, nursing homes or long-term care facilities.[46]

- "More than 80 percent of patients wish to avoid hospitaliza-tion and intensive care during the terminal phase of illness, but those wishes are often overridden by other factors."[47]

- Eighty-nine percent of American think doctors should discuss end-of-life care with patients. Only 17 percent of Americans have discussed end-of-life care preferences with physicians.[48]

The majority of Americans do not receive end-of-life care consis-tent with their values and goals. Absent clear direction, the American medical system adopts an all-necessary-measures approach that gener-ates excessive treatment, high costs and reduced quality of life. Rather than end life on their own terms, patients die overburdened in institu-tional settings. Life's final passage becomes a nightmare journey into oblivion. Everyone suffers.

Supported by a payment system that reimburses all "justifiable" care, the U.S. health system goes full out to prevent death. Chronic dis-ease patients in their last two years of life account for over 30 percent of Medicare spending, much of it going toward physician and hospi-tal fees associated with repeated and unnecessary hospitalizations and treatments. "The average rehab stay costs $30,000," observes Fields, the primary care physician in Houston. He continues, "Too often it's spent on people who realistically are not rehab candidates. They're

44   Huffington Post, *Top 10 Reasons People Go Bankrupt*, May 24, 2015

45   Time Magazine, *A Kinder, Gentler Death*, John Cloud, September 18, 2000

46   Centers for Disease Control, Deaths by Place, 2005

47   The Dartmouth Atlas

48   Kaiser Family Foundation, *Kaiser Health Tracking Poll*, September 30, 2015

older, chronically ill patients who would benefit more from home visits than hospitalizations."

Even the recent upswing in palliative and hospice care hasn't significantly dented end-of-life healthcare spending. In her post "The Cost and Quality Conundrum of American End-of-Life Care,"[49] Helen Adamopoulos cites a February 2013 study published in *JAMA* that found fewer individuals die in hospitals and more receive hospice care. Despite this positive trend, "more patients are receiving care in an intensive care unit in their last month of life and a growing number are shuffled around between different care sites in their final three months." These intensive treatments rarely benefit patients, consume enormous resources and often diminish their humanity.

Exploitive Healthcare Pricing

Medicare decides how much it will pay for specific treatments according to complex formulas that incorporate multiple variables. Commercial insurers generally follow Medicare guidelines but pay at higher levels. Hospitals and doctors exploit this formulaic pricing methodology to optimize revenues in the following two ways: By providing more treatment than is necessary (i.e. overtreatment) and receiving payment for these unnecessary treatments; and by coding each treatment for the highest-allowable reimbursement payment.

Both schemes enable providers to receive excessive payment. Providers, commercial insurers and the government spend billions of dollars each year to monitor and regulate payment compliance. Despite this significant investment in regulatory compliance, the healthcare payment system is rife with abuse. At its best, the current payment system invites manipulation; at its worst, it encourages fraud. A February 2015 investigative report by the *Wall Street Journal* found that long-term acute-care hospitals disproportionately discharge patients to optimize their Medicare payments—a clear sign that payment

---

49 The Medicare NewsGroup, June 3, 2013

incentives influence patient care.[50] Overtreatment and aggressive coding add significant costs to an already profligate delivery system.

For more than 20 years, the Dartmouth Atlas of Health Care has tracked Medicare payment and outcomes data. Its scholars have documented significant and unwarranted variations in utilization and pricing of medical resources. Their analyses demonstrate that more healthcare treatments do not generate better health outcomes. Higher payments, however, do correlate with greater treatment levels for similar medical conditions. Over time, physician practice patterns that support excessive treatment become entrenched and difficult to change.

Entrenched physician practice patterns create pricing variations that resist standardization and raise the cost of healthcare. The result, as Elisabeth Rosenthal, healthcare reporter for the *New York Times* chronicled, is significant price variation for even routine procedures.[51] Rosenthal described three colonoscopies with vastly different charges: $6,385 in Merrick, NY; $7,564 in Keene, NH; and $19,438 in Durham, NC. Despite their widespread application, predictability and necessity, colonoscopies defy pricing standardization. It gets worse. Castlight, a new company that provides price and outcomes transparency, analyzed claims data and found that colonoscopy prices in just *one* San Francisco zip code ranged from $500 to $9,800.

Taken together, these spending patterns and perverse economics illustrate a fundamental flaw in the U.S. healthcare system: A build-it-and-they-will-come mentality has created an expensive, inflexible asset-heavy healthcare industry where the best predictor of cardiac procedures is the number of licensed cardiologists, not patient need.[52]

Roemer's Law Revisited

Chapter 1 introduced professor Milton Roemer and his 1960s prediction that third-party reimbursement for healthcare services (i.e. American healthcare's current payment model) would create its

50 Wall Street Journal, February 17, 2015
51 *The $2.7 Trillion Medical Bill: Colonoscopies Explain Why U.S. Leads he World in Health Expenditures*, Elisabeth Rosenthal, originally published June 1, 2013
52 Dartmouth Atlas

own demand and lead to excessive healthcare expenditure. This supply-driven demand economic model requires abundant facility investment to optimize provider revenue. Roemer was more right than he ever could have realized. U.S. healthcare has an overbuilt and underused acute care infrastructure that maximizes provider revenue.

After rising steadily and more than doubling in eight years, annual healthcare construction peaked in 2008 before declining and holding at or around $40 billion through 2015 (see chart below).

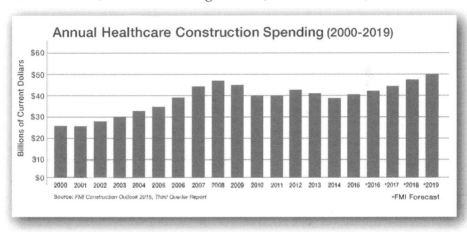

Health systems are building again. A July 21, 2015, *Modern Healthcare* article[53] highlights a surge in new facility construction. Increased bond issuance[54] for new projects provides conclusive proof. FMI's 2015 third quarter "Construction Outlook"[55] forecasts healthcare construction increasing to $50 billion annually by 2019, based on demographics, needed facility modernization and greater demand for outpatient services. This is wishful thinking. Acute facility over-investment combined with more treatment accountability, value-based purchasing and game-changing technologies have created a sizable asset bubble.

---

53 http://www.modernhealthcare.com/article/20150721/NEWS/150729959
54 *Id.*
55 http://www.fminet.com/media/pdf/forecasts/Outlook_2015Q3_FMI.pdf

Acute-Care Facility Asset Bubble

In *The Ascent of Money*, Niall Ferguson chronicles 400 years of financial bubbles. Bubbles happen frequently and have five distinct stages:

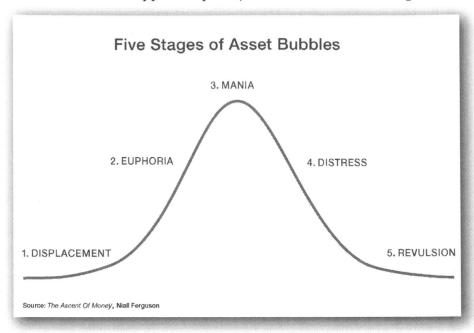

1. **Displacement:** A change in economic circumstances creates a profit-making opportunity;

2. **Euphoria:** A positive feedback loop emerges where rising expected profits lead to a rapid investment growth;

3. **Mania (or bubble):** The prospect of easy profits turbocharges investment and inflates valuations;

4. **Distress:** Insiders discern that expected profits cannot continue and begin to liquidate their positions; and

5. **Revulsion:** Valuations fall as owners stampede to sell causing the bubble to burst.

Applying Ferguson's five-stage formula to hospitals reveals a classic asset bubble:

1. **Displacement:** Entering the new millennium, consumer resentment against HMOs, consolidation-driven pricing leverage, the specialty-hospital moratorium and breakthrough surgical and imaging technologies increase hospital profits and stimulate demand for new facilities.

2. **Euphoria:** As healthcare consumes an ever-larger percentage of the economy, health systems invest heavily in new facilities. Hospital volumes and profitability increase. Capital access through the debt markets expands. Complex hedging strategies reduce borrowing costs. Bond insurance is plentiful. Credit metrics improve.

3. **Mania:** Cost per bed skyrockets to over $1 million. Hospitals compete with new facilities, specialized care centers and hotel-like amenities. *Metropolitan Chicago invests over $8 billion in new hospitals despite flat population growth.*

4. **Distress (where the market is now):** The financial crisis triggers severe investment and hedging losses. Philanthropy diminishes. The Affordable Care Act and exploding government deficits increase operating uncertainty. Stagnant revenue growth. Increasing industry consolidation. Extensive market-based reform. Companies explore narrow network contracts (General Electric), sole-sourced specialty care (Boeing) and defined contribution health plans (Sears). Increasing pricing transparency limits cost shifting.

5. **Revulsion (where the market's going):** The market shifts to population-based health. Narrow networks predominate. Health insurance exchanges drive pricing and transparency. Evidenced-based medicine, prevention, chronic disease

management and predictive analytics reduce acute-care volume. Hospitals become cost centers, not revenue generators. Full price transparency eliminates cost shifting. The end result is diminished medical education and research funding, bond defaults and health system restructuring.

Established to regulate the construction of new healthcare facilities, state-based certificate of need (CON) programs have not controlled the overbuilding of acute care facilities. Political support for new healthcare facilities overcomes regulatory arguments for restricting their growth. Given their ineffectiveness, many states have eliminated CON approvals altogether. Unfortunately, remaining CON approvals are often perfunctory and sometimes vulnerable to political shenanigans. For example, Illinois attorney Stuart Levine received a five-year prison sentence in 2012 for using his seat on the Illinois Health Facilities Planning board to shakedown hospitals for kickbacks.

More is Less

Ironically, as the asset bubble inflates, U.S. healthcare becomes less stable, less efficient and less effective. Justifications for ever-greater facility investment wither under scrutiny. Not only is there excess demand, there's an excessive facility base to treat that demand. Factors influencing this facility oversupply include the following:

Overtreatment/Waste: In an April 2012 *JAMA* article, Donald Berwick and Andrew Hackbarth estimate that 21 to 47 percent of annual health U.S. healthcare spending is wasteful—adds cost without improving outcomes. Their mid-point estimate of 34 percent represents $910 billion of unnecessary healthcare spending in 2011.[56]

Preventable Medical Admissions: The current system rarely helps patients manage their chronic disease. Instead, it treats

56 http://jama.jamanetwork.com/article.aspx?articleid=1148376

chronic disease symptoms when they emerge. This generates high levels of preventable admissions for congestive heart failure, diabetes, hypertension and other prevalent chronic diseases.

Underutilized Operating Rooms: Hospitals typically run one operating- room shift daily and only on four or five days per week. Scheduling responds to surgeons' demands for weekday appointments. Given their very high cost to build, hospitals should run multiple OR shifts daily to accommodate incremental demand.

Inappropriate Emergency Room Care: Too many consumers use emergency rooms rather than clinics or urgent care centers for routine ailments, such as strep throat and ear infections. Inappropriate ER care multiplies treatment costs, reduces ER responsiveness and inconveniences customers. Achieving better facility alignment for emergency and routine care will lower costs and improve outcomes.

The unfortunate consequence of America's build-it-and-they-will-come approach is too many underutilized facilities catering to too many specialized physicians performing too many procedures with too little standardization and too much variation in pricing and outcomes. America's current healthcare business model generates artificial demand for private rooms and high-end amenities while incentivizing overtreatment and aggressive coding to optimize revenue generation for hospitals and doctors.

Fifty-plus years of supply-driven demand for healthcare services have generated excessive treatment levels, excessive treatment variation, excessive facility investment and excessive health expenditure. Turbocharging this wasteful and excessive health expenditure is a toxic combination of centrally managed healthcare regulation and a ferocious private-sector appetite for optimizing profits by exploiting perverse financial incentives.

CHAPTER 3

HEALTHCARE'S PRODUCTIVITY PARADOX

Nothing is less productive than to make more efficient what should not be done at all.
PETER DRUCKER

It is not enough to be industrious; so are the ants. What are you industrious about?
HENRY DAVID THOREAU

L as Vegas is a strange place to attend a medical conference. In June 2014, the Healthcare Financial Management Association (HFMA) convened its Annual National Institute (ANI) at the Venetian Hotel and Casino. Several thousand healthcare finance professionals assembled to network and improve their business acumen. I was there to speak on hospital affiliations and acquisitions.

Here's something not seen every day: ANI attendees intermingled with almost 200,000 young people attending the Electric Daisy Carnival at the Las Vegas Speedway. They wore lots of makeup, danced all night in their underwear and consumed untold amounts of illegal substances. Three people died. Hundreds stumbled through the casino each morning bumping into straight-laced consultants. What happens in Vegas....

Upon arrival, I wandered through the massive exhibit floor. The number of revenue cycle companies exhibiting was staggering. My rough estimate was three-fourths of the exhibitors. Later that day, the official program kicked off with six hospitals winning awards— big trophies— for revenue cycle excellence. The audience exploded with applause. Clearly, revenue rules in modern American healthcare. Fifty years after Medicare's creation, Roemer's law is thriving and more electric than a Las Vegas rave.

This chapter unravels U.S. healthcare's profound productivity paradox. Private company exploitation of activity-based payment mechanisms distorts care delivery protocols and misuses care resources. Perhaps even worse, activity-based payments disconnect healthcare consumers from healthcare providers. Fee-for-service payment fragments patient-care provider relationships, which are the central feature of effective healthcare delivery. This chapter also investigates the dominant role that nonprofit health companies play in U.S. healthcare delivery. While nonprofit healthcare organizations have many virtues, their governance, cultures and operating models too often suppress productivity improvement, resist consolidation and promote facility overbuilding.

Feed Me Revenues

U.S. healthcare has a voracious appetite for billable treatments and reimbursement revenue. It trumps everything else. As price transparency and high-deductible health plans increase, providers are doubling down on pricing and collection strategies that maximize revenues. And why not? It's worked for decades. Dr. Atul Gawande presented a version of the following chart during his ANI keynote address.[57] The blue line depicts patient mortality rates between 1821 and 2010 at Massachusetts General Hospital, where Gawande practices medicine. The green line depicts Mass General's cost per discharge in today's dollars for the same period.

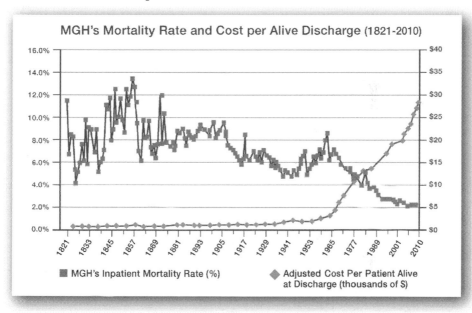

Two hundred years ago, the current average cost was $997. Obviously, many more patients died at the hospital in the 1800s than today. With advances in infection control, antibiotics and surgical intervention, mortality rates plummeted after World War II. Costs spiked upward in the mid-1960s with the advent of Medicare and cost-plus reimbursement. In the past 10 years, Mass General's mortality rates have flattened but discharge costs have increased by $10,000. While mortality is an imperfect quality measure, the correlation between mortality

---

57 http://www.nejm.org/doi/full/10.1056/NEJMp1202628

and costs is spot-on: healthcare costs spiral upward without a commensurate increase in quality outcomes.

Unlike other industries, healthcare's prices disconnect from its products and services. Mass General's pattern of outcomes and expenditures replicates itself in almost all American hospitals. The best regulatory structures minimize damage by aligning market incentives to deliver desired results. Unfortunately, the U.S. healthcare system's current payment policies invite manipulation (legal but unethical) and fraud (illegal and unethical). Here is an example of each:

Case Study 1 - Manipulation: A New York man undergoes neck surgery. He has commercial insurance and anticipates he'll have a costly out-of-pocket payment for the surgeon, anesthesiologist and hospital. What he didn't expect was the $117,000 bill from another doctor "attending" his procedure. Imagine his shock upon receiving the mystery surgeon's bill. By contrast, Medicare pays $600 (one two-hundredth of the cost) for the same service. Hospitals and doctors are like bank robber Willy Sutton: they "go where the money is." As part of her ongoing "Paying Till It Hurts," series,[58] Rosenthal, the *New York Times* reporter, detailed this shocking episode of "drive-by doctoring." It occurs when doctors, assistants and other hospital employees charge patients and/or their insurance companies substantial fees for non-disclosed services. This gross manipulation is a toxic consequence of activity-based payment.

Case Study 2 - Fraud: From the late 1980s through mid 2000s, two cardiologists at the California Heart Institute of the Redding Medical Center in Northern California, performed tens of thousands of cardiac procedures. They distinguished themselves and amassed substantial wealth. They committed fraud. A local primary care physician became the whistleblower after his patients received unnecessary treatments. Department of Justice and F.B.I. investigations uncovered substantial amounts

---

58 http://www.nytimes.com/2014/09/21/us/drive-by-doctoring-surprise-medical-bills. html?)r=0

of unnecessary treatments, including many that caused death. Tenet Healthcare, the hospital's owner, paid multimillion-dollar fines and sold Redding Medical Center as part of the settlement.[59/60]

Is it in the water? Now owned by Prime Healthcare and named Shasta Regional Medical Center, this same hospital is in trouble again. In early 2009, Shasta Regional Medical Center diagnosed 1,030 cases of kwashiorkor—70 times the state average of 0.2 percent. (Shasta treated only eight cases in all of 2008.)[61] The surge was particularly startling given kwashiorkor is a nutritional disorder that "almost exclusively effects impoverished children in developing countries."[62] It also garnishes hefty reimbursement bonuses from Medicare. Federal agencies are investigating whether the hospital illegally upcoded its treatments. Upcoding is the practice of intentionally inflating medical bills. It is rampant in American healthcare, very difficult to prosecute and costs healthcare payers billions of dollars annually. Upcoding is U.S. healthcare's productivity paradox in action.

Healthcare separates from other industries in its pursuit of revenues over value. In competitive markets, companies that provide value to customers see rewards. Sales increase. Profits climb. High-performance companies employ constant productivity improvement to improve quality and lower prices on products customers want. Not healthcare. Doctors and hospitals receive payment for treatment activity, not health outcomes (products). Their accounting systems optimize billing and revenue generation over cost-effectiveness and productivity.

---

59   http://www.highbeam.com/doc/1G1-115480370.html

60   Hospital Partners of America paid approximately $60 million. When HPA declared bankruptcy in 2008, Prime Healthcare Services bought Shasta Regional Medical Center.

61   Lance Williams, Christina Jewett and Stephen K. Dolg, *Hospital chain, already under scrutiny, reports high malnutrition rates*, California Watch, February 19, 20111; http://californiawatch.org/health-and-welfare/hospital-chain-already-under-scrutiny-reports-high-malnutrition-rates-8786

62   *Id.*

The resulting productivity paradox creates high treatment costs with mediocre health outcomes.

Health systems in other advanced economies centrally manage treatment pricing and the overall budget for health expenditures. While far from perfect, this approach controls health expenditures. In America, Medicare manages pricing centrally but has no control over treatment activity. As long as providers can demonstrate medically necessity (a loose standard), Medicare pays for all treatments. Commercial programs follow Medicare's payment approach (codes for approved procedures) but pay premium prices for the same treatments. As a result, activity-based payment systems create toxic incentives that encourage overtreatment, excessive billing and fraud. Healthcare entrepreneurs make money by creating companies that exploit perverse financial incentives. This drives up U.S. healthcare costs without improving outcomes.

The Price of Tin

Capitalism's inherent beauty is its ability to allocate resources efficiently among market participants. Outcomes, not process, triumph. Confession time: I'm addicted to the Great Courses program. On a drive through Indiana several years ago, I listened to a lecture by Macalester College professor Timothy Taylor on the Austrian economist Friedrich Hayek. Little did I expect to gain insight into centralized health systems.

Born in Vienna in 1899, Friedrich Hayek was a leading mid-century economist who championed liberal democracy and free-market capitalism. He taught at the University of Chicago, won the Nobel Prize in 1974 and debated socialist theorists on markets, government's role in the economy and social planning. Hayek maintained that markets and competition were the best mechanisms for calculating and coordinating economic choice. He believed that prices contain sufficient information to guide and adjust economic decisions. He stressed that decentralized planning by individuals and companies is the most effective system for allocating resources and generating wealth. To illustrate, Hayek contrasted how free-market enterprise and market socialism respond to increasing tin prices in the chart below.

Free-Market Capitalism vs. Market Socialism

Tin Prices Increase

Free-Market Capitalism	Market Socialism
• Price contains meaningful information	• Central planners study factors driving price increase
• Marginal users find substitutes	• Determine priorities for tin usage
• Essential users adjust	• Assign and enforce prices
	• Very complex
• Correlated product prices increase	• Never have complete information
	• Prone to mistakes
• Market stabilizes and functions efficiently	• Retards economic growth
	• Stimulates "black market" trade

Under free-market capitalism with decentralized planning, primary and marginal users of tin "read" the pricing information and adjust consumption accordingly. In response, manufacturers substitute materials, improve production mechanics and/or adjust prices. The cycle repeats until the market stabilizes. In contrast, market socialism with centralized planning requires complex protocols to determine why the price of tin increased, establish priorities for its use, assign prices and enforce market acceptance. Before long, complexity overwhelms managerial capabilities and it's easy to make mistakes, such as manufacturers producing too many gutters and too few pans. Managed economies create imbalances in supply and demand, impede economic growth and stimulate black-market trading activity.

While listening to Taylor's lecture, I had an epiphany. Medicare is market socialism. Its centrally managed practices for pricing, regulating and policing healthcare services distort market function, create imbalances in supply and demand and stimulate black-market behavior. By this point in my drive, I was approaching Indianapolis, where health systems were constructing four new cardiac surgical centers even as new therapies were reducing the need for cardiac surgery. Centralized administration breeds mistakes. Remember the former Soviet Union's remarkably consistent record of missing its five-year economic forecasts? It wasn't much better at manufacturing. An old joke makes the point: Car owners could double the value of their Lada, the Soviet Union's marque automobile, by putting a liter of petrol in its gas tank.

Despite global success with free-market capitalism, the U.S. government relies on centralized planning (a.k.a. Medicare) to design, administer and police healthcare services. Medicare's centralized operating model is contrary to American trust in competitive markets. Native distrust of bigger government is a core reason lawmakers' attempts to create a national health system in the U.S. have failed.

When Process Trumps Outcomes

Noted Princeton economist Ewe Reinhardt uses the diagram below[63] to depict the complex analytic methodology Medicare uses to calculate treatment payments. Medicare's actual methodology is even more complex. The payment process begins by calculating an average inpatient case rate sufficient to cover operating and capital costs for efficient facilities. In 2014[64], the operating base rate was $5,370 and the capital base rate was $429.

---

63 Source: *How Medicare Sets Hospital Prices: A Primer*, By Uwe E. Reinhardt, November 26, 2010, http://economix.blogs.nytimes.com/2010/11/26/how-medicare-sets-hospital-prices-a-primer/?_r=0

64 http://www.cms.gov/Medicare/Medicare-Fee-for-Service-Payment/AcuteInpatientPPS/FY2014-IPPS-Final-Rule-Home-Page.html

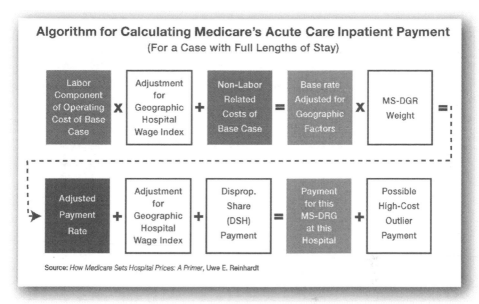

Medicare adjusts this base rate for geographic variation in labor and non-labor costs as well as treatment complexity based on the primary diagnosis, coexisting medical conditions and complications. The adjusted payment rate incorporates these geographic and care-intensity factors. Then, Medicare adds payments to compensate hospitals for medical education and indigent care costs. It also makes an allowance for high-cost, outlier cases.[65]

Medicare's payment algorithm incorporates multiple factors, homogenizes complex relationships and requires massive data entry for processing. Notably absent from Medicare's algorithm is payment for superior outcomes and penalties for inferior outcomes. To its credit, Medicare now incorporates some value-based payments and hospital readmission penalties into care reimbursement. Some employers and commercial insurers also are creating incentives for better care management, but it's still small potatoes. In his book *Healthcare Beyond Reform,* Joe Flower identifies the two core rules of [healthcare] economics:

---

65 Section 1886(d)(5)(A) of the [Medicare?] [AC] Act gives "background" on Outlier Payments. The section runs almost 550 words, 3000 characters, long.

- Rule 1: People do what you pay them to do; and
- Rule 2: People do *exactly* what you pay them to do.

Flower's assessment is harsh but directionally right. Healthcare won't change until payment incentives change. Process wins. Outcomes lose.

Hayek observed that resource-allocation mistakes occur when central planners manage complex business sectors with incomplete information. His insight certainly applies to Medicare. Mistakes abound. It takes years to plan and construct new acute care facilities. The Indianapolis health systems planned and built new cardiac centers to maximize reimbursement payments for cardiac care predicated on existing treatment patterns and payment rates. They didn't envision the emergence of new cardiovascular drugs that would reduce the need for surgical intervention. Overbuilding leads to overtreating. To make up for lost volume and income, cardiologists overtreat by performing justifiable, but unnecessary, procedures.

In yet another payment quirk, the American Medical Association ("AMA") influences the design of Medicare's reimbursement system. Talk about the fox guarding the hen house. An AMA committee annually reviews Medicare billing codes and rates to recommend appropriate rates for primary and specialty procedures. Medicare typically accepts the AMA panel's recommendations. Medical specialty associations devote considerable resources to lobbying the committee. The medical association lobby is more politics than medicine. Strong specialty associations, such as the American Society of Cardiology, overwhelm primary care advocates. As a consequence, Medicare, Medicaid and commercial reimbursement payments disproportionately benefit specialists.

If "Deep Throat" were a mole in "Healthgate," he would say, "Follow the reimbursement." Healthcare's payment complexity enables hospitals and doctors to optimize payment by seeking the highest reimbursement within allowable guidelines (hence the importance of revenue cycle management). The government, commercial payers and health systems invest enormous resources to prevent, identify, investigate, negotiate and settle payment disputes.

Based in Irving, Texas, CHRISTUS Health is a nonprofit health system with more than 60 hospitals and long-term care facilities, 175 clinics and outpatient centers and dozens of other health ministries and ventures.[66] I was a long-serving member of CHRISTUS Health's Audit Committee. Our committee spent over half of its time assessing regulatory compliance issues, including self-identified instances where the company inappropriately billed for services. By necessity, we focused on how well the company was complying with established reimbursement guidelines, not on how the company could implement best care practices. While regulatory compliance is vital, it does not advance healthcare delivery. Imagine what CHRISTUS and other health systems could achieve if they directed all of their considerable capabilities toward achieving superior clinical outcomes and improving community health.

Medicare has no official estimate of how much it loses annually to fraudulent billing practices. The FBI estimates 3 to 10 percent of all healthcare billings are fraudulent.[67] That represents a wide range. Even at the low end of the range, fraudulent billing is a huge cost (almost $100 billion) for a $3 trillion industry. Officials concede that billions more tax dollars are misspent every year because doctors and hospitals exaggerate their patients' illnesses when billing for treatment.[68]

Prices and Outcomes: "What, Me Correlated?"

The media is becoming more critical of U.S. healthcare's revenue-first operating model. In the now famous 2013 *Time Magazine* feature story, "A Bitter Pill: Why Medical Bills are Killing Us," author Steven Brill argued eloquently that healthcare reform "changed the rules related to who pays for what, but we haven't done much to change the prices we pay."[69] Brill tears into the Byzantine way hospitals set prices to maximize

---

66 http://en.wikipedia.org/wiki/CHRISTUS_Health

67 www.medicarenewsgroup.com

68 http://www.kpbs.org/news/2014/nov/04/more-scrutiny-coming-for-medicare-advantage/

69 Steven Brill, *A Bitter Pill: Why Medical Bills are Killing Us*, Time Magazine, February 20, 2013

revenue generation. Here's a dirty secret: Prices bear little relationship to actual costs and often don't support the best care practices.

Brill shares the story of oncologists at Memorial Sloan Kettering Cancer Center who stood up against high-cost cancer drugs that offered no incremental benefit. In an op-ed to *The New York Times*, the physicians describe their decision to switch from a specific colorectal-cancer drug that cost $11,063 per month to one that cost $5,000. The drugs were equally effective, so there was no need to burden patients with the extra cost.[70] A month later, the manufacturer of the more expensive drug cut its price in half to remain competitive. As Justice Lewis Brandeis observed, "sunshine is the best disinfectant." Transparency has its benefits, but should it require a *New York Times* article to change inappropriate business behavior?

A distinguishing feature of American healthcare is that hospitals and doctors charge different prices for the same treatments. Medicare reimburses hospitals and doctors using the predetermined methodology outlined above. By contrast, providers negotiate directly with commercial insurance companies for procedure-specific reimbursement rates that are usually higher than Medicare rates. This differential-pricing strategy enables hospitals to cost shift, offsetting lower Medicare payments by charging insurance companies more for the same treatments. A hospital's "chargemaster," its confidential price list for everything from bandages to brain surgery, forms the basis for these negotiations but receives little, if any, public scrutiny. Hospitals defend this secrecy. As Brill notes in "A Bitter Pill", hospital administrators and public relations employees alike dodged his questions about chargemaster prices, even claiming they were irrelevant.

The chargemaster controversy encapsulates the larger issue confronting American hospitals and doctors. Providers depend upon cost shifting to generate profits. It's easier to raise prices than cut costs. Brill observes:

---

70 *id.*

That so few consumers seem to be aware of the chargemaster, demon-strates how well the health care industry has steered the debate from why bills are so high to who should pay them.[71]

The U.S. system places principal emphasis on revenue generation, not efficient operations.

Value, What Value?

In comparison to other industries, healthcare's operating model has changed relatively little during the last 50 years. Americans rely on doctors and hospitals to distribute healthcare services in accordance with predetermined fee schedules. What about value? Given complex Medicare reimbursement formulas and undisclosed chargemasters, it's challenging for consumers to align healthcare products with their prices. Instead, consumers make healthcare decisions anecdotally, querying friends and/or Internet resources to find care providers and facilities.

America's activity-based, fee-for-service reimbursement system has conditioned providers to optimize revenues through agile manipula-tion of coding and treatment guidelines. This has created hospitals with robust revenue-cycle capabilities but little understanding of per-unit revenue and cost relationships. Most hospitals allocate their costs in relationship to their charges, which provides no useful information to guide efficient use of labor, supplies and capital.

Health companies' intense focus on optimizing revenue has atro-phied their ability to understand and manage operating costs. This operating deficiency poses a serious challenge for health companies as the market moves toward value-based purchasing. Moreover, few health companies have the organizational cultures necessary to improve qual-ity and efficiency while reducing costs. This is a big problem. It's im-possible to assess and deliver value-based healthcare services without a solid understanding of organizational cost structure.

---

71 *id.*

Unique Character and Challenges of Nonprofit Health Companies

Society establishes nonprofit organizations for permanence. Think museums, cultural institutions and foundations. Nonprofit governance models reflect this. They tend to be large, community-based, strategically conservative, uncompensated and philanthropically oriented. Nonprofit organizations exist to fulfill a charitable purpose or mission. It's a historical quirk that charitable healthcare activities center on delivery, not insurance. This anomaly reflects healthcare's early history when health insurance didn't exist and charitable organizations provided care to those who could not pay.

Society bestows considerable financial benefits upon nonprofit health companies (no income taxes, no property taxes, access to lower-cost tax-exempt debt and philanthropic support) in exchange for funding some or all of the care costs for indigent patients. It's a popular contract: approximately 80 percent of U.S. hospitals have a nonprofit or governmental ownership structure. These include all the famous brands, such as Mayo Clinic, Johns Hopkins and Mass General. Nonprofit health companies employ community-based governance, are mission oriented, care for the medically indigent, train doctors, educate the community and conduct basic research. They are large community-focused employers.

At the same time, nonprofit health systems must access the public debt markets to fund new capital investments. Health systems' ability to access the debt markets is a function of their profitability, balance-sheet strength and market position. This creates an inherent conflict between mission and margin that does not exist in for-profit companies. Nonprofit health systems must operate simultaneously to fulfill charitable obligations and meet competitive market requirements. A short phrase, "no margin, no mission" captures this tension. Managing conflicts between mission and margin can compromise organizational effectiveness. As a consequence, nonprofit health companies can become parochial, inefficient and/or facility-centric.

In 2007, the IRS revised its Form 990 to require hospitals to report charity care and other community benefit information, beginning in 2009. Community benefit reporting varies substantially across health companies. Some companies even include operating losses from treating Medicare and Medicaid patients in their calculations. Communities want to believe their hospitals and doctors act in their best interests at all times; however, it's hard to get accurate data to support that conclusion.

Harvard Professor Clay Christensen, the noted expert on market disruption, believes there are no inherent differences between non-profit and for-profit healthcare systems. Each provide the same services, operate within the same regulatory scheme and need to generate profits for long-term sustainability. It's also true that most consumers don't know whether their local hospital is nonprofit or for-profit. While true that nonprofit and for-profit healthcare systems essentially provide the same services, unique governance and operating characteristics inhibit the organizational effectiveness of nonprofit healthcare companies in the following areas: resource allocation, board accountability, major capital programs and ownership change.

Resource Allocation: Most nonprofit health systems experience public criticism when profit margins climb above 5 percent. Demands for charitable services increase and regulators question the need for tax-exempt status. As a result, most nonprofit health systems accept constrained profitability and tolerate greater operating inefficiencies. Labor is a hospital's largest expense. Payroll costs as a percentage of revenues are significantly higher for nonprofit hospitals. Nonprofit hospitals also are less efficient at managing supply costs and revenue collection. Some nonprofit proponents claim higher expense levels are necessary to fund mission-related activities. While true to some extent, less efficient operations explain most of the performance differential.

Board Accountability: There are over 3,000 nonprofit hospitals in the U.S. They are *private* enterprises, and their boards of trustees have minimal accountability to the broader body politic. Nonprofit boards tend to be large, voluntary and uncompensated. Often, local business leaders with vested interests in a hospital's operations serve as part of its governance structure. Not surprisingly, there is enormous variability in the caliber and capabilities of hospital governing boards. Many, perhaps most, nonprofit organizations lack engaged boards that hold management accountable for operational and strategic performance. As a result, management exercises disproportionate control over organizational decision-making. This compromises organizational effectiveness, particularly when managers conflate their individual interests with broader organizational goals.

Major Capital Programs: Return on investment (ROI) is the lifeblood of for-profit companies. Consistent failure to meet ROI targets leads to bankruptcy. Given their high cost, major capital programs must generate adequate returns to merit investment. Capital investment is more nuanced in nonprofit organizations. While nonprofit health companies forecast expected returns, their decision criteria focus more on market access and "affordability" than projected returns. A major capital program's affordability is primarily a function of organizational profitability, balance sheet strength and philanthropic support. Nonprofit boards also consider qualitative project-approval factors. Trustees believe their doctors, researchers and patients deserve state-of-the-art facilities *irrespective of whether or not there is sufficient market demand for them.*

Ownership Change: Nonprofit boards tend to be community-centric and committed to institutional preservation. Local bias poses incremental hurdles for organizations that want to consolidate hospitals. The currency in nonprofit hospital mergers is board seats and managerial positions. There isn't the clarity between buyer and seller that occurs in for-profit mergers and acquisitions. Mergers often fail because CEOs can't agree on who will lead the combined organization. Cultural and religious factors have disproportionate influence in negotiating agreements. Attachment makes it hard to relinquish control of local institutions even when it is financially and strategically beneficial to do so. Many trustees believe selling to out-of-town or for-profit buyers violates fiduciary responsibilities. Too often, boards demand reserve powers or super-majority decision-making that compromises organizational effectiveness. The unfortunate conclusion is that nonprofit hospital governance makes asset rationalization more difficult.

Houston is home to Texas Medical Center (TMC). TMC is the world's largest single-campus medical enterprise with 54 medicine-related institutions: 21 hospitals; eight specialty institutions; eight academic and research institutions; three medical schools; six nursing schools; and schools of dentistry, public health, pharmacy and other health-related practices. Despite all 54 institutions being nonprofit, Fields, the Houston physician I introduced in Chapter 2, asserts, "There is no such thing as nonprofit and for-profit. It is either non-tax or for-tax." Fields wonders why nonprofit organizations that receive tax breaks charge the same or more for healthcare services as for-profit hospitals. For the record, the highest grossing hospital in 2013 was the University of Pittsburgh Medical Center (UPMC) at $11.87 billion.[72] UPMC's nonprofit tax status amounts to tens of millions in foregone income, property and ad-valorem taxes. In March 2013, the city of Pittsburgh sued to remove UPMC's tax-exempt status, alleging the medical center should pay approximately $20 million annually in additional payroll taxes and property taxes.[73] Expect these types of battles to increase as cash-strapped governments seek new revenues, particularly since the number of Americans without health insurance is declining under Obamacare.

While for-profit and nonprofit hospitals provide the same services, they operate with different mythologies. The chart below illustrates their differing worldviews.

---

72 Molly Gamble, *100 Top-Grossing Hospitals in America,* Becker's Hospital Review, June 24, 2013

73 Elizabeth Rosenthal, *Benefits Questioned in Tax Breaks for Nonprofit Hospitals,* December 16, 2013, http://aid-us.org/benefits-questioned-in-tax-breaks-for-nonprofit-hospitals

Healthcare Culture Clash
Non-Profit vs. For-Profit Delivery

Non-profit Mythology	For-profit Mythology
For profit providers are: • Greedy • Unconcerned with quality • Answerable only to shareholders • Not sensitive to community needs	Non-profit providers are: • Over-staffed • Inefficient • Secretive • Small-minded
Non-profit Competitive Advantages	**For-profit Competitive Advantages**
• No taxes • No dividends to shareholders • Lower-cost financing • Strong community support • Less market scrutiny	• Equity capital • Broad range of financing vehicles • Greater access capital • More focused operating profile • More expansive partnership structures

This is increasingly a debate without distinctions. As industry consolidation continues and health companies take more health insurance risk, the lines between for-profit and nonprofit activities increasingly blur. Given their different operating orientations, market-based metrics make it more challenging for nonprofit organizations to justify the substantial subsidies they receive. Nonprofit healthcare's societal compact is beginning to unravel.

Washington Roulette

Maintaining regulatory privileges for health companies requires commitment and lots of money. According to *Modern Healthcare,* "Healthcare special interests spend roughly half a billion dollars a year to influence the regulatory and policymaking process, making them one of the largest lobbying presences in the nation's capital."[74]

---

74 Paul Demko, *How healthcare's Washington lobbying machine gets the job done,* July 18, 2014

By mid-July of the 2014 mid-term elections, the American Hospital Association's PAC had already spent nearly $1 million on political ads. That was three months before the election. "That's roughly as much as the association spent on radio and TV advertising during the entire 2012 election cycle," according to the PAC's filings with the Federal Election Commission.[75]

The 2010 census data revealed that metropolitan Washington, D.C. had seven of the ten wealthiest counties in the United States. That is not good news. The principal business in Washington is nudging federal governmental expenditures in clients' interests. When it comes to healthcare, a small regulatory change can determine success or failure, winners and losers. This is why health companies spend hundreds of millions to influence government decision-making. They're good at it, and reap benefits for themselves at the expense of American taxpayers.

In 2012, the Centers for Medicare and Medicaid Services (CMS) released new rates for hospital and non-hospital radiation-therapy treatments. CMS proposed increasing hospital rates by 9 percent and slashing non-hospital rates by over 20 percent. Each side employed highly educated, well-paid researchers to produce detailed position papers supporting their cases and lobbied relevant officials, legislators and staff. Between the associations, the government and think tanks, lobbying for radiation-therapy reimbursement created enough activity to employ at least 50 professionals with advanced degrees. This is the economic equivalent of digging a hole and refilling it. The task requires work, skill and perseverance but doesn't generate incremental value.

Walden Pond Revisited

The U.S. health system costs too much and delivers sub-par outcomes because it combines centralized reimbursement analytics with ferocious private-market pursuit of formulaic reimbursement payments. This is healthcare's productivity paradox. Activity-based, fee-for-service payment is its weapon of mass value destruction.

---

75 *id.*

In 1845, writer and philosopher Henry David Thoreau moved to a small cabin on Walden Pond in Concord, MA, to "live deliberately," experience the "essential facts of life" and learn "what they had to teach."[76] Like a stone thrown into his Walden Pond, Thoreau's observations on nature, minimalism, politics and and civil disobedience have rippled through the ages and influenced leaders from Gandhi to Frank Lloyd Wright to Martin Luther King.

Thoreau believed that activity without creating value was purposeless. Thoreau made this point quite elegantly in an 1857 letter to a friend,

> *It is not enough to be industrious; so are the ants. What are you industrious about?*[77]

American healthcare is too "industrious" in its pursuit of revenues. As currently constituted, it exerts an enormous drag on the overall U.S. economy.

---

76 Henry David Thoreau, <u>Walden or A Life in the Woods</u>, *Where I Lived, and What I Lived For*, 1854

77 Henry David Thoreau, Letter to Harrison Blake, November 16, 1857

CHAPTER 4

IT'S A DRAG

We cannot continue. Our pension costs and health care costs for our employees are going to bankrupt this city.
MICHAEL BLOOMBERG, MAYOR OF NEW YORK CITY

Health care costs are eating the Defense Department alive.
ROBERT GATES, SECRETARY OF DEFENSE

If you find yourself in a hole, stop digging.
WILL RODGERS

In early 2004, I attended an intimate Global Connections dinner sponsored by the Chicago Council on Global Affairs. William Lewis was the evening's featured speaker. Lewis was the founding director of the McKinsey Global Institute (the Institute), launched in 1990 to study globalization and assess its impact on the world economy. Lewis spoke that evening about his just-published book, *The Power of Productivity*, which explores the relative wealth of national economies. Lewis' methodology for assessing national productivity and wealth provides a powerful way to evaluate U.S. healthcare's relative effectiveness.

The McKinsey Institute assesses a country's economy by studying its individual industry sectors, such as retailing, manufacturing and telecommunications. In essence, national economies are the sum of these industry sectors and national wealth reflects their relative productivity. The Institute's approach enables it to compare the strengths and weaknesses of industrial sectors across nations. This differs from typical macroeconomic analysis that seeks correlation within massive data sets to explain economic behaviors. As any statistician will explain, correlation does not equal causation. It expresses opinion. In contrast, the Institute's industry-specific approach identifies causal factors influencing the performance of individual economies, e.g. Japan's mom and pop retailers are significantly less productive (as measured by sales, turnover and inventory costs) than America's big box retailers. Several key insights emerge from the Institute's "bottom-up" analytic methodology:

- National wealth is a function of productivity. The core metric for measuring wealth is per capita GNP (Gross National Product) adjusted for purchasing equivalency. Higher productivity enables higher compensation and greater consumption. Together they stimulate incremental economic activity and wealth creation. Using productivity-based analytics enables the institute to explain the wealth disparity among nations where conventional macroeconomic explanations fail.

- Unfettered consumerism drives markets toward value creation spurred by continuous productivity improvement. Consumers maximize their purchasing power and increase their wealth by rewarding companies that deliver desirable goods and services at the lowest prices.

- Inefficient industry sectors create a drag on national economies.

- Economies prosper when more productive enterprises replace less productive ones. Capitalism's creative/destructive cycle creates turnover as consumption patterns reward more efficient producers of goods and services. Underlying this regenerative process is an implicit belief that competitive markets use labor and capital more efficiently.

- Governmental support (e.g. through regulation, favorable tax policies and subsidies) of underperforming industry sectors reduces national productivity and wealth. It tilts the competitive playing field in favor of inefficient incumbents and stifles innovation.

The United States ranks among the world's richest countries as measured by GNP per capita.[78] America's impressive wealth comes despite a very expensive and inefficient healthcare system. According to World Bank data, healthcare consumed almost 18 percent of the U.S. economy in 2012, over 50 percent higher than France (11.7 percent), the next highest-spender among large developed economies. Yet, Americans are less healthy than their peers in almost all developed nations. The U.S. spends more and gets less. Using the McKinsey Global Institute's analytic framework, it's clear that the U.S. healthcare sector exacts a toll on the nation's economy. Employing the same logic, a more productive U.S. healthcare system would generate positive economic growth and wealth creation.

This chapter explores the negative drag healthcare exerts on the U.S. economy. It quantifies the inefficiency and details its effect on real wage growth for average American workers. Inefficient healthcare spending depresses real wages, crowds out investment in productive industries, explodes government budgets and reduces America's living standard.

---

78 World Bank data

America's "Adjustment" Challenge: Smaller Slice of a Bigger Pie

The global economy is experiencing unprecedented redistribution between developed and developing nations. As chronicled by the World Bank, global GNP expanded from $32.2 trillion in 2001 to $69.9 trillion in 2011. U.S. GNP grew 46 percent during this same period, but the American share of global GNP shrank from 32 to 22 percent.

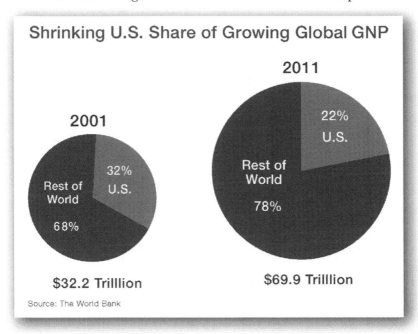

Shrinking U.S. Share of Growing Global GNP

2001

32% U.S.

Rest of World

68%

$32.2 Trilllion

2011

22% U.S.

Rest of World

78%

$69.9 Trilllion

Source: The World Bank

This economic repositioning occurred within a short 10-year period. With roughly 4.5 percent of the world's population, it's logical that the U.S. percentage of the global economy will shrink as developing economies, particularly China and India, advance. An expanding global economy is good news. New markets for American products create new jobs in export-oriented industries but achieving competitive advantage in a "flat world" is hard. The U.S. no longer has the luxury of being so wealthy that it can absorb the cost of underperforming industries and inefficient government programs. To maintain our living standard, the U.S. must excel within a much larger, more efficient global economy. Coming to terms with this new economic reality will force Americans to rethink tax policy, infrastructure investment, defense spending, social welfare benefits, education and, of course, healthcare.

A more efficient, globalizing economy presents two profound challenges for the U.S. healthcare system. First, the system itself must become more competitive. It needs to cost less while delivering comparable or superior treatment outcomes. To the extent the U.S. healthcare system is less productive than healthcare systems in other countries, it exerts a negative drag on the overall U.S. economy. Secondly, America's obesity and chronic disease epidemics weaken labor force productivity. In a globalizing economy, the U.S. requires a healthier, fitter workforce to advance national living standards.

U.S. Healthcare's $1 Trillion Productivity Problem

The World Bank classifies countries as low, middle or high income based on per capital GNP. The U.S. stands among the world leaders with a 2013 per capita GNP of $53,042. Despite this robust figure, America's costly and inefficient healthcare system prevents the country from achieving even higher prosperity.

The Organisation of Economic Co-operation and Development ("OECD") collects comparative healthcare data from 34 of the world's most advanced economies. By contrasting America's healthcare expenditure, life expectancy and obesity statistics with the OECD's five highest per capita healthcare spenders,[79] several key insights emerge.

On a relative basis, the U.S. spends over $1.1 trillion more for equivalent healthcare than this five-country OECD cohort. Overspending on healthcare steals investment from more productive industries and reduces consumers' purchasing power. The non-medical costs of shorter life expectancy, obesity and chronic disease are manifold. They include lost human potential, lower worker productivity and non-compensated caregiving. The following analysis chronicles the magnitude of America's underperforming health sector:

---

79 Austria, Canada, Germany, Norway, Switzerland. Excludes the United States.

- **Per capita total expenditure on health:** The U.S. spent $7,662 per capita on health expenditure in 2012. The OECD's next five highest-expenditure countries (Austria, Canada, Germany, Norway and Switzerland) spent $4,275. That is $3,327 less per capita than the U.S. That aggregates to just over $1 trillion of waste when multiplied by the current U.S. population of 320 million. Despite lower per capita spending, 2012 life expectancy at birth for these countries is almost three years longer (81.6 years vs. 78.7 years) than it is in the United States.

In their 2012 *JAMA* article,[80] Berwick and Hackbarth identified between $558 billion and $1.264 trillion in wasteful healthcare spending that occurs each year. They place the types of wasteful spending into the following six categories: 1) failures in care delivery, $102 billion to $154 billion; 2) failures of care coordination, $25 billion to $45 billion; 3) overtreatment, $158 billion to $226 billion; 4) administrative complexity, $107 billion to $389 billion; 5) pricing failures, $84 billion to $178 billion; and 6) fraud and abuse, $82 billion to $272 billion.

However it's calculated, there is enormous waste embedded in U.S. healthcare delivery. Berwick and Hackbarth observe that eliminating waste (i.e. non-value added practices) yields meaningful healthcare savings faster and more sustainably than reducing services and/or payments.[81]

- **Measured obese population:** The U.S. has the world's largest percentage of obese adults by a considerable margin. In 2012, the U.S. adult-obesity percentage was 35.5 percent. By contrast, the adult-obesity percentage (14.6 percent) for the OECD's highest healthcare spenders was 58.6 percent lower. Obesity generates non-healthcare costs that

---

80 Author's note: please see Berwick's original article for sources used to calculate per-category waste

81 Berwick and Hackbarth, *"Eliminating Waste in U.S. Health Care,"* JAMA. 2012;307(14):1513-1516; Published online March 14, 2012. doi:10.1001/jama.20;

reduce America's economic vitality. In 2011, the Society of Actuaries issued a seminal report, *Obesity and its Relation to Mortality and Morbidity Costs.*[82] The report estimates that obesity annually costs the U.S. approximately $148 billion in lost productivity due to higher death rates and disability payments. This generates a per capita cost of $461 ($148 billion divided by 320 million people). Assuming similar levels of non-healthcare obesity costs, the U.S. spends $270 more per capita than the OECD cohort because of its significantly higher obesity rate.

Other non-medical costs related to obesity include non-compensated time for caregiving and even increased fuel costs. Engineer Sheldon Jackson of the University of Illinois estimates that American obesity increases annual fuel consumption by approximately 1 billion gallons. Carrying that extra weight steals $4 billion annually from household and corporate budgets.

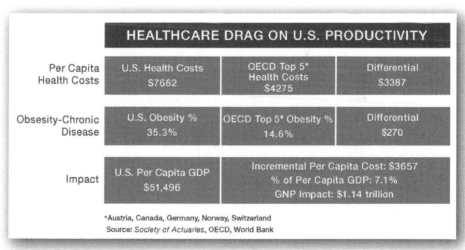

HEALTHCARE DRAG ON U.S. PRODUCTIVITY

Per Capita Health Costs	U.S. Health Costs $7662	OECD Top 5* Health Costs $4275	Differential $3387
Obsesity-Chronic Disease	U.S. Obesity % 35.3%	OECD Top 5* Obesity % 14.6%	Differential $270
Impact	U.S. Per Capita GDP $51,496	Incremental Per Capita Cost: $3657 % of Per Capita GDP: 7.1% GNP Impact: $1.14 trillion	

*Austria, Canada, Germany, Norway, Switzerland
Source: *Society of Actuaries*, OECD, World Bank

In America, higher per capita healthcare expenditure and non-medical costs related to sub-par health outcomes total $3,657. This

---

82 https://www.soa.org/News-and-Publications/Newsroom/Press Releases/New-Society-of-Actuaries-Study-Estimates-$300-Billion-Economic-Cost-Due-to-Overweight-and-Obesity.aspx

translates into an unnecessary $1.14 trillion increase in national healthcare costs. Even a country as wealthy as the United States cannot sustain this level of drag in today's competitive global economy. Over time, redirecting inefficient healthcare spending into more productive enterprises will enhance national competitiveness, create wealth and increase household incomes.

A Mighty Anchor: Healthcare's Drag on Federal Spending

In his insightful book, *After the Music Stopped,* about the financial crisis and its aftermath, noted Princeton economist Alan S. Blinder examines the 2012 Congressional Budget Office's ("CBO") long-term forecast and concludes controlling healthcare spending is the U.S. government's central fiscal challenge. The forecast projects 75 years into the future, through 2087. This isn't really a forecast but an extrapolation of current spending patterns.

During this time period, interest payments to service the national debt soar. Revenues at current tax rates are woefully insufficient to cover government spending on defense, healthcare, social security and all other non-interest expenditures. The government terms this *primary spending.* As a result, the increasing primary-spending deficit in combination with increasing interest payments push the overall national debt ever upward to almost 80 percent of GNP from 20 percent today. Even more terrifying, increasing healthcare expenditure fundamentally redistributes primary spending in the following two ways:

1. Primary spending rises to greater than 30 percent of GNP, fueled by increasing healthcare expenditure.

2. All non-healthcare primary spending (defense, social security and everything else) *declines* to just over 10 percent of GNP. By the end of the forecast period, healthcare is *double* the cost of all other governmental activities combined.

Blinder concludes his analysis with this providential warning:

The implication for budgeteers is clear: If we can somehow solve the health care cost problem, we will also solve the long-run deficit problem. But if we can't control health care costs, the long-run deficit problem is insoluble. Simple, right? Impossible? We'd better hope not.[83]

Blinder's analysis focuses only on the federal government's healthcare expenditures. Private employers, individuals and state governments confront the same runaway healthcare costs. Published in October 2014, CMS's 2013–2023 national health-expenditure forecast projects that overall health spending will exceed $5 trillion and consume almost 20 percent of national GNP (vs. $3 trillion and almost 18 percent of GNP today). Wow. How bad can it get? If you believe these forecasts, it could get really, really, really bad.

Healthcare's Toll on Average Workers

The U.S. boasts the world's most productive workforce. High worker productivity creates wealth and sustains high living standards. The U.S. outspends all countries on healthcare services. Logic suggests that generous health spending enhances national productivity, competitiveness and wealth creation. The opposite is true. As just presented, America's health status is lower than that in other developed economies. The costs and ineffectiveness of the U.S. healthcare system fall disproportionately on middle- and low-income families, who experience this burden in the form of stagnant wages and increasing health disparity.

Historically, there has been a tight correlation between improving productivity and median household income. This is wealth creation in action. The benefits of higher productivity went directly to American workers through increased wages. This historic pattern changed for the worse as America entered the new millennium. The chart below details the sobering trend.

---

83 Alan Binder, *After the Music Stopped*, Chapter 15

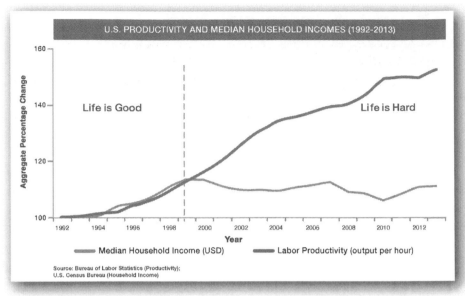

On an inflation-adjusted basis (using 2010 dollars), U.S. median household income peaked in 1999 at $53,250 and has declined slowly since then to $49,450. During the same period, U.S. productivity continued its upward march. While two recessions and technological advances have influenced this divergence, globalization has been its driving force. The expansion of the global workforce by over 2 billion individuals has diminished labor's value in lower-skilled occupations. Overall, Americans have struggled to maintain current living standards.

Unfortunately, increasing health insurance premiums also have contributed to wage stagnation. The *2011 Health Benefits Report* from the Kaiser Family Foundation (KFF) estimates that health insurance premiums increased three times faster than workers' earnings between 1999 and 2011. The average 2014 health insurance premium for a family plan was substantial: $16,834 with the employee paying $4,823. It's a double whammy on wages. Workers pay more for health insurance, decreasing out-of-pocket spending. Meanwhile, escalating health insurance costs limit employers' ability to increase wages. The net result: Workers pay more for health insurance and receive lower pay increases because employers are also paying more for employee health insurance. Lowering healthcare costs would translate into lower insurance premiums, more take-home pay and more out-of-pocket spending money. Escalating healthcare costs will continue depressing workers' incomes.

The KFF survey estimates that employer-sponsored insurance plans cover approximately 149 million non-elderly Americans.[84] The survey's good news is average 2014 premium increases rose only slightly more than wages (3 percent vs. 2.3 percent). Unfortunately, insurance premiums spiked upward in 2015 and 2016 by 5 to 6 percent on average.[85] This is not good news for average workers.

There's more bad news for workers. Employees' out-of-pocket healthcare costs have increased as employers have shifted costs to employees through higher deductibles and co-pays. Moreover, individual enrollees in high-deductible health plans (including Obamacare enrollees) means more Americans are paying an increasing percentage of their healthcare costs. Not only is the amount of household income available for healthcare expenses shrinking, the remaining portion of income actually buys less care. In 2014, consumers could afford 15 percent less healthcare than in 2000 due to rising healthcare costs and stagnant wages.[86]

While competitive pricing in electronics and clothing has helped American households manage family finances, the opposite is true in healthcare. In a clever post-Thanksgiving analysis of healthcare costs, Scott Andes and Mark Muro from the Brookings Institution calculated how much less Black Friday shoppers could buy if electronic and clothing prices had risen at the same rate as healthcare spending. Their unsurprising conclusion: Consumers would buy 52 percent less clothing, 78 percent fewer computers and 40 percent fewer video games.[87]

---

84   *2014 Employer Health Benefits Survey*, The Henry J. Kaiser Family Foundation, September 10, 2014; http://kff.org/report-section/ehbs-2014-summary-of-findings/

85   http://www.npr.org/sections/health-shots/2015/06/12/413073921/health-insurance-premiums-will-go-up-in-2016-but-by-how-much

86   Scott Andes and Mark Muro, *When will We Get Black Friday Deals for Health Care?* The Avenue, Brookings Institute, December 30, 2014; http://www.brookings.edu/blogs/the-avenue/posts/2014/1#recent/

87   *Ibid.*

According to the Bureau of Labor Statistics, most of the major components of household spending decreased in 2013; the only major components to increase were healthcare (2.1 percent), housing (1.5 percent), and transportation (0.1 percent).[88] Remarkably, the U.S. achieves high productivity despite its underperforming, high-cost healthcare system. Imagine the boost to U.S. productivity if the healthcare system delivered outcomes and costs equivalent to those achieved by other advanced economies.

Healthcare Pathologies

U.S. healthcare is sick. Its symptoms include excessively high costs, suboptimal treatment outcomes and sub-par health status. Collectively, they weaken the U.S. economy and threaten its long-term vitality. Pathology is the study of disease. It isolates the sources of disease, so researchers can investigate cures. U.S. healthcare has three primary pathologies: information asymmetry, process-based payment and inadequate care management.

#1: Information Asymmetry

This occurs in transactions where either the buyer or seller has better information than the other party. In markets where asymmetric information exists, bad outcomes and market failure result. Millions of healthcare transactions occur each day in America. In the vast majority of these transactions, care providers (doctors and nurses) have more information than patients. Where information asymmetry goes, market failure is sure to follow. A Nobel-Prize-winning analysis reveals why.

As an assistant professor at Berkley in 1967, George Akerlof wrote an article, "The Market for 'Lemons': Quality, Uncertainty and the Market Mechanism." Highlighting used-car sales, Akerlof's 13-page paper examined why market failure occurs when used-car sellers have more information than used-car buyers. Several economic journals rejected Akerlof's paper referencing its triviality and judgment errors.

---

88 http://www.bls.gov/news.release/cesan.nr0.htm.

Their mistake. With his article's 1970 publication by *The Quarterly Journal of Economics,* Akerlof expanded market analysis beyond the concept of perfect competition to include powerful exogenous variables. Today, economic scholars recognize Akerlof's seminal contribution to modern economic theory and have cited his paper in over 8,500 academic articles. Fittingly, "The Market for 'Lemons'" won Akerlof the 2001 Nobel Prize in Economic Sciences.

Akerlof begins his analysis by observing the gaping price differences between new and used cars. Going beyond "the joy of being a new-car owner," he explores the market forces driving this pricing disparity. When an individual purchases a new car, neither the buyer nor the seller knows whether the vehicle is a good car or a lemon. That reality emerges over time as the new owner drives the car. When ready to sell the car, the new owner knows whether it is a good car or a lemon. A prospective buyer knows only that some cars are good and some are lemons. This creates an asymmetric information relationship between the car's seller and any prospective buyer. In essence, the seller has inside information that distorts the negotiating process. Let's assume a good car is worth $10,000; a lemon is worthless, and there's a 50 percent probability that this car is a lemon. Here's what happens:

- The expected value of the car is $5,000 (50 percent times $10,000);

- The owner of a good car requires $10,000 to sell the car;

- There is no mechanism for the owner of a good car to demonstrate its worth to a prospective buyer;

- The owner of a lemon would be delighted to receive $5,000 for the car;

- A buyer will never pay more than $5,000 (and probably less) given the 50 percent probability of purchasing a lemon;

- Given information asymmetry, the owner of a good car cannot find buyers willing to purchase the car for its $10,000 value and does not sell the car; and

- As sellers of good cars leave the market, only lemons remain available for purchase.

Here's how Akerlof explains asymmetric market failure:

...bad cars drive out the good because they sell at the same price as good cars... the bad cars sell at the same price as good cars since it is impossible for a buyer to tell the difference between a good and a bad car; only the seller knows.[89]

Inside information compromises the symmetry required for proper market functioning. Sellers become predatory. Buyers become defensive. Potential transactions dissolve. Given these dynamics, it's not surprising that used-car salesmen have achieved iconic status in American culture as unscrupulous, fast-talking charlatans. As Akerlof observes, "dishonest dealings tend to drive honest dealings out of the marketplace."[90]

Preventable bad outcomes are healthcare's lemons. Asymmetric information exchange between providers and patients contributes to medical errors, overtreatment and undertreatment in the following three ways:

1. Doctors and other care providers overwhelm patients with information and deliver unnecessary treatments;

2. Doctors and other care providers fail to provide necessary care and/or make preventable mistakes (e.g. prescribe a harmful drug); and

---

89 George Akerlof, *The Market for "Lemons": Quality Uncertainty and the Market Mechanism*, The Quarterly Journal of Economics, Volume 84, Issue 3 (August, 1970), page 490.
90 Akerlof, *The Market for "Lemons*, Page 495.

3. Uninformed patients demand unnecessary treatments based on anecdotal experience, social-media conversations or Internet research.

In the same way that used-car buyers question a seller's motivation, Americans increasingly question whether providers act in patients' best interests. They turn first to websites, not doctors, to find answers for their medical questions. They exhibit higher levels of distrust toward providers. Negative media coverage, like *Time Magazine's* 2013 "Bitter Pill" cover story, fuels consumer distrust. Healthcare's inability to execute even-handed medical transactions increases consumer distrust, distorts market behavior and contributes to healthcare's upward spiraling costs.

#2:*Process-Based Payment*

As discussed in Chapter 3, fee-for-service payment perversely rewards doctors and hospitals for services performed rather than outcomes delivered. At its worst, the system pays providers for medical errors, incremental care related to those errors and care required to correct the medical errors. Providers' intense focus on optimizing revenue has atrophied their ability to understand and manage entire episodes of care. Healthcare's inability to offer fixed prices and performance guarantees for routine treatments limits accountability, increases costs and delivers inferior outcomes.

Fee-for-service reimbursement is a ludicrous payment method for healthcare services. It is the equivalent of paying individually for each component of a car's manufacturing process rather than buying the whole car for a single price. Harvard Business School Professor Michael Porter argues for value-based healthcare, emphasizing the economic and clinical risks of an entrenched process-over-outcome operating orientation. Porter observes the following:

> *Without understanding the true costs of care for patient conditions, much less how costs are related to outcomes, health care organizations are flying blind in deciding how to improve processes and redesign care.*[91]

91   Michael E. Porter and Thomas H. Lee, *The Big Idea: The Strategy That Will Fix Healthcare*, Harvard Business Review, October 2013, p. 12

A by-product of process-based payment is exceptionally high administrative costs (insurance overhead, hospital administration, nursing home administration and physicians' billing and overhead expenses.) In 2010, the Institute of Medicine (IOM) reported that the United States spent $361 billion annually on administrative costs. As such, Americans spent two and three-times as much on healthcare administrative costs as they did on heart disease and cancer treatments respectively.[92] The IOM characterized more than half of healthcare costs as unnecessary.

The principal driver of high administrative costs is the health system's practice of charging different prices for the same procedures. Armies of administrative professionals bill, approve, pay, challenge, defend and police claims. They navigate a convoluted path of calculating the proper bill for each procedure and paying each provider their contracted rates. Errors abound. The bills themselves are often unintelligible and bear little correlation to the final payment. Moreover, patients bear ultimate legal responsibility for payment despite insurance coverage.[93] This creates confusion, multiple billing cycles, deep consumer frustration and delays in billing and payment processes. Process-based payment is a cancer that prevents providers from designing and delivering value-driven healthcare treatments to patients.

#3: Inadequate Care Management
Despite remarkable medical advances, Americans are sicker today than ever. Addressing obesity and the chronic disease it spawns is America's principal health challenge. A factsheet by the Partnership to Fight Chronic Disease details the magnitude and impact on American health and healthcare costs. One hundred thirty-three million Americans have chronic disease. It accounts for 81 percent of hospital

---

92 David Cutler, Ph.D., Elizabeth Wikler, B.A., and Peter Basch, M.D. *Reducing Administrative Costs and Improving the Health Care System,* N Engl J Med 2012; 367:1875-1878November 15, 2012DOI: http://www.nejm.org/doi/full/10.1056/NEJMp120971110.1056/NEJMp1209711

93 *Redefining Competition in Health Care,* Michael E. Porter and Elizabeth Olmsted Teisberg, Harvard Business Review, June 2004.

admissions, 91 percent of prescriptions and 76 percent of physician visits. As chronic disease swells, healthcare spending climbs, national productivity declines and income inequality expands.

Unfortunately, the U.S. system lacks the care management capabilities to fight obesity and diminish chronic disease. Fee-for-service payment favors acute treatments over prevention and chronic disease management. There is ample funding in the system to amputate a foot but little to manage the diabetes that led to the amputation. As a result, U.S. healthcare lacks the capabilities needed to proactively manage the care of large populations. Providers focus on treatments and seek payment from government and commercial payers. Commercial payers largely process claims on behalf of self-funded employers. Medicare pays for treatments in accordance with predetermined fee schedules. The system's costs swell, in large measure, because the system's providers have not developed the tools, business models and expertise to build relationship-based primary care practices that promote wellness, prevent chronic disease and treat at-risk patients before they require hospitalization.

The 1990s: As Good as It Gets?

As the 1990s began, President George H.W. Bush was riding an 80 percent approval rating fueled by the Soviet Union's demise and by America's decisive victory in the First Gulf War. His re-election in 1992 seemed preordained. A mild recession created a window for little-known Arkansas governor Bill Clinton to defeat Bush. In his own words, Clinton "focused like a laser beam" on the economy. James Carville, Clinton's colorful campaign manager, posted the now famous "It's the economy, stupid" sign in the campaign's war room to keep staff on point. Clinton's eight years in office ignited partisan conflict but also coincided with strong economic growth, deficit reduction, job creation and real wage increases.

During Clinton's 8-year term (1993–2000),[94] healthcare expenditures remained constant at roughly 13.4 percent of GNP. Since

---

94 Committee on Ways and Means, Medicare and Healthcare Chartbook, 106th congress

Medicare's passage in 1965, this is the only sustained period when healthcare expenditures didn't grow faster than the overall economy. Is it coincidental that job growth and real-wage increases correlated with moderating health expenditures? The answer is: No, it's not.

Before taking office, President-elect Clinton prioritized economic growth. In December 1992, he convened an economic conference in Little Rock to assess the state of the American economy. Middle- and lower-income workers were vulnerable. Real average hourly earnings were lower than they had been when President Regan took office in 1981. During the same period, healthcare costs had risen more than 20 percent.[95] At Clinton's economic summit, Ford Motor president Harold Poling complained about rising health insurance costs, "Ford spends as much on healthcare as it does on steel. Health care providers are our largest supplier."[96]

Under Hillary Clinton's leadership, the Clinton Administration made heathcare reform its top legislative priority. Despite a massive task force, a fierce public relations campaign and strong majorities in both houses of Congress, "Hillarycare" never won public support. Its enabling legislation died in a House committee chaired by Michigan Democrat John Dingell, a passionate supporter of healthcare reform. Led by Newt Gingrich and his "Contract with America," Republicans made the 1994 mid-term elections a referendum on big government. They won a sweeping mandate that included control of the U.S. House of Representatives for the first time since the Eisenhower administration.

After Clinton's healthcare reform program collapsed, enrollment in health maintenance organizations ("HMOs") skyrocketed. To keep costs under control, HMOs created limited provider networks that employed primary care physicians as gatekeepers to guide care and limit unnecessary treatments. HMOs helped moderate healthcare expenditures throughout the 1990s, but their cost-control mechanisms were

---

95 *"Power of Progressive Economics: The Clinton Years,* Center for American Progress, October 28, 2011

96 *THE TRANSITION; Excerpts From Clinton's Conference on State of the Economy,* The New York Times, December 2015; http://www.nytimes.com/1992/12/15/us/the-transition-excerpts-from-clinton-s-conference-on-state-of-the-economy.html

crude. Delays, denials and voluminous paperwork were routine. Some HMOs even paid bonuses to gatekeepers to encourage care denials.

Consumer frustration mounted and then exploded. In 1998, Actress Helen Hunt won an Oscar for her performance in *As Good as It Gets*. Hunt plays a single mother whose son suffers from chronic asthma. In a pivotal scene, Hunt's character launches into a profanity-laden rant against HMOs. Audiences in movie theaters across the country broke into spontaneous applause. Just like that, HMOs largely vanished. As President George W. Bush entered the Oval Office in 2001, healthcare costs began another upward climb. By 2011, healthcare consumed 17.9 percent of GNP.

During the 1990s, the U.S. experienced sustained prosperity, job growth and real income increases. Most economists attribute these achievements to productivity improvements created by the tech boom and big box retailing. Restrained healthcare spending rarely receives mention as a positive contributor; yet, lower health insurance premiums enabled workers to put more cash in their pockets and improve their living standard. As companies reduced their healthcare spending, they were able to redirect resources into more productive enterprises that stimulated innovation, improved profitability and increased workers' take-home pay.

Unfortunately, the moderate healthcare spending in the 1990s came primarily from care rationing, not better care management. For too many, the lessons learned from the 1990s were that healthcare costs are uncontrollable, and that it's politically dangerous to restrict access to healthcare services.

Are America's healthcare choices limited to either runaway healthcare spending or care rationing? Is this as good as it gets? Of course not. Inefficient healthcare delivery is not America's destiny. U.S. healthcare is highly fragmented and contains correctable inefficiencies. It's time for consumers and the marketplace to demand greater value. It's time for health companies to meet societal demands for better, more convenient healthcare services at lower prices.

SECTION II: Align

LIFE, LIBERTY AND THE PURSUIT OF VALUE

The purpose of business is to create and keep customers.

PETER DRUCKER

- Chapter 5: Value Rules
- Chapter 6: Data is as Data Does
- Chapter 7: It's the Customer, Stupid!

Management guru Peter Drucker's observation that customers are the lifeblood of business is a non-sequitur for hospital executives. Most don't even like the word "customer." When they pursue alignment, it's almost always with physicians. And why not? Physicians generate hospital revenues through diagnostic services, treatments and surgeries. Without physician referrals, hospitals would be out of business. As a consequence, established business concepts relating to price, value and customer satisfaction have limited relevance in healthcare operations.

Physicians, in turn, receive reimbursement payments for services provided irrespective of whether their treatments lead to positive health outcomes. Physicians are dependent upon hospitals to provide facilities and services that support their treatment activities. Treatments lead to payments that lead to more treatments. This circular productivity paradox spins ever upward, generating more revenues for the medical-industrial complex and increasing its $1trillion drag on the U.S. economy.

Breaking this cycle requires hospitals and doctors to end their artificial economic relationship and meet market demands for better, more affordable and more convenient healthcare services. They must overcome counter-productive behaviors to deliver higher-value, customer-focused healthcare services. This is the essence of *sustaining innovation*. Healthcare companies must improve core competencies to succeed in post-reform healthcare. This means listening to patients, providing appropriate treatments in lowest-cost settings, reducing medical errors and improving care transitions. To remain competitive, physicians and hospitals must align with patient and employer needs.

Section II, *Align,* tackles sustaining innovation, the massive challenge of aligning the delivery system's performance with market demands for better and more convenient healthcare at lower prices.

- Chapter 5, ***Value Rules***, describes how winning healthcare providers differentiate their services through value-based delivery (better health outcomes at lower costs).

- Chapter 6, **Data Is as Data Does**, explores healthcare data's ups and downs. Getting the data right is essential to delivering value-based care. Big data has enormous potential to advance care delivery but comes with significant risks.

- Chapter 7, *It's the Customer, Stupid,* details how unfettered consumerism will drive U.S. healthcare toward value creation.

Consumer spending drives the U.S. economy. At 68 percent of GNP in 2013, U.S. consumer spending is substantially higher than other advanced economies.[97] Consumer consumption patterns change industries. Despite reported support for mom and pop hardware stores, American consumers put them out of business by flocking to big box retailers, like Walmart, that offered more selection and lower prices.

To date, American healthcare has resisted consumerism's power to reshape supply and demand relationships. Regardless of healthcare's inherent flaws, most Americans support the current delivery model and like their nurses, doctors and hospitals. Since employers and the government have largely paid for healthcare, consumers have focused more on access to healthcare services than their cost.

In contrast, consumers revolted against managed-care insurance plans and their implicit care rationing in the 1990s. Freed from managed care's cost restraints, American healthcare spending regained its profligate character, digesting an ever-larger percentage of the national economy.

While consumer behavior is understandable, it is surprising how little value employers have demanded from doctors, hospitals and health insurers. Employers complain about high healthcare costs but tolerate the never-ending cost increases. Rather than becoming better purchasers of healthcare services, employers have largely passed healthcare's increased costs to their customers and their employees.

---

97   Source: World Bank Data

Passive consumer and employer behavior in the face of rising healthcare expenditures is un-American and won't continue. Pursuing value is as American as pursuing happiness. Value rules. In the long run, this American character trait will prevail over healthcare's artificial economics and embedded inefficiencies.

CHAPTER 5

VALUE RULES

Price is what you pay. Value is what you get.
WARREN BUFFETT

For over a decade I've plodded up and down the Chicago lake-front with the same group of idiotic runners. Through wind, sun, snow and rain we babble about anything that comes to mind. There isn't much we don't know about one another. Except for mine, the jokes are terrible.

On consecutive weeks in 2015, two members of our running crew required emergency care. "Big Daddy" (he's not that big) smashed his foot running in Tokyo. The week after Big Daddy's ordeal, Paulie Wally had searing chest pain and momentarily collapsed. Big Daddy is in his early 50s and Paulie Wally is in his late 40s. These are their stories in their words. Both emerged from emergency care in great shape, but their experiences were dramatically different.

Toe Story: Big Daddy Runs Aground in Tokyo

So, I am in Tokyo and decide to go for an early-morning run. Two days earlier I had discovered a scenic route over a bridge and along a river toward Tokyo Bay. Nice trees, river on one side, monorail going by, paved path . . .

BAM!

My foot hits something and I go down, catching my fall on a guardrail. Almost fell into traffic. Turns out the thing I hit was a concrete base jutting out into the sidewalk.

One of my toes hurt. Bad.

I finish the run, get back to my hotel, take off my shoes and see that the middle toe on my right foot is swollen. By the end of day, my toe is seriously ugly. Quite swollen, a deep purple hue. Every step hurts. I am in Tokyo for another week. Is it broken? What do I do if it is?

So, here's my story of healthcare in a foreign land . . .

I call the number on the back of my credit card. Pretty quickly, the operator retrieves emergency medical information from the American Embassy. I go to their recommended website and find a number for an English-speaking service that identifies English-speaking health care providers. I call the service, which is free.

From that free call, I get the number of a doctor less than a mile from my current location (Midtown Tokyo). I call his office at 4:15 in the afternoon. Receptionist puts me directly through to the doctor. The doctor! Literally within 10 minutes of starting the process, I am speaking with an orthopedist in Japan who speaks English. He tells me to come in, gives me the address in a way he is sure the cab driver will understand. Cab driver (no English) understands. I am there by 4:30.

By 4:35, I'm meeting with the doctor—no long intake forms, doesn't even take my medical insurance card, doesn't even check ID. By 4:40, he's taking x-rays. Personally. In his office. By 4:45 we are looking at the x-rays together on his computer screen. No fracture. Just a bad bruise. He gives me a set of patches with some sort of analgesic for the pain ("it's fine," I tell him, but the patches really did help). I am back in a cab by 5. At dinner with clients by 5:30.

The bill? 13,000 Yen—about $107. I paid in cash. "Want a receipt?" "Nah," I say, "I can't imagine trying to get BlueCross/BlueShield to pay any of that. Or the massive headache involved in trying."

So in less than an hour from start to finish, I identify, speak with, get an appointment, register, get x-rayed, get diagnosed, get pain relief, pay the full and total cost and am on my way. For $107. All by a real doctor in the world's largest city where English is not commonly spoken.

Take that, American Healthcare System.

I don't have to imagine better healthcare. I just had it.

Big Daddy goes to Tokyo, crushes his toe and receives timely ortho-pedic care in the world's most expensive city. His total outlay was less than the cost of a nice sushi dinner. In Sweet Home Chicago, it was Paulie Wally's turn for emergency care.

Hospital America: Paulie Wally Checks In But Can Never Leave

> *I missed the group run last Saturday. Woke up in plenty of time and was looking forward to 8 miles. At 6:50 or so, my son called me to get him out of bed. I grabbed his clothes, pulled off his diaper and WHAM, my chest is on fire. Pain stretching from one side to the other. I get dizzy, drop to my knees and try to collect myself. At some point, I pass out. Pain is gone, but I'm out. My wife got up (I must have called her), found me on the floor and called an ambulance. Ambulance arrives quickly.*

> *The ambulance has a trainee kid, who takes vitals and then sticks me in an attempt to get an IV going. Swing and a miss. My vitals are great, I'm totally fine at this point, the only pain I'm feeling is the botched IV line. The real paramedic tells him to skip the line, they aren't going to give me nitro. The paramedic gives me 4 baby aspirin to chew on, just in case. The ambulance is the cleanest thing I've ever seen. I was its FIRST passenger.*

> *We head to the local hospital ER. ETA two minutes. They asked why my heart rate was so low—because I'm a distance runner. I sit in the ER for 2 hours, then receive one simple blood test. They were looking for heart attack markers and stroke markers. None found. They talked about giving me a stress test. No medicine given.*

> *Then they truck me to a room. Looks like I'm being admitted. The plan was to monitor my condition for 6 hours, draw blood again, make sure all was well and release me. They need 6 hours between tests because sometimes it takes that long for the markers to show up. But, the attending physician didn't want to be passive, so he set up an echo-cardiogram and CT scan. Both fine. Heart is strong, no leakage, no dissection in heart valves or neck (carotid).*

The attending then set up a Doppler Test on my neck to rule out that dissection possibility. It was close to 4pm at this point. I'm still calm, but starting to realize that getting home that night would be unlikely. All fine, if they had any real concerns. Did they? I was left to guess. The doctor who saw me at 10am and ordered the tests was the invisible man the rest of the day. No test results discussed. Still, not a drop of medicine administered.

They scheduled the Doppler Test, but the staff wasn't available to administer until Sunday. I'm overnight with no consultation and no explanation. Now I'm pretty unhappy. Next morning, still no updates from anyone. New nurse checks in, and I told her I needed to know my test and discharge schedule. "Oh, it's Sunday. We don't do Doppler Tests on Sunday." I kid you not.

This is when I became my own patient's rights advocate and demanded to see my doctor. Still no medicine administered, so I am certain everything is perfectly fine. Doctor comes in 2 hours later, tells me he is releasing me, no Doppler required. Wait, so I spent the night waiting for this obviously very important test (must be important if they won't release me, won't allow me to do it as outpatient, etc.), so important that the hospital doesn't have any staff to provide the test on the day it was ordered.... So important that, well, forget it, you don't need that test.

I'm positive I was kept overnight to fill an empty bed (in a private room, mind you!). I can't wait to see the bills for this. Probably 20k, 30k? Insured, of course, so not much skin of my back... But THIS is what is wrong with healthcare in America. 30 hours at the hospital to be released with NO findings, and NO required follow-up, for what could have been a 6 hour observation since the blood tests were sufficient to tell them what the Echo and CT and non-Doppler confirmed.

So what happened? I stretched a chest muscle and felt 30 seconds of pain. I spent 30 hours in the hospital ruling out heart and blood-clot concerns. Might as well have stubbed my toe.

Stopped by the fire station yesterday to give them a signed dollar bill to tape on the ambulance wall. FIRST CUSTOMER!

What/Who Gives?

For the last several months, Paulie Wally and I have been trying to figure out how much his unfortunate medical odyssey cost. His initial estimates were high. We still don't have final numbers, but hospital and physician charges approximate $18,250. Insurance has paid roughly $11,000. Paulie Wally has paid $550, including the full $300 cost (not sure why) for the echo-cardiogram. Had Paulie Wally not confronted his doctor on Sunday, he undoubtedly would have spent another night in the hospital and received the Doppler test on Monday. That would have added thousands of dollars to his already sky-high bill.

Like Paulie Wally, almost every American has a horrific healthcare story to share. Each one stains the industry's image. Patients aren't cash registers. Like Big Daddy's emergency care in Tokyo, patients deserve the right care at the right time in the right place at the right price. Value isn't ephemeral. It's as concrete as the guardrail base that smashed Big Daddy's foot.

Why Should Customers Buy Our Car?

James C. Tyree grew up a Chicago south-sider. He earned undergraduate and MBA degrees from Illinois State University. After graduation in 1980, he joined Chicago-based Mesirow Financial as a research assistant and never left. Ten years later he was president; then chairman and CEO in 1994. Under his leadership, Mesirow catapulted from a financial boutique to a major investment house. How did Tyree push his company toward greatness? By constantly asking himself and Mesirow employees, "Why should customers buy our car?"

During an offsite retreat in 2010 for my investment bank, Tyree made a compelling presentation on organizational transformation to my firm's leadership team. After his presentation, our CEO asked Tyree to comment on changing business models and remaining competitive in investment banking. What I recall most was his incessant focus on value. He answered his own question, adamantly stating, "If you can't give customers reasons to buy your car, they shouldn't buy it." He added, "What's most important in business is seeing the pictures in customers' heads." Tyree believed "in his bones" that companies succeed by knowing and meeting customer needs. This requires a solid understanding of competitive advantages, communicating winning value propositions and constantly improving performance.

Tyree shared the story of a good friend with pancreatic cancer. He almost died because his hospital would not admit its limitations. For weeks, the hospital's doctors considered every option except moving their patient to a better-equipped facility. As the patient's condition deteriorated, his wife found a specialty hospital that could provide the necessary, last-chance surgery. She pressed the hospital's administrators until they approved the transfer. Only then did Tyree's friend receive the life-saving surgery.

To Tyree, the hospital had failed on multiple levels. It didn't understand its strengths and weaknesses; it wouldn't admit deficiencies; it wasn't transparent; and (by default) it tolerated unacceptable patient care to avoid losing business or bruising egos. Most importantly, the hospital didn't put his friend's interests first. This represents a foundational statement about delivering value in healthcare, made more poignant by Tyree's untimely 2011 death at age 53 due to a medical error.[98]

Mental Models: "Market" vs. "Regulatory" Mindsets

In Tyree's view, the customer always comes first. His fundamental question—Why should people buy our car?—distills the essence of a *market mindset* where companies maximize sales by finding optimal relationships between price and value. Customer needs and perceptions are the principal considerations. Understanding and building upon a company's competitive advantages is the foundation of value

---

98 http://www.chicagobusiness.com/article/20110318/NEWS01/110319843/meshow-chief-james-tyrees-death-accidental-caused-by-air-embolism

creation. Apple has become the world's largest company by making its products desirable, affordable and accessible.

By and large, America's healthcare industry is miles away from building value-based processes that deliver value to customers. Most health companies employ a *regulatory mindset* where the managerial objective is to maximize revenues. Customer needs are secondary considerations.

Gilead Science's pricing strategy for its breakthrough drug Solvaldi illustrates the point. Solvaldi cures Hepatitis C, a remarkable accomplishment. Gilead charges a breathtaking $1,000 per pill ($84,000 for a 12-week protocol in the U.S.) for Sovaldi.[99] They market Solvaldi as a specialty drug and assert that its limited use, high efficacy and complicated manufacturing justify its exorbitant price.[100] When logic fails, public explanations turn emotional, i.e. "you can't put a price on health." Gilead's 2014 Q1 earnings were a stunning $2.3 billion, driven by record Solvaldi sales.[101] Unfortunately, Solvaldi's high price tag busts payer budgets and limits access to many people who need the drug.

Gilead's managerial mindset centers on maximizing reimbursement revenues, not sales, because the U.S. does not inject value into its drug approval process. The Food and Drug Administration's (FDA) statutory standard for product approval is whether a drug or medical device is "safe and effective."[102] The product's benefit relative to price is not part of the federal evaluation and approval process. Absent market competition from other pharmaceutical companies, Gilead can basically charge what it wants irrespective of patient needs, payer complaints and/or the traditional market forces of supply and demand. Pharma wins. Society loses.

---

99 Margot Sanger-Katz, *Why the Price of Sovaldi is a Shock to the System,* The New York Times.com, August 6, 2014; http://www.nytimes.com/2014/08/07/upshot/why-the-price-of-sovaldi-is-a-shock-to-the-system.html?_r=0&abt=0002&abg=1

100 Sanger-Katz reported Gilead Sciences generated $5.1billion revenue by August, 2014

101 http://www.nytimes.com/2014/04/27/sunday-review/it-will-save-lives-but-whats-th-cost.html?_r=0

102 http://www.nytimes.com/2014/04/27/sunday-review/it-will-save-lives-but-whats-the-cost.html?_r=0

Historically, healthcare insiders have never asked, "What's our value proposition?" Market-based competition is nudging the healthcare companies closer to Jim Tyree's way of thinking by pushing for better, more affordable products and services. Under pressure, innovative providers deliver better, more customer-centric care at lower costs, particularly for routine procedures. Better data lifts the murk. Prices and outcomes become transparent and fair.

Successful businesses deliver value. Healthcare executives must shift their managerial focus from maximizing reimbursement revenues (irrespective of costs and outcomes) to finding, identifying and creating more value. This chapter explores different approaches healthcare organizations employ to answer Tyree's provocative question—in essence, how to *manufacture* healthcare efficiently and cost effectively, so customers will want to buy *our care* (car with an "e") without dreading either the process or the outcome.

Defining Value in Healthcare

Healthcare's importance often crowds out value considerations for those receiving care. In the moment of medical need, patients want curative treatments irrespective of cost. Water costs less than diamonds, but ask California's drought-stricken residents which one they value more. Like healthcare, water is life-giving but diamonds are not. Americans don't pay exorbitant prices for water. They shouldn't have to pay exorbitant prices for healthcare.

Clay Christensen, the Harvard Business School professor and noted scholar on market disruption, defines value as the ability of a good or service to satisfy a customer's "jobs to be done." To illustrate, Christensen describes a convenience store researching why customers buy milkshakes. When surveyed, customers said they "hired" milkshakes to relieve the tedium of long commutes. Understanding the customers' job to be done, the store increased sales by making its milkshakes thicker (so they would last longer), quicker to buy and part of a targeted rewards program.

As the Gilead example highlights, healthcare's principal job to be done is optimizing revenues. In fee-for-service medicine, quality becomes less important than volume and reimbursement. That must change for American healthcare to realize its potential. *Market mindsets must replace regulatory mindsets.*

According to Porter and Thomas Lee, who wrote the Harvard Business Review article "The Strategy That Will Fix Healthcare", value in healthcare is the relationship between positive health outcomes and their cost. Most hospitals currently allocate costs based on revenue not actual per-unit costs. Porter and Lee explain the risk in this approach:

> *Existing costing systems are fine for overall department budgeting, but they provide only crude and misleading estimates for actual costs of service for individual patients and conditions...Without understanding the true costs of care for patient conditions, much less how costs are related to outcomes, health care organizations are flying blind in deciding how to improve processes and redesign care.*[103]

Cost accounting is essential to delivering value-based healthcare. Porter and cost-accounting guru, Robert Kaplan, assess healthcare value by measuring outcomes achieved relative to dollars spent. This outcome-cost paradigm is the secret sauce that will transform healthcare delivery. It translates into lower, transparent and competitive prices for healthcare services. Enlightened health companies are figuring this out.

Sunshine is the Best Disinfectant

Hoag Orthopedic Institute (HOI) in Irvine, California, is a for-profit hospital specializing in orthopedic surgeries. It was the brainchild of Dr. James Cailloutte, an orthopedic surgeon at Newport Orthopedic Institute; Dr. Richard Afable, CEO at Hoag Memorial Hospital Presbyterian in Newport Beach, California; and Steve Jones, Hoag's chairman of the board. Inspired by Porter's value framework, the three sought a competitive edge in an orthopedic market dominated by Kaiser Permanente. They committed HOI to taking full risk for the cost and outcomes of its surgical procedures. Cailloutte explains,

---

103 Michael E. Porter and Thomas H. Lee, *The Strategy That Will Fix Healthcare*, Harvard Business Review, October 2012

Our only competitive option was to become more efficient than competitors. If we owned the hospital, we could combine physician decision-making around optimal patient care with a hospital's focus on efficiency and productivity. Alignment would be the key. We could align physicians, hospital leadership, and front-line employees.[104]

HOI hired Dereesa Purtell Reid, CPA, MBA, to become HOI's first president in 2011. With a cost-accounting background and deep surgical-hospital experience in the free-wheeling Texas market, Reid was the ideal leader to shape a high-performance, cost-based operating culture at HOI. Per-unit revenues needed to align with per-unit costs. With Kaplan's help, Reid implemented time-driven activity-based costing (TDABC).[105] She wanted to "...compare activity costs across physicians, reduce variation among physicians, use the more accurate costs to inform the pricing of existing bundles, and develop new best practices."[106]

HOI accomplished these and other objectives. Cost information enabled HOI to quantify potential savings from process-improvement initiatives. Cost and outcome data drove decision-making. Through process standardization, rigorous performance monitoring and physician accountability, HOI reduced variance, improved outcomes and lowered costs. HOI also embraced transparency, annually publishing outcomes data. HOI's leaders believe transparency enhances accountability and performance improvement. They're right.

HOI isn't alone. The Surgery Center of Oklahoma City (SCOC) uses transparent prices to persuade domestic and international patients to undergo procedures at its facilities. [107] SCOC proves that U.S. consumers don't have to leave the country to practice medical tour-

---

104 Robert S. Kaplan and Jonathan Warsh, *Hoag Orthopedic Institute,* Field Case: Harvard Business School November 24, 2014.

105 Robert S. Kaplan and Steven R. Anderson, *Time-Driven Activity-Based Costing,* Harvard Business Review, November 20014; Michael E. Porter and Thomas H. Lee, *The Strategy That Will Fix Healthcare,* Harvard Business Review, October 2012. TDABC measures 1) the unit cost of supplying capacity and 2) the time required to perform a transaction or an activity.

106 Robert S. Kaplan and Steven R. Anderson, *Time-Driven Activity-Based Costing,* Harvard Business Review, November 20014

107 http://opinionator.blogs.nytimes.com/2013/07/31/a-new-health-care-approach-dont-hide-the-price/

ism. SCOC's transparent prices have forced its Oklahoma competitors to do the same. According to co-founder Keith Smith, patients in other states even used the surgery center's pricing to bargain for lower costs at their local hospitals.[108] By linking prices to outcomes, the Surgery Center of Oklahoma presents a clear and transparent value proposition for potential customers. Its success speaks to America's pent-up demand for value-based care delivery.

Lean In: Constant Process Improvement

Healthcare's *regulatory mindset* has blinded health company managers to strategies that optimize value in other industries. Management guru W. Edwards Deming preached that higher quality results from eliminating waste and inefficiency. The counter-intuitive result is that higher quality products cost less to manufacture.

Deming put his theories to work in post-war Japan as a statistician working with General Douglas MacArthur to rebuild Japanese industry. Focused on quality improvement, Deming demonstrated how manufacturers could employ statistics and process controls to improve both efficiency and product quality. His comprehensive methodology engaged all employees in process standardization, variance reduction, waste reduction and constant quality improvement. The Japanese labeled Deming's methodology *Kaizen*, or change for the better, and it spread like wildfire.

The results were stunning and brought American manufacturers to their knees. By employing *target-based pricing* (TBP) across multiple industry sectors, Japanese manufacturers routed their American competitors. TBP reverse-engineers the manufacturing process to build high-quality products to sell at predetermined low prices (Sales Price – Target Profit = Target Cost). Up to that point, manufacturers added profit margins to organically generated costs. Facing an adapt-or-die moment, American manufacturers transformed their operations by focusing on outcomes and value (better products at lower prices). Today, American manufacturers are global leaders in productivity, quality control and constant process improvement.

---

108   *Ibid.*

Healthcare delivery, like auto manufacturing, is a process-driven, component-heavy production enterprise. Waste manifests through medical errors, overtreatment and hospital-acquired illness. Efficient resource utilization enhances patient care. Similar to manufacturing, there are discoverable costs for tonsillectomies, hip replacements and ER visits. Healthcare can benefit enormously from the same lean, reverse-engineering processes that transformed the American auto industry.

Not surprisingly, there is a connection between process improvement and sales growth. Toyota wrote the book on it, literally, in 1990.[109] The Toyota Production System[110] (known simply as Lean) builds on Kaizen principles and Henry Ford's original production-line design. Ford's approach optimized mass production of one product. Toyota expanded Ford's concept to producing multiple types of vehicles without compromising production time, quality or cost. Toyota's capacity to discover and implement value-driven process improvement rocketed the company to the world's top-selling brand. Global manufacturing took notice, followed by service industries.[111] Eventually, healthcare organizations in the U.S., Canada, the United Kingdom and Australia[112] began applying Lean principles to increase efficiency and improve patient experience.

Kaizen and Virginia Mason Medical Center

Returning from Japan to Seattle in 2000, Virginia Mason CEO Gary Kaplan found himself seated next to Toyota's CEO. By the end of the 10-plus hour flight, Kaplan had concluded that Virginia Mason could create a distinct competitive advantage by applying Toyota's Lean principles to healthcare delivery. This effort became the groundbreaking Virginia Mason Production System (VMPS). VMPS employs constant process improvement to design and implement zero-defect protocols. It

109 James P. Womack, Daniel T. Jones, Daniel Roos and Donna Sammons Carpenter, *The Machine That Changed the World: The Story of Lean Production—Toyota's Secret Weapon in the Global Car Wars That Is Now Revolutionizing World Industry*, Free Press, a division of Simon & Schuster, 1990.

110 http://www.lean.org/WhatsLean/History.cfm

111 http://healthydebate.ca/2014/09/topic/lean

112 *Ibid.*

first determines costs associated with each activity. These include labor, supplies, procedure duration and turnaround times. VPMS standardizes processes and staffing based on actual costs and outcomes. The results are higher-quality care, fewer medical errors and reduced financial risk.

Virginia Mason was the first healthcare system to integrate Toyota's management system throughout its entire organization.[113] The healthcare system now runs its own Lean Master Class. Established in 2008, the goal of the Virginia Mason Institute's trainers is "to advance quality, safety and value by sharing our knowledge and experience."[114] The institute introduces clinicians and administrators from around the world to VPMS. Ironically, even Japanese providers fly to Seattle to study what Virginia Mason learned from Toyota.[115]

Virginia Mason captured national attention in September 2014 when it introduced 90-day warranties for hip and knee replacements. Warranties cover the full-treatment cycle (diagnosis, surgery and rehabilitation) when the patient receives all services within the Virginia Mason system. Progressive companies, like HOI and Virginia Mason, have shifted market prices lower for joint replacement surgery. Between 2012 and 2013, median prices for total hip replacements in U.S. hospitals declined by 34 percent, from $40,364 to $26,489.[116] Prices will likely fall even lower as Medicare implements bundled payments for joint replacements in 75 markets nationwide. Hip surgery with lower costs, fixed prices, better outcomes *and 90-day warranties?* Hip Hip Hooray!

Target-based Pricing at CHRISTUS Health

Under CFO Jay Herron, CHRISTUS launched a price-led costing process in 2010 to become profitable on Medicare business, which accounted for over 50 percent of CHRISTUS' revenues. Herron used

---

113 https://www.virginiamason.org/vmps

114 http://www.virginiamasoninstitute.org/about

115 as quoted in http://www.amnhealthcare.com/latest-healthcare-news/hospitals-turning-lean-six-sigma-performance-improvement/

116 The International Federation of Health Plans reported this decrease in their 2013 and 2014 "Comparative Price Reports," an annual listing of procedure prices by country.

cost accounting to unpack the ratio between CHRISTUS' costs and Medicare reimbursement for high-frequency DRG (Diagnostic Related Group) codes. He examined cases with surgical implants where the ratio between the procedure's supply cost and DRG non-labor reimbursement exceeded 30 percent. In all of those cases, Herron found that implant costs alone were higher than the non-labor component of the DRG payment. The news got worse. Herron observed, "As I recall, we found cases where our cost for the supply exceeded the entire DRG payment. Physicians were often shocked to hear about the high prices for the implants they used. Many never knew."

The evaluation also revealed that CHRISTUS' surgeons used multiple implants for the same procedure. Physician preference rather than cost, quality or device appropriateness drove this practice variation. What began as a fiscal exercise to stem its Medicare losses, stimulated CHRISTUS to overhaul its surgical operations. This led to protocol standardization for high-volume procedures, greater efficiency, enhanced vendor management, lower costs and higher profitability.

Necessity Turbo-Charges Productivity at Cleveland Clinic Florida

Coming into 2015, Ozzie Delgado confronted a thorny problem. Cleveland Clinic Florida was experiencing expansive demand for surgical services. Occupancy was already at 92% and there would be no capacity relief until 2018. That's when a $300 million capital project will add inpatient beds, three operating suites, an expanded Emergency Department and incremental diagnostic services (e.g. imaging, laboratory).

As the organization's Chief Operating Officer, Delgado's challenge was to accommodate volume growth and maintain superior quality/safety standards until the new facilities come on-line. There were no obvious solutions. Cleveland Clinic Florida was already efficient. Its average length of stay was 9% lower than UHC's benchmark database on the "Observed to Expected Ratio." Delgado is among a new generation of health company leaders that understand the current system is not sustainable, fear it could collapse on their watch and are pro-actively working to transform it from the inside. They're fearless and relentless. Like heat-seeking missiles, they find and exploit opportunities for value creation (better outcomes at lower costs). This is their story.

Along with the Chief of Medical Operations, Dr. Fabio Potenti, and Chief Nursing Officer, Kerry Major, Delgado developed a portfolio approach to productivity improvement. A year later, the results are spectacular. Despite higher surgical volumes, Cleveland Clinic Florida's occupancy percentage has decreased to 88% even as its treatment intensity magnified. The hospital's case mix index jumped from 1.86 to 2.13. Embedded within the Cleveland Clinic Florida narrative are important lessons regarding productivity improvement, consumerism, competitiveness and facility design.

America's Most Intensive Small Hospital

Despite having only 155 beds, Cleveland Clinic Florida performed over 150 heart, liver and kidney transplants in 2015. Its 240-plus physicians encompass 40 specialties and subspecialties. Physicians have primary appointments in Florida and secondary appointments in Cleveland. They practice advanced care protocols developed through Cleveland Clinic's institutes. Next to the Clinic's flagship hospital in Cleveland, Cleveland Clinic Florida has the system's second highest case mix index.

Cleveland Clinic Florida operates in a tough market. Excess acute capacity in the greater Ft. Lauderdale markets limits pricing flexibility. Cut-throat competition from physician groups, for-profit providers and public hospitals keeps margins tight. The 2015 National Chartbook of Health Care Prices[117] reports that Florida has some of the lowest prices for healthcare services in the nation. Paraphrasing Frank Sinatra, if you can make it there, you can make it anywhere. Despite tough reimbursement, Cleveland Clinic Florida achieves healthy operating margins. Cleveland Clinic Florida is experiencing the future of healthcare delivery today and thriving.

---

117 http://www.healthcostinstitute.org/news-and-events/some-states-pay-twice-price-health-care-finds-new-report

Consumers shape demand in Southeast Florida. The vast majority of Cleveland Clinic Florida's patients self-refer to the facility. Consequently, the organization invests significant resources to promote access to its physicians and facilities. Customers can "call-in, walk-in or click-in." Cleveland Clinic Florida offers extended hours and express care for common medical conditions. It practices expansive tele-health. Pound-for-pound, Cleveland Clinic Florida may be America's most intensive, efficient and customer-centric small hospital. It's a model for competitive positioning in post-reform healthcare.

Portfolio Approach to Strategy

To attack their hospital's near-term capacity challenge, the executive team evaluated 20 initiatives within the following four categories: 1. Emergency Room Capacity Management; 2. Surgical Operations Streamlining; 3. Transitions of Care and 4. Partnerships. All options were on the table. These included relocating services, "renting" capacity at competing institutions and transferring patients.

The beauty of a portfolio approach to strategy is that it doesn't predetermine outcomes or overweight favored approaches. It supports constant process improvement. It's adaptive. It enables solutions to emerge as the organization addresses its productivity challenges. This portfolio approach enabled the Cleveland Clinic Florida team to reinforce successful initiatives and jettison or delay others. Here's what worked:

> **Better Emergency Room Management:** Everything in the ER works on a stopwatch: door-to-doctor; doctor-to-disposition; disposition-to-discharge. The pressure is always on to move patients through the system. This causes some unnecessary patient admissions. By improving patient triage, staging and follow-up, the hospital's ER physicians reduced unnecessary admissions and created incremental capacity for surgical admissions.

> **Better Patient Discharge:** upon examination, the hospital's standard discharge protocols and processes created a severe

"bottleneck." Addressing this bottleneck became a multi-faceted challenge. The hospital hired a discharge hospitalist who arrives at 3 am to initiate discharge protocols. As discharge paperwork finalized earlier, management discovered that the nursing staff and patients weren't prepared for quicker discharges. However, clearer communications, enhanced patient transportation and hard checkout times increased early morning discharges. This freed-up inpatient beds for patients recovering from early-morning surgeries.

Leveling Surgical Hours: like most hospitals, Cleveland Clinic Florida used block scheduling to accommodate surgeons' preferences. The hospital extended its operating room hours until 9:30 pm and "leveled" surgical volume to accommodate more efficient discharge planning. Some physician unwilling to expedite discharges received Friday surgical assignments which necessitated Saturday discharges. "Walking the talk" requires determination, consistency and resolution.

Predictive Analytics: Delgado's team now employs sophisticated algorithms to predict census, recovery times and resource requirements. Management uses this information to adjust staffing levels and optimize facility usage. Learning organizations receive continuous feedback, experiment, adjust and perform better. Like all effective process improvement, the hospital's employees are learning as the capacity initiative unfolds. Eliminating waste improves quality and efficiency while reducing costs.

In business speak, surgical operations at Cleveland Clinic Florida are a *complex adaptive system.* As such, constructive change is "bottom-up," ongoing and engages all employees. Expect more change and performance improvement as the hospital's capacity initiatives evolve during 2016 and 2017. Management still has several strategies (e.g. Saturday surgeries) in reserve that it can implement under the right circumstances.

Predictive Disruption

Cleveland Clinic Florida has a well-articulated strategic vision. Delgado expects Cleveland Clinic Florida to become "Southeast Florida's solution for complex care." He's not content to relax once the hospital's new capacity comes on-line in 2018. Rather, he sees this interim period as an incredible opportunity to "force efficiency" and "drive quality."

Like many emerging health leaders, Delgado understands the disruptive forces roiling traditional business practices in healthcare. Rather than resist consumer demands for greater value, he's embracing that challenge with energy and infectious enthusiasm. Healthcare needs more leaders like Delgado, Potenti and Major pushing their organizations hard to achieve greater quality, efficiency and productivity.

Complex care combines high outcome uncertainty and ongoing treatment. Most complex care occurs in large, high-cost centralized locations. Cleveland Clinic Florida's business model suggests that smaller, focused facilities can deliver high-quality, customer-friendly complex care more efficiently. Expect other health systems to replicate this high-performance strategy. Value rules in post-reform healthcare. Cleveland Clinic Florida exemplifies market-driven reform in action. The question isn't whether the Cleveland Clinic Florida will increase surgical volume and market share. It's by how much.

Mass Production Surgery at Narayana Health

Before Dr. Devi Shetty founded Narayana Health in Bangalore, India, he was Mother Teresa's cardiologist. Her compassion for India's poor inspired him to work to improve their quality of life. Shetty recognized that there was huge demand for quality healthcare and surgery in India and the rest of the developing world, and that high prices were the primary barrier to accessing care.

The Indian constitution guarantees universal healthcare coverage, but the reality is less than ideal. Access to quality care relates directly to economic status. Private healthcare spending is three-to-four times greater than public spending, concentrated among India's affluent citizens, and based primarily on price and brand recognition. Since these customers have choice, hospital companies must deliver customer-friendly healthcare at competitive prices. Maintaining profitability requires increasing efficiency and lowering per-unit costs. Indian doctors work longer hours and perform more procedures than their American counterparts. Likewise, Indian hospitals run more intensely. Full Saturday surgical schedules are routine.

Given India's market-oriented healthcare environment, Shetty realized that increasing access to necessary surgeries for India's poor required low prices. In 2001, he launched Narayana Health (NH) to carry forward Mother Teresa's belief in human dignity and a hands-on commitment to the poor. From day one, he employed mass-production techniques to deliver high-volume quality care at low prices.[118] I toured NH's flagship facility in March 2014. Every Narayana Health employee understands that lower per-unit costs increase surgical access for India's poor. How's that for mission? Here's what I saw:

- Operating rooms run daily from 7:00 a.m. until all cases are completed (as opposed to U.S. facilities that operate one shift per day on four or five days per week);

- Salaried doctors increase surgical levels and reduce per-unit costs (as opposed to U.S. facilities where operating rooms left vacant increase per-unit costs);

- Dialysis centers run 24/7 (unlike U.S. facilities that follow traditional 9:00 a.m. to 5:00 p.m. schedules regardless of need);

- Operational engineers continuously extend equipment life, improve throughput and substitute less-costly technologies, e.g. digital imaging instead of film;

- NH uses low-cost medical and diagnostic equipment wherever possible;

118 Narayana Health was the subject of a Harvard Business School Case Study: *Narayana Heart Hospital; Cardiac Care for the Poor,* "Tarun Khanna, V. Kasturi Rangan and Merlina Manocaran, August 26, 2011.

- A single-line of visible ICU beds with centralized nursing stations and individual tablet screens enable efficient and effective patient monitoring; and

- Patients move from room to surgery to recovery without changing beds.

Most importantly, NH's health outcomes are equivalent or better than those achieved at the world's most prestigious medical centers. High volumes and constant process improvement do translate into lower prices and higher quality. Somewhere, Deming is smiling.

These efficiencies translate into remarkably low prices. For example, cardiac bypass surgery costs $2,500 (compared to average price of $75,000 in the U.S.) with subsidies for those who cannot pay. Aligning existing surgical services with proven manufacturing efficiencies enabled Narayana to reduce per-unit costs, specialize in high-end surgical services and revolutionize outcome benchmarks.

By 2014, Narayana Health had grown from one 225-bed facility to a healthcare conglomerate with 7,500 beds in 29 hospitals across 17 cities in India. A lean approach and commitment to accessible, affordable care built Narayana Health's global brand as a leading low-cost, high-quality healthcare provider.

While India is on the other side of the world from the U.S., the Cayman Islands is a one-hour flight from Miami. Amid much local fanfare, over 2,000 people gathered in February 2014 to celebrate the grand opening of Health City Cayman Islands. Phase I consists of a 140-bed joint-venture hospital between India-based Narayana Health and Ascension Health, America's largest not-for-profit health system. When finished, Health City will encompass a 2,000-bed multi-specialty medical center, 1,500 assisted-living units, medical and nursing schools for 3,000 students and a biotech research park. Most importantly, the project comes with Narayana Health's mass-production business model that delivers low-cost, high-quality surgical care around the clock. For example, Health City will offer cardiac bypass surgery for a fraction of the average U.S. cost of $75,000.

Interestingly, Health City's grand opening has received scant American media coverage in either the general or medical press. An excellent Forbes blog[119] by Kaiser Permanente's Dr. Robert Pearl was the exception. The Cayman Islands' government set its sights on the potentially lucrative U.S. medical tourism market. It granted the land and will make the infrastructure investment necessary for Health City to realize its expansive vision. Unlike Caribbean pirates of old, Health City expects to capture its treasure (patient volume) fairly—by providing better care at lower prices. As Pearl observes, "If I were the CEO of a hospital in Florida, I would be rushing to match [Health City's] outstanding clinical outcomes and low prices today… [before it's] too late."

Care Redesign: Tele-ICUs Deliver Better Care at Lower Costs

As in other industries, technology can improve healthcare outcomes while lowering costs. Tele-ICUs, which use teleconferencing to monitor ICU patients remotely, provide a textbook example. ICUs have hospitals' highest mortality rates and can consume 30 percent of their operating costs.[120] Nationally, critical care accounts for 1 percent of national GNP and 20 percent of all healthcare costs.[121] ICUs are complex environments that require care providers to filter data continuously and act instantly. Lack of process standardization and inconsistent performance measurement in ICU care increases risk of patient harm.

ICUs nationwide, particularly in small hospitals, lack enough specialty care coverage. Board-certified intensivists, physicians who specialize in inpatient care, are also in short supply. Decreasing reimbursement and career attrition further complicate ICU staffing.[122] The solution to limited ICU coverage lies in using intensivist resources more efficiently. Enter tele-ICUs.

---

119 http://www.forbes.com/sites/robertpearl/2014/03/27/offshoring-american-health-care-higher-quality-at-lower-costs/

120 http://www.icumedicine.com/hospitals/whyactnow

121 http://www.livescience.com/39510-icu-treatment-overused.html

122 www.leapfrog.org; informs Americans on hospital safety and quality. They established and continuously update the ISP Standard, the benchmark for ICU care management.

The concept of remote ICUs surfaced in the 1970s. Two decades later, VISICU (virtual ICU) recognized the value in standardizing ICU care and developed a prototype. VISICU maintains a centrally located remote bunker staffed 24/7 by ICU physicians who monitor multiple ICUs around the country. Two-way cameras put expertise at the bedside. Onsite physicians can consult with VISICU staff to maintain a high level of care.

Acceptance of tele-ICUs grew over the next 20 years, and they gained critical mass. By 2011, 41 tele-ICU command centers monitored almost 6,000 ICU beds in 249 locations.[123] Their numbers continue to grow. Leapfrog studies underscore the value of the approach, reporting that tele-intensivists reduce ICU mortality by 15 to 30 percent[124].

St. Louis-based Advanced-ICU is the nation's largest independent, tele-ICU company. It monitors ICUs across midsized hospitals. The University of Massachusetts Memorial Medical Center as well as The University of Minnesota and Fairview Health System run their own centralized ICU command centers. These tele-ICU units provide a higher ICU standard of care at significantly lower per-unit costs. A 2010 comparison of 10,000 ICU patients (5,397 with advanced ICU tele-care; 4,612 control group) yielded the following results:

- 40 percent lower mortality;
- 25 percent lower length of stay; and
- 17 percent more ICU cases (by avoiding transfer and allowing patients to receive treatment at local hospitals).

Studies estimate that by 2030, ICU hospital beds will increase from the current 10 to 40 percent.[125] Centralizing ICU monitoring demonstrates how thinking differently about how to allocate resources can generate superior outcomes.

---

123 http://perspectives.ahima.org/tele-icu-efficacy-and-cost-effectiveness-of-remotely-managing-critical-care/#.VXM1XaavIfk

124 www.leapfrog.org

125 *Crossing the Technology Chasm: Tele-ICUs Save Lives and Money,* David Johnson, July 2013 http://4sighthealth.com/crossing-technology-chasm-tele-icus-save-lives-money/

Rethinking Addiction Treatment

On average, over 700,000 Americans seek treatment for alcohol or drug addiction every day.[126] Treatment prices and effectiveness vary depending upon whether the program is inpatient or outpatient, privately or state-funded or has minimal or many services and amenities. High-end luxury programs can cost as much as $120,000 a month.[127] While a majority of Americans (80 percent) have positive views about prevention and recovery from substance use, the journey is personal.[128] A key first step is finding the right rehab path.

Almost 15 percent of patients prescribed painkillers become addicted to them. Current protocols suggest a 30-day inpatient stay in a rehabilitation hospital is the most effective treatment. It isn't. Brain science has discovered it takes a minimum of 8 to 10 weeks to develop neural pathways strong enough to overcome addictive habits. A 30-day rehab stint by itself rarely works and is remarkably expensive.

Recovery Ways is an early-stage behavioral health company with a better idea. It has developed evidence-based protocols that use brain science to cure addiction at two-thirds of the cost of 30-day inpatient programs. Patients stay in hospitals just long enough to stabilize. Their treatment continues with rigorous outpatient counseling supported by frequent Skype sessions. Recovery Ways' singular goal is to achieve better outcomes, not maximize revenues. It embodies Porter's value equation of establishing a positive relationship between outcomes and their costs.

It's worth noting that Recovery Ways is a private, venture-funded company. Venture investment in provider-based services startups is increasing. Smart money is flowing toward companies that deliver low-cost, high-quality healthcare solutions.

Competitive Advantage: Good, Better, Best

Health companies have a culture of offering comprehensive services, owning assets and valuing control. This operating orientation reflects

---

126 http://www.reneweveryday.com/resources/addiction-recovery-facts/
127 http://alcoholism.about.com/od/pro/a/blsam040527.htm
128 http://www.reneweveryday.com/resources/addiction-recovery-facts/

a regulatory mindset where benefits accrue to those providing the most, not the best, services. As healthcare becomes more consumer and value-oriented, meeting customer demands will require rigorous examination of corporate capabilities along with proactive partnering and outsourcing to strengthen product offerings.

All businesses have inputs and outputs. Companies with market mindsets focus on outcomes and efficient resource allocation. They are agnostic with regard to whether they own, partner or outsource capabilities. The chart below outlines the flow of healthcare inputs to outputs and the resource-allocation alternatives (own, partner, outsource) within health networks. It also depicts the key channels (brand, price, consumerism) that differentiate superior product offerings. Winning health companies understand their strengths (why customers will buy their cars) and the risks they should own. They relinquish control to partners and/or vendors that add value and generate better outcomes. Competitive advantage is the mechanism through which companies evaluate and make effective resource-allocation decisions.

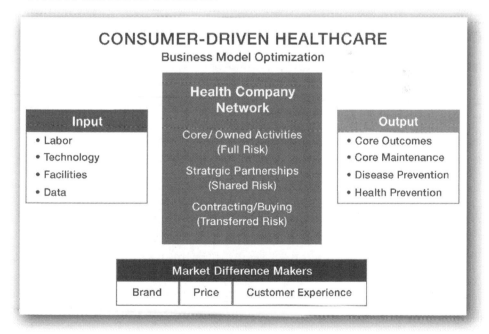

Owned Activities

The best companies become synonymous with superior products and services: Ritz Carlton and customer service; Toyota and cars; Starbucks and coffee; Cleveland Clinic and cardiology. These companies own the intellectual property, service delivery and performance accountability for their essential products and services. The Ritz Carlton mantra (*"Ladies and Gentlemen Serving Ladies and Gentlemen"*) captures the benefits of a powerful service orientation to guide employee behavior. A *market mindset* requires these companies to operate at the highest performance levels to maximize sales. They cannot compromise quality. They cannot risk customer loyalty. They cannot weaken their brands.

Most healthcare is local, but a few national brands have emerged. For 20 consecutive years, *U.S. News & World Report* has ranked the Cleveland Clinic number one in cardiology and heart surgery. The clinic leverages its expertise, labor, technologies, facilities and data to develop protocols, conduct research and deliver superior care. The world comes to Cleveland Clinic for cardiac care. To capitalize on their competitive advantage in cardiology, the clinic formed the National Cardiology Network in 1994 to offer their cardiac expertise to hospital affiliates nationwide. Cleveland Clinic physicians train local health systems in the clinic's protocols and provide second opinions as needed. The sickest patients come to Cleveland Clinic while others receive treatment locally in accordance with the clinic's protocols. The network now operates with 17 affiliates across 10 states and Washington, DC.

In 2010, Cleveland Clinic expanded the network model to provide direct care to corporate customers, including a program with Lowe's Home Hardware, headquartered in Mooresville, NC. The clinic provides heart surgery at predetermined rates to insured Lowe's employees. Lowe's covers all medical costs, including deductibles and co-pays, for the patient and travel expenses for the patient and one companion.[129] As its national network has expanded, the clinic has expanded its direct contracting relationships with seven large employers, in-

---

129 http://www.beckershospitalreview.com/hospital-physician-relationships/7-points-about-cleveland-clinics-bundled-payment-program-for-lowes-employees.html

cluding Wal-Mart and Boeing.[130] By *owning* its cardiology service line, Cleveland Clinic now delivers superior cardiology care well beyond its traditional northeast Ohio service area.

Strategic Partnerships

Health companies should pursue strategic partnerships when prospective partners bring expertise, capabilities and/or capital that enhances performance and improves outcomes. The ideal strategic partnerships align customer and service-provider interests. The parties are on the same side of the table, pursuing agreed-upon objectives and winning or losing together. This requires the following four elements: 1. A mutual focus on client objectives, not transactions or processes; 2. Incentive-based compensation tied to clearly-defined outcomes (e.g. reduced costs, higher sales, fewer errors); 3. A shared commitment to mutual learning and adaptive program evolution; and 4. Honest and regular program assessment (what's working, what's not, how to be better, new win-win opportunities, should the engagement continue).

Strategic Surgical Partnership: Surgical Care Affiliates and Florida Hospital Carrollwood

Representing approximately 30 percent of commercial health-insurance spending, surgery is a highly profitable business. However, inefficient scheduling, slow operating room turnaround, hospital and physician misalignment and a lack of standardization reduces productivity, stifles growth, increases patient risk, frustrates physicians and diminishes profitability.

Surgical Care Affiliates ("SCA") partners with hospitals to improve perioperative services. SCA begins with a rigorous diagnostic review of a hospital's surgical operations. It then works with hospital management and surgeons to design and implement data-driven solutions. According to Gerry Biala, SCA's head of perioperative services, "It's

---

130 https://www.advisory.com/daily-briefing/2012/10/22/boeing-cleveland-clinic-strike-bundled-payment-deal

not enough to offer tools; we have to change behavior." Breakthrough performance improvement requires changing governance, engaging surgeons on strategy, flexible scheduling and constant re-engineering (see chart below).

SCA Program for Perioperative Surgical Improvement

Rapid Assessment	SCA Solutions	Scalable Management
• Assessment of one or more surgery departments • Focus on efficiency, case mix, profitability and case quality • Develop recommended action plan	• Physician Engagement • Schedule Optimization • Labor Optimization • Supply Chain Management • Case Profitability • Market Expansion	• Integrate full management services for surgery departments and off-site facilities • Leverage and complement existing delivery model • Provide interim and transition leadership

Source: Surgical Care Affiliates

Florida Hospital Carrollwood in Tampa was marginally profitable and in danger of losing its largest surgical group. In 2013, the hospital partnered with SCA to improve surgical operations. After an eight-day, on-site assessment, the partnership created a shared decision-making governance council with hospital and physician representatives to address utilization, scheduling, staffing and growth. Together they designed and implemented a performance improvement plan. The results were impressive:

- Surgical volume increased 10 percent with no additional staffing
- Operating Room ("OR") utilization increased from 53 to 73 percent
- OR turnover time decreased from 35 to 16 minutes
- On-time starts increased from 36 to 93 percent
- Case cancellations dropped from 12 to 3 percent
- Patient satisfaction increased from the 28th to the 70th percentile
- Infection rates decreased from 2.7 to 0.8 percent
- Profitability surged

The best strategic partnerships not only deliver superior outcomes, they excite and energize partners to explore, experiment and strive together.

Contracting/Buying

Many organizational functions from revenue cycle to food services to facilities management are neither core competencies nor critical to corporate identity. Companies don't need to *own* these functions. When lacking internal expertise, it's best to purchase these types of services from companies that specialize in delivering them. Purchasing routine, non-core services improves productivity, reduces costs and increases accountability. Companies can always replace underperforming vendors. The right question for management to ask is not "What functions can we purchase?" but rather "Which functions can't we purchase?" When the goal is superior outcomes, productivity is the singular performance measure for non-core functions. More often than not, purchasing competitively-priced services generates higher productivity.

Real estate and facility management, for example, are typically a health system's largest expenditures after payroll and supplies. Yet health systems lack effective facilities management or real estate expertise. Service redundancy, overstaffing and suboptimal leasing abound. Outsourcing facility and real estate management to experts can generate significant cost savings.

Beaumont Health is a $4 billion health system serving metropolitan Detroit with multiple hospital campuses and numerous ambulatory and clinical sites. Until 2011, Beaumont Services Corporation (BSC) managed the company's real estate operations. Operating BSC gave Beaumont's leadership insight into the benefits of centralized management and led them to seek a national partner to achieve greater efficiencies. After a competitive process, Beaumont selected Jones Lange LaSalle (JLL) to become equal partners with BSC in managing their real estate operations. At that time, Beaumont's long-term goal was to outsource facilities management entirely to JLL.

The initiative generated immediate savings that average $16 million annually. JLL discovered a third of Beaumont's real estate expenditures weren't included in BSC's budget. Coordinated planning eliminated 95 percent of vacant lease space. JLL has also brokered third-party service contracts and provides operational input on quality and safety issues. Using scale, specialized expertise and execution ability, JLL transformed Beaumont's facility maintenance, energy management and purchased services. This is a perfect illustration of how purchased services can generate economic value,

Modernizing Healthcare Anti-Trust Regulation

U.S. healthcare operates within a fragmented, bureaucratic and outdated anti-trust regulatory infrastructure. No regulatory body considers the entire eco-system. As a consequence, current anti-trust regulators are unable to evaluate business models that blend payer and provider functions to meet the market demands for coordinated, outcomes-based care delivery. Like blind men describing elephants, government agencies only regulate what they feel and touch. They miss the bigger picture. While the Federal Trade Commission regulates hospitals, state insurance commissions regulate health insurers. Inadequate regulatory oversight compromises the ability of enlightened health companies to deliver more holistic and cost-effective healthcare services.

Anti-Competitive Monopsony Behavior

Depending on the market, monopsony payer and/or provider companies can emerge. With enough market concentration, dominant payers and providers use their clout to distort pricing for their benefit. For example, BlueCross BlueShield of Illinois controls almost 75 percent of the state's lucrative commercial insurance business. With its quasi-monopolistic market position, BlueCross essentially sets provider reimbursement rates and payment procedures. Doctors and hospitals have little choice but to accept BlueCross' payment terms. Not surprisingly, these payment terms favor BlueCross.

In almost all of its commercial contracts, BlueCross administers healthcare benefits on behalf of self-insured employers. Since employers pay healthcare costs for their covered employees, BlueCross benefits when those employees consume healthcare services in the following two ways:

1. Self-insured employers pay BlueCross a percentage of claims administered. Higher claims mean higher fees; and/or

2. BlueCross manipulates provider reimbursement through complex pre-payment and discounting strategies. These "strategies" accelerate co-pay/deductible capture, facilitate claim denials, optimize profitability and complicate payment reconciliation.

BlueCross scores beauty points with employers by lowering some contract rates. Under pressure from some employers, BlueCross created a lower-cost narrow network for the 2016 coverage year. They euphemistically named this plan "Blue Choice." Blue Choice excludes the region's most prestigious and higher-cost health companies, including Advocate, NorthShore, Northwestern, Rush and University of Chicago. In addition, BlueCross uses "soft steerage" to direct members to lower-cost treatments and diagnostic services. Narrow networks and soft steerage reduce per-unit costs of healthcare services, but do little to reduce unnecessary medical treatments.

BlueCross' profitability emanates from financial contracting, not patient care. The company is expert at shifting "treatment risk" and its costs to individuals, employers and providers. By contrast, traditional payers are not effective at managing the care of large populations. Large commercial insurers are losing billions insuring new exchange members under Obamacare. Care costs have overwhelmed premium revenues.

Health Care Services Corporation ("HCSC") is the parent company of BlueCross affiliates in Illinois and four other states. It is struggling to adapt to new marketplace dynamics. HCSC lost almost $2.3 billion on individual policies in 2014 and 2015. To compensate, it eliminated popular PPO plans and stopped paying broker commissions. In Illinois this sent 173,000 Illinois members scrambling for new 2016 health insurance coverage.

Regulatory Blindness

Despite healthcare's changing market dynamics, the Federal Trade Commission still applies narrow and outdated 1990s-era methodologies to identify and break-up anti-competitive hospital networks. The FTC's decision to oppose the proposed merger in Illinois between Advocate Health Care and NorthShore University Health System illustrates the point. The combined company's consolidated network would provide healthcare services throughout the Metropolitan-Chicago region. In opposing the merger, the FTC argued that the new company's concentration of hospitals in Chicago's North Shore would stifle competition, raise prices and reduce service quality for North Shore residents.

Upon examination, the FTC's conclusions regarding the proposed Advocate-NorthShore merger appear pre-determined. The agency structured its analysis to portray the merger in the most anti-competitive terms possible. Consider the following:

- The FTC used a "gerrymandered" North Shore service area to create a "highly concentrated" (greater than 50 percent) combined marketshare. Their analysis excludes the closest competing hospital (2.9 miles away) from NorthShore's flagship institution. More expansive regional analyses peg the combined marketshare between 23 percent and 28 percent.

- They examined only inpatient admission and price data. Most healthcare treatments occur in outpatient settings and physician offices. Relying exclusively on inpatient data is equivalent to assessing phone-company concentration by counting land lines.

- They did not consider Advocate's care management capabilities or the merged company's potential to deliver higher-quality, lower-cost care Metro-wide.

- They focused exclusively on per-unit hospital prices. They did not consider incremental costs associated with unnecessary treatments, medical errors or readmissions. The FTC even rejected Advocate-NorthShore's offer to cap post-merger hospital prices.

- They did not consider non-hospital competitors offering equivalent services at lower prices.

- They did not consider BlueCross' market dominance and "price-setting" power in evaluating Advocate-NorthShore's potential pricing leverage.

Using this tortured methodology, the FTC reached this inaccurate and meaningless conclusion: the proposed merger "will generate significant harm" to North Shore consumers of "general acute care inpatient hospital services."

State insurance commissions vary in their ability to monitor anti-competitive health insurance behavior and evaluate the relative benefit of integrated business models that combine health insurance and health delivery. In Illinois, for example, obtaining a health insurance license is difficult. Health companies, like Advocate, wishing to offer insurance products must partner with a licensed insurance provider. These operating realities limit competitive health insurance competition in Illinois. BlueCross' dominance reflects Illinois' inadequate regulation of the state's health insurance marketplace.

Modernizing Healthcare Regulation

As U.S. healthcare moves toward integrated delivery and managing the care of large populations, its regulatory infrastructure must adapt to assess anti-competitive integrated healthcare service providers. This argues for a regulatory body or bodies able to evaluate each market's entire eco-system for healthcare payment and delivery across all traditional and non-traditional participants based on cost, quality, outcomes and availability. In addition, reducing state-specific regulatory variation would foster more efficient service provision, promote competition and facilitate logical consolidation. Freeing health companies from unnecessary, burdensome and anti-competitive regulation will free them to focus on value-based care provision: better, more convenient, less expensive healthcare services.

Value Rules

Enlightened health companies are embracing value-based service delivery to prosper in post-reform healthcare. It will take years of focused effort to overturn entrenched business models and heads-in-the-beds operating cultures. The new post-reform playbook has the following five Value Rules:

Rule #1. Quality is Job 1: Trying to overcome a planned-obsolescence managerial mindset and respond to voracious Japanese competition, Ford Motor Company launched its "Quality is Job 1" campaign in the early 1980s, transformed operations, started building great cars again and turned the company around. By definition, there can only be one "Job 1." Health companies that don't give quality primacy can never hit targeted quality, safety and outcomes metrics. Left unopposed, the energy generated from optimizing revenues (Job 1 at most health systems) overwhelms well-meaning quality initiatives. There is no wiggle room in pursuing quality.

Rule #2. Care Episodes, Not Treatment Codes: As more care becomes routine (episodic with high outcome certainty), customer assessment of quality shifts to price, convenience and customer experience. Most treatments, even surgical procedures, are increasingly routine and potentially vulnerable to commodity pricing from retail competitors. Piecemeal treatment activity is the principal revenue driver for hospitals and doctors. As delivery migrates toward value, entire patient-care episodes will emerge as the logical units of outcome measurement and payment. Providers will bundle all pre-acute, acute and post-acute activity into single cohesive treatment regimens that incorporate relevant clinical, operational and financial data. Reducing performance and pricing variation, particularly in post-acute care, will differentiate high-performing health systems.

Rule #3. Price Matters: Third-party reimbursement for treatment activity has protected health companies from traditional market forces governing supply and demand. Increasing transparency regarding treatment outcomes and prices is reshaping market dynamics. When reimbursement payments are higher than market prices for routine treatments, it creates opportunities for independent entities to disintermediate traditional relationships between patients and providers. Over time, market forces will drive payments for routine care to lower price points. Expect value-driven behavior to shape pricing and service delivery for insurance products, diagnostic procedures and routine treatments. Using programs like SmartShoppers, employers offer payment incentives to direct employees to lower-cost, high-quality treatment centers.

Rule #4: Data is as Data Does: Data informs decision-making when metrics and analytics support desired outcomes. Health companies have excellent data for measuring treatment volume, payment flow and revenue optimization. Unfortunately, they have not developed effective metrics and analytics for optimizing care management and outcomes. As big data evolves, precision searching of massive data sets informed by cutting-edge analytics will give external reviewers the ability to assess and rank health system performance. For better or worse, every healthcare provider and procedure will have a score. The race is on. Data must support quality and cost-effective delivery. Healthcare companies that advance value-based care delivery will develop enhanced data capabilities, earn external praise and gain market share. Paraphrasing Warren Buffett,

"Time is the friend of value-driven companies and the enemy of revenue-driven ones."

Rule #5: It's the Customer, Stupid! As the healthcare marketplace becomes more individualized, consumers will exercise more control over medical decision-making. Unleashed, consumers become value-seeking machines, rewarding companies that offer more selection, lower prices, greater convenience and better customer experience. Businesses only exist to serve customers. Beyond providing appropriate care, health companies must engage customers through individually tailored programs, shared medical decision-making and meaningful second opinions. Health companies that help customers navigate healthcare's complex pathways will earn their loyalty. A good marketing campaign isn't sufficient. Rhetoric and performance must align or valuable customers will seek care services elsewhere.

The Oracle Speaks

Pundits affectionately describe Warren Buffett as the "Oracle of Omaha." Buffett's common sense, value-focused approach toward investment has generated enormous wealth and returns for his shareholders. His business aphorisms are insightful and popular. For example, Buffett once observed, "Only when the tide goes out do you discover who's been swimming naked."

Real value in healthcare is delivering the best outcomes at the lowest prices. As the fee-for-service tide recedes, America will discover which health companies are prepared for the value-driven demands of the post-reform marketplace. Winning health companies will employ a new playbook that emphasizes quality, embraces transparency, optimizes performance and, most importantly, embraces customers. As Warren Buffet shrewdly observed, "Price is what you pay. Value is what you get." Health companies that follow the value rules will rule their markets.

CHAPTER 6

DATA IS AS DATA DOES

In God we trust, all others must bring data.
W. EDWARDS DEMING

*Not everything that can be counted counts, and
not everything that counts can be counted.*
ALBERT EINSTEIN

Between finishing my Peace Corps service in Africa and beginning graduate school at Harvard, I worked as a general laborer for near-minimum wage at an electronics supply company in Providence, RI. It was not glamorous. I spent most of my time in the wire room filling customer orders for electric wire, but I also did janitorial work and drove a delivery truck. The work was hard. I gained 10 pounds of muscle lifting heavy wire spools on and off of storage shelves.

I studied calculus during my lunch break in a cubbyhole above the wire room. My fellow workers thought I was nuts, but knew I needed the money. Despite frequent ribbing, they gave me space to prepare for graduate school and my math skills soon came in handy. Billy, the wire room manager, struggled with a remnant problem. When a customer's wire order was less than a standard 100-foot spool, we'd cut the order and store the residual wire (the remnants) in scattered piles around the wire room. Over time the piles grew. It became impossible for us to fill custom orders from our remnant inventory.

A restless mind is a terrible thing to waste. For several weeks, I measured, sorted, stored and chronicled hundreds of remnant wire segments. Billy and I kept handwritten records in a blue college-ruled notebook. The results were spectacular:

- We filled customs order, when possible, from remnant inventory;

- We created a system for cataloguing new remnants;

- As we sold remnants, we reduced our storage needs and streamlined our order-filling process; and

- We saved the company thousands of dollars.

In recognition of my contribution, I received a wage increase of 25 cents per hour and an offer of full-time employment with potential for promotion. I declined graciously, cleaned a few more bathrooms and headed to Harvard. As a going-away gift, Ollie, the foreman, gave me a multi-ink pen, so I could "take better notes"—one of the best gifts I've ever received. I still have that pen, my "Dave" work shirt and a wire remnant to remind me that it's impossible to improve quality, efficiency and outcomes without the right data.

Data vs. Big Data

Before organizations can incorporate big data's capabilities, they first need data systems and organizational processes that enhance the jobs to be done. My wire room saga illustrates how a simple process improvement solved an inefficient inventory problem. Better data in combination with enhanced inventory storage enabled Billy and me to become more productive, deliver greater value to our employer and earn more money.

Health companies cannot benefit from big data's enhanced analytic, storage and computing properties until they properly identify their "jobs to be done" and develop complementary data and performance measurement systems. As discussed in the "Productivity Paradox" chapter, the principal "job to be done" at almost all health companies is optimizing revenues. Current provider data and management systems support revenue optimization quite well. Key metrics focus on occupancy, payer mix, surgical volume and patient turnover. Red flags appear when these key metrics decline because poor performance in these areas imperils profitability, credit standing and capital access.

Attaching quality and customer-engagement metrics to revenue-driven business models is the equivalent of putting seat belts in Indy 500 cars. They increase safety, but they cannot alter the inherent dangers embedded in racing packs of high-performance cars around tight oval speedways. Quality and customer-engagement metrics will never have enough organizational gravity to change incumbent behaviors as long as the jobs to be done center on revenue maximization.

To quote Hamlet, "There's the rub." Incumbent health companies cannot generate data and performance systems that both maximize revenues and deliver better, lower-cost healthcare services. These objectives conflict with one another. This inherent conflict between maximizing revenues and delivering value-based care explains why the industry's hodge-podge of data systems underperform. Despite billions spent on electronic medical records (EMRs), the systems have not demonstrably improved quality outcomes or transformed the patient experience. Commercial EMRs emphasize treatment billing as much or more than they do clinical care. It's complex to mix these functions and the result is suboptimal care delivery.

Data, even big data, is agnostic and follows function. Designers apply data systems to achieve specific outcomes. Health companies design data systems to achieve multiple outcomes, including revenue optimization or enhanced clinical care. Indeed, health companies invest more of their resources optimizing revenue than care delivery. Exploiting this market need, revenue cycle companies are investing heavily in big data capabilities to enhance collections from payers and patients. For example, they're using natural language processing to interpret doctors' notes to optimize billing codes. The same technology could optimize clinical protocols, but there is limited market demand for this capability.

Quality is Job 1

Paraphrasing the 1980s Ford ad: There's only one Job 1. Organizational vision cannot serve two masters. If a health company's Job 1 is maximizing revenues, the quality of its care suffers. It will underperform on quality and customer-engagement metrics. Data and performance measurement systems respond to organizational imperative. If health companies embrace consumerism and quality outcomes as their Job 1, effective data systems will follow.

Walled Gardens vs. Town Commons

Epic Systems dominates the commercial EMR market, covering 54 percent of U.S. patients.[131] Despite governmental mandates to share relevant health information, Epic's business model builds a walled garden around patient data for its health company clients. Its closed platform customizes and tightly controls software installations and ongoing platform development. Epic is under enormous pressure to share medical

---

131 http://host.madison.com/news/local/govt-and-politics/epic-systems-draws-on-litera-ture-greats-for-its-next-expansion/article_4d1cf67c-2abf-5cfd-8ce1-2da60ed84194.html

information more broadly.[132] Despite other commercial EMR companies (notably Cerner and McKesson) pursuing greater interoperability, Epic continues to gain market share. It's unclear when its garden wall will crack.

In contrast, the Veterans Administration employs VistA, a secure, open-source EMR. Unlike commercial EMRs that combine clinical and billing functions, VistA focuses solely on patient care, incorporates all relevant patient records, operates on a national platform and shares patient data easily with other EMR systems. Veterans and their care providers can access patient records at all VA facilities worldwide. Since the U.S. government funded VistA's development, the VA offers its award-winning VistA software for free on its website. VistA's intrinsic inter-operability facilitates care coordination, improves outcomes and reduces costs.[133]

A March 2014 RAND study[134] compared Epic and VistA. Even though they use the same underlying MUMPS source code, their different business models lead to strikingly different applications. RAND describes VistA as "the archetype of an enterprisewide EHR solution" supporting the "the largest integrated delivery system in the United States." It credits VistA with dramatically improving the health of America's veterans through better data dissemination and care coordination. Despite its open source platform, effectiveness and low cost, OpenVista (VistA's commercial product) has limited market penetration. Despite its high cost, Epic's closed platform is the preferred choice for America's large health systems with over 260 installations. It's gold-plated customer base includes the Cleveland Clinic, Johns Hopkins and Kaiser Permanente. The company has built a reputation for flawless execution of its customized installations. Epic gets the job done, although there is debate regarding the platform's clinical effectiveness.[135]

Epic's large health-system clients share Epic's ambivalence on interoperability. Controlling patient data creates market power. The RAND study highlights this market reality:

132 http://www.modernhealthcare.com/article/20141001/NEWS/310019945
133 http://www.healthcareitnews.com/blog/vista-epic-tale-two-systems
134 http://www.rand.org/content/dam/rand/pubs/research_reports/RR300/RR308/RAND_RR308.casestudies
135 *Ibid.*

The shift [to interoperability] will be less welcome to large legacy vendors because it will blur the competitive edge they currently enjoy. Health care systems may be less-than-enthusiastic adopters because functional health information exchanges will make it easier for patients to see non-affiliated healthcare providers or switch to a competing healthcare system.[136]

Healthcare is not the only industry to confront the dichotomy between open and closed systems and see advantages to both sides. With smartphones, operating systems like Android are open source while Apple is strictly proprietary; yet both perform exceptionally well in the marketplace. In healthcare, however, the consequences of a closed system's tight data control is antithetical to the intent of Congress when it passed HITECH (Health Information Technology for Economic and Clinical Health Act) in 2009, which committed $28 billion to digitize health records, accelerate EMR adoption and promote interoperability.

The lack of data interoperability blocks data sharing among providers and inhibits clinical care coordination and care transitions in appropriate, lower-cost settings like Minute Clinics, local pharmacies or e-visits. Today, only 39 percent of office-based providers share patient information with other providers within the same health system.[137] Even fewer, 15 percent, share outside their organizations. Within systems, roughly 50 percent of hospitals notify primary care physicians when their patients enter an emergency room; only 24 percent of hospitals notify primary care physicians outside of their system.[138] Unlike the VA's fully integrated care network, the rest of America's care delivery system fails to coordinate care consistently.

In 2013, a number of Epic's competitors joined forces in a group called the CommonWell Health Alliance to advance the cause of

---

136 *Ibid. p. 31*

137 http://healthitinteroperability.com/news/office-based-docs-lag-in-outward-health-information-exchange

138 http://dashboard.healthit.gov/quickstats/pages/FIG-Hospital-Routine-Electronic-Notification.php

interoperability. No doubt this initiative represents a competitive response to Epic's dominance, but it's also smart and aligns with value-based care delivery. The alliance's goal is to build a vendor-neutral service that facilitates health data exchange through common standards and protocols. Theoretically, a patient could walk into any care setting nationwide and access their patient records. In the long run, inter-operability will win. As the walled gardens come tumbling down and patient data flows freely, American healthcare will emerge stronger, better and more patient-centric.

Data Connections

The best way to picture data is as the middle layer of a three-part success hierarchy. Data flows to and from this middle tier to inform value-based operations (the bottom tier) and fully engaged customers (the top tier). The chart below captures these flows.

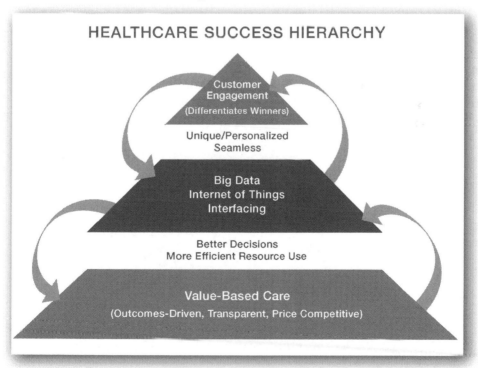

Bottom Tier: Value-Based Care

In post-reform healthcare, winning health companies will employ data to generate consistent high-quality outcomes, reduce performance variation and improve operational efficiency. Data inputs flow to and from operations to improve care design and execution. At the individual level, all relevant data from all sources flows into algorithms that optimize diagnosis and treatment. As data proliferates and analytics advance, individual genetic and environmental characteristics will lead to more personalized and less population-based therapies; more precision and less trial-and-error care. At the individual disease level, all relevant information from all sources flows into data systems advancing medical research and protocol development. Pricing and outcomes data will be transparent and available.

Top Tier: Customer Engagement

Unfortunately, getting the medical treatments right will not be sufficient to win in post-reform healthcare. Health companies also must engage customers to gain their trust, confidence and loyalty. This requires understanding customer needs, listening and responding to customer preferences and delivering user-friendly healthcare services. The winning health companies will offer unique, personalized, seamless, thoughtful and caring services.

None of this should be a surprise. Consumer purchasing drives 70 percent of the U.S. economy. Companies succeed and fail based on their ability to read and respond to consumers' sentiments. Consumer-oriented companies spend billions of dollars on polling, focus groups and test marketing to enhance their product offerings. Companies can't tell consumers what to do, they persuade. Leading through persuasion is antithetical to the cultures at most health companies where physicians make medical decisions on behalf of their patients. But a doctor-knows-best approach doesn't work for market-savvy American consumers.

Big data analytics are essential for understanding consumer preferences. Collecting, measuring and evaluating consumer data drive strategic growth and customer acquisition. Companies use big data to design appealing products and services. Health companies must develop the metrics, training and experiential learning to create customer-driven operations. Expect Ritz Carlton's and Disney's healthcare consulting practices to boom. Great customer service takes time, effort and investment.

Big Data's Promise, Peril and Creepiness

Big data changes everything it touches. It has enormous power to advance and harm civilization. Having the right data at the right time is essential for value-based care delivery and customer engagement. The application of big data, the Internet of things (connected devices) and interfacing (digital service connectivity, think Uber) into healthcare will revolutionize service delivery, business models and consumer behaviors. Buckle up. It's going to be an exciting, fast-paced, bumpy ride.

Before digging deeper, let's frame the discussion with two examples of big data's profound capabilities wrapped around a cyber-threat analysis. One story is inspiring, the other creepy; the filling in between is stomach-churning.

Analytics-Boosted Performance[139]

After finishing a distant 10th at the World Championships in 2012, the U.S. women's cycling team knew it had to improve its performance to compete for medals at the upcoming London Olympics. The struggling team turned to former Olympian cyclist Sky Christopherson. Disgusted with cycling's doping culture, Christopherson had developed an analytics-based training programed named "Optimized Athlete." His mantra was "data not drugs."

In the three months leading up to the Olympic Games, team members became big data repositories. Computers analyzed reams of nutrition, endurance, bio-physical, environmental and micro-performance

---

139   Forbes Magazine, *Big Data Not Doping*, Bernard Marr, June 8, 2015

measures. Small adjustments turbocharged individual performance. Here's an example:

> ...one cyclist, Jenny Reed, performed much better in training if she had slept at a lower temperature the night before. So she was provided with a temperature water-cooled mattress to keep her body at an exact temperature throughout the night. This had the effect of giving her better deep sleep, which is when the body releases human growth hormone and testosterone naturally...[140]

Big data analytics supported precision training by quantifying factors that influence performance. These included training loads, recovery cycles and muscle regeneration. The program also sensed stressors and minimized injuries. The data eliminated guesswork and primed the athletes for peak performance. They were ready for London.

Training hard and smart with data-driven performance adjustments propelled the U.S. women's cycling team to Olympic glory. Surprising the cycling world, the U.S. team captured the silver medal. Big data geeks around the world celebrated with the victorious U.S. women.

Healthcare's Ominous Cyber Threat[141]

Healthcare is a target-rich environment for cyber criminals. Digitized data passing through cyberspace invites unwanted guests. According to the *New York Times*, there were 750 major breaches at healthcare organizations from 2010 to 2015 involving electronic information on 29 million people. Attacks on Anthem and Premera Blue Cross insurance companies compromised the personal information of one in four Americans. Anthem alone had 80 million records accessed. The breach in Anthem's advanced security defenses remained undetected for months.

---

140 *Ibid.*
141 David Johnson, *Deep Web Rising: Healthcare's Looming Cyber Threat,* June 10, 2015

Crime pays. Accessing health information facilitates identity theft. Identity thieves crave robust medical records with birth dates, addresses, social security numbers, etc. Criminals can get $50 on the street for a full set of medical information on a person. By contrast, a credit card number is often worth just $4 or $5.[142]

Foreign governments (e.g. China, Russia) increasingly initiate attacks. Their expansive programs operate with impunity. They apply "advanced persistent threats" (APTs) that are patient, careful, nuanced and widespread—focusing on employees, sub-contractors and suppliers.

These cyber attacks aren't going away. The current defenses are leaky. Cyber security requires significant tradeoffs between protecting data and maintaining privacy; between data exchange and organizational productivity. Health companies must appreciate these tradeoffs, increase vigilance and confront the emerging cyber threat head-on. Awareness and employee education are essential. Aware employees spot atypical data patterns that identify cyber attacks. Appropriate encryption, hack-a-thons and health-system collaboration make sense. Adopting policies of least privilege (proactive data access) and assumed compromise (people are suspect until proven otherwise) are cost-effective methods for bolstering cyber defense.

There are two kinds of health companies. Those that have been hacked and those that don't know they've been hacked. Ignorance isn't a defense. Utilizing big data's capabilities comes with the responsibility to protect sensitive information.

Papa Don't Preach

Like many retailers, Target collects voluminous data on its customer purchasing patterns. Most shopping is habitual, but big life events, like getting married, shift buying habits. Retailers use big data analytics to identify customers experiencing a big life event, so they can lure them into their stores with personalized incentives. There is no bigger life event than having a baby. With that in mind, Target developed a

---

142 NY Times, *Anthem Hacking Points to Security Vulnerability of the Health Care Industry*, Feb. 5, 2015

model that assigns a pregnancy- prediction score based on purchases of 25 products during the first 20 weeks of pregnancy. The model also predicts the prospective birth date, which enables Target to send sequenced coupons at predetermined stages of the women's pregnancy (e.g. baby stroller coupon at seven months). Their model worked really well, perhaps too well.

A year after the pregnancy prediction model went live, a father stormed into his local Target store in Minneapolis demanding to see the manager. His teenage daughter was receiving coupons for baby clothes and cribs. The father wanted to know if Target was encouraging his daughter to become pregnant. The manager apologized and said he'd look into the matter. He called the man a few days later to apologize again. This time the man was contrite. During an emotional conversation with his daughter, he had learned she was pregnant and his future grandchild was due that August. Through big data analytics, Target discovered the man's daughter was pregnant before he did.[143]

Inevitably, companies and governments will mash healthcare data together with other data about purchases, food choices, exercise, work and personal finances to make predictions and judgments about specific individuals. Everyone and everything will have scores. Each person's digital footprint will shape his or her external interactions, often with no discernable indication that this is occurring. This will influence job hunting, dating, lending and, perhaps, access to healthcare services. Like any new technology, this has potential beneficial and destructive uses. Managing digital reputations and navigating digitized environments are new human experiences. Are we ready?

Digging into Big Data

McKinsey's January 2013 study *Big Data Revolution in Healthcare* estimates the U.S. healthcare system could reduce annual health expenditure by $300 billion to $450 billion through data-driven health

---

143 New York Times, *How Companies Learn Your Secrets*, Charles Duhigg, February 16, 2012

prevention, delivery, payment and innovation. Their research identified over 200 new healthcare information companies launched since 2010.[144] The federal government is allocating $40 billion to accelerate hospital adoption of EMRs and also is posting Medicare outcome, payment and customer satisfaction data. Premier, the provider-owned group purchasing organization, has created a for-profit subsidiary and issued stock to commercialize its member hospitals' data.

Mining massive data sets has the potential to personalize medicine, pre-empt disease and eliminate treatment redundancy. Google co-founder Larry Page extols the research benefits to be gained by sharing anonymous healthcare data with doctors and scientists.[145] Dr. Richard Platt, a drug-risk researcher at the FDA, estimates that giving researchers access to patients' health records would have reduced Vioxx-induced heart-attack deaths by 27,000 to 55,000.[146] Capturing the "evolution of patient's illnesses over time," Intel medical director, Dr. John Sotos, argues, will make doctors smarter about treating specific patient subsets.[147] However, big data also increases complexity, statistical noise and processing requirements. Big data's promise will materialize unevenly and require changing human behaviors (never easy).

Big Data's Promise

In *The Creative Destruction of Medicine*, renowned cardiologist Dr. Eric Topol asserts, "medicine is about to go through the biggest shakeup in its history." In Topol's world, informed consumers receive personalized therapies tailored to their genomes, informed by biosensors and delivered close to home. The following chart captures the super convergence of forces that Topol believes will transform medicine.

---

144 *The "Big Data" revolution in healthcare*, McKinsey & Company, Center for US Health System Reform, Business Technology Office, January 2013

145 http://www.businessinsider.com/larry-page-on-medical-records-and-sharing-information-2014-3

146 http://blogs.law.harvard.edu/infolaw/2012/06/22/death-by-hipaa/

147 http://blogs.wsj.com/experts/2015/03/24/how-big-data-can-make-your-doctor-smarter/

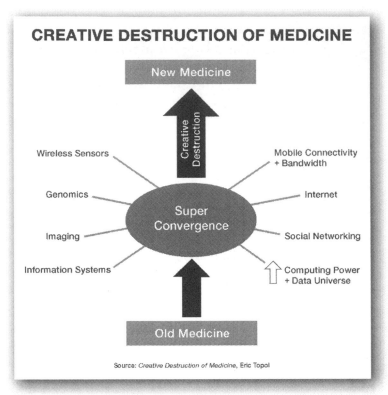

Source: *Creative Destruction of Medicine*, Eric Topol

To achieve Topol's vision, scientists will analyze massive data sets to predict disease, simulate treatments and reengineer protocols. Efficiency, precision and tailored delivery will optimize outcomes while minimizing impairment and cost. Hints of big data's potential are numerous: genetic markers for some cancers, more reliable patient screening, digital performance tracking of care professionals and identification of new environmental and behavioral disease triggers.

Bigger Haystacks

When aggregated, big data's health information (treatment histories, personalized medical data, individual genomes, digitized images and behavioral and environmental factors) creates data sets too large to comprehend. Topol says researchers sift through ever bigger "haystacks" (how much is a quintillion?) to discover a finite number of "needles" (i.e. meaningful relationships). In medicine, doctors require access to clinical data in real time to make appropriate treatment decisions. Health systems link clinical activity to patient bills. These are highly complex processes dependent on rapid, accurate filtering of massive, dynamic data sets.

In *The Signal and the Noise*, political forecaster Nate Silver explores why "prediction in the era of big data is not going very well" as evidenced by failure to foresee the September 11 attacks, the banking crisis and the Fukushima nuclear plant's vulnerability. Silver identifies several factors that make connecting the dots difficult in a big data environment:

Complexity: Computers make fast calculations and work best when simple rules govern. That's why IBM's Deep Blue computer could defeat chess grandmaster Gary Kasparov. Computer science has improved its predictive abilities with some dynamic systems (e.g. a hurricane's likely path). It is less effective in predicting outcomes for more complex systems. This is not a new realization. In the 1980s, Alan Greenspan observed that the global economy's complexity was increasing at a greater rate than our ability to model its behavior. The biological complexity of different cancers illustrates the point. Medical science has conquered some cancers (testicular cancer) while others (pancreatic cancer) defy understanding and cure.

Productivity Paradox: Productivity declines when information growth exceeds our ability to process it. This occurred in the 1980s with the emergence of desktop computing. Nobel economist Robert Solow observed in 1987 that "you could see the computer age everywhere except in the productivity statistics." Once systems could process computerized data efficiently, productivity exploded.

A January 2013 RAND study highlights the failure of EMRs to achieve their potential. This finding was notable because a

2005 RAND study was instrumental in garnering funding for EMR development. The study's abstract identifies the causes of failure as follows:

> *Sluggish adoption of health IT systems, coupled with the choice of systems that are neither interoperable nor easy to use; and the failure of health care providers and institutions to reengineer care processes to reap the full benefits of health IT."*

This is the productivity paradox at work.

More False Positives: As the amount of information expands so does the number of observed correlations and hypotheses to explain these correlations. As any statistician will shout: correlation does not mean causation. Wearing purple in Minneapolis doen't automatically make one a Minnesota Vikings fan. False positives are the statistical equivalents of fool's gold. Their explanatory power diasppears on closer examination. In *Naked Statistics*, economist Charles Wheelan highlights the damage caused by observed but unsubstantiated correlations between childhood vaccines and autism.[148] Despite categorical disproof of any linkage, thousands of parents chose not to vaccinate their children, many of whom then contracted and spread measles, mumps and other preventable diseases.

As big data analytics expand, false positives skyrocket. This is particularly damaging in medicine where small percentages of people carry specific diseases. For example, only 1.4 percent of women in their 40's (14 out of 1000) have breast cancer. Mammography identifies 75 percent of those cases accurately. Mammography misdiagnoses breast cancer (false positives) in 10 percent of the other 98.6 percent of women. Overall, only 10 percent of positive mammograms (11 out of 110 tests) accurately diagnose breast cancer. The other 90 percent are false positives.

---

148   Charles Wheelan, *Naked Statistics*, Conclusion, 2013

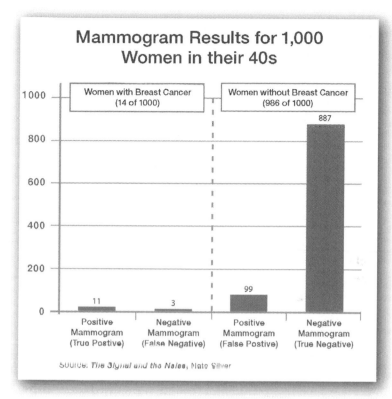

Mammogram Results for 1,000 Women in their 40s

Source: *The Signal and the Noise*, Nate Silver

A November 2012 *New England Journal of Medicine* study[149] estimates that 1.3 million American women received false-positive diagnoses for breast cancer in the past 30 years–leading these women to seek treatment for diseases they never had. The emotional and financial toll created by medical false-positives is catastrophic.

The Human Element

Although counterintuitive, big data's biggest challenges are human. Humans are pattern-seeking machines. At conscious and unconscious levels, people strive to understand and predict outcomes from sensory data. Most judgments are correct: People know when they're in danger; whom to trust and what to eat. But instinctive judgments

---

149 http://www.nejm.org/doi/full/10.1056/NEJMoa1206809?viewType=Print&viewClass=Print

are not always right. Bias infects decision-making through risk aversion, overconfidence, embedded memories, recent experience and so on. These cognitive biases also influence data interpretation: highlighting supportive data, ignoring important facts, overemphasizing unimportant data, missing obvious patterns and seeing nonexistent patterns.

Data-driven predictions can be either right or wrong. With more data comes more noise. In Silver's terminology, it's harder to find the "signal." Big data magnifies potential damage from human error in the same way that losing computer files with patient data is exponentially more damaging than losing paper medical records. For big data to realize its potential, medical researchers must develop evidenced-based systems that overcome human bias in diagnosis and treatment—not impossible but not easy either.

Extending pregnancy to term (usually 39 weeks) results in healthier babies, fewer Cesarean deliveries and significantly less neonatal care. Yet, many hospitals struggle to achieve full-term deliveries consistently because patients and physicians sometimes opt to induce an early delivery for non-medical reasons, such as convenience. Intermountain Healthcare has instituted evidenced-based protocols that result in full-term deliveries in almost all cases. Doctors Bryan Oshiro and Ware Branch have led development and implementation of Intermountain's elective induction protocols. Like all doctors, obstetricians believe they follow best practices and express surprise when evidence reveals otherwise. Knowing what to do is step one. Changing behavior is the other necessary and often more difficult step.

Medicine will realize big data's enormous potential over time as computer processing and human management capabilities coalesce. Successes will be intermittent and there will be failures. Big data's early wins will come less from the breakthrough discoveries Topol envisions and more from applying Intermountain-like discipline to build statistical evidence for established treatment protocols (e.g. limiting induced births).

The Internet of Things

The Internet of Things ("IoT") refers to the network of devices and systems that autonomously communicate and exchange digitized information. The IoT is at work when cars tell drivers that tire pressure is low. MarketResearch.com reports that the healthcare IoT market will reach $117 billion by 2020.[150] IoT services will include fall prevention/detection systems, monitoring devices, medical refrigerators, medication management and fitness wearables.

The Internet of Things will facilitate care coordination. Constant monitoring of patients with diabetes or hypertension will alert care providers to worrying anomalies. Earlier interventions and preventive care strategies will become more prevalent and effective. Interactive systems combined with sensors will improve treatment adherence. It's entirely possible that future Apple watches will become interactive health platforms that guide individuals toward healthy behaviors—at least when they're not guiding people toward cheesier pizza.

Interfacing Changes Everything

More suits aggregate in downtown San Francisco each January for JP Morgan's Healthcare Conference than the rest of the year combined. A month before the 2014 conference, I searched for lodging. Talk about sticker shock. No rooms were available for less than $1,000 per night. Out of desperation (or inspiration), I browsed the Vacation Rentals by Owner ("VRBO") website and rented a well-located, one-bedroom apartment for $200 a night.

VRBO is a phenomenal service. We rent Lake Michigan vacation cottages every August through its website. VRBO offers abundant choice, competitive prices and incredible convenience. Here's the thing: Like Airbnb, VRBO doesn't own or manage any properties. It connects customers like me with property owners looking for short-term renters. VRBO is a classic interface company—those that use sophisticated software to connect people with other people or services online.

---

150 http://www.forbes.com/sites/tjmccue/2015/04/22/117-billion-market-for-internet-of-things-in-healthcare-by-2020/

Interface companies are the fastest-growing, most profitable companies in history. Think Uber, Facebook, Google, Twitter, Airbnb, YouTube, Priceline. Their value resides in interfacing software, not in owning hard assets. In a fascinating *TechCrunch* article,[151] Tom Goodwin describes this new breed of company:

> *These companies are indescribably thin layers that sit on top of vast supply systems (where the costs are) and interface with a huge number of people (where the money is). There is no better business to be in.*

It's a great business model because the best interface companies own valuable customer relationships at very low operating costs. Like heat-seeking missiles, interfacing companies target and exploit market inefficiencies with precision and deadly effect. Armed with abundant supply and price flexibility, interface companies compete with the big brands for customer loyalty (think Expedia vs. Marriott). Strong brands expand their loyalty programs (at great cost) to compete.

Healthcare Interfacing

Like many disruptive innovations, interfacing is attacking healthcare later in its development cycle. Regulatory barriers, opaque pricing and complex supplier relationships make healthcare a tough industry to penetrate. It is perhaps fitting that by-products of healthcare's protective barriers (asset-heavy providers, revenue-centric business models, ineffective cost control) make incumbent health companies particularly vulnerable to value-based attacks. Interfacing technologies will attack vulnerabilies embedded within entrenched business models in the following ways:

- Centralized, overbuilt and underutilized acute-centric facilities: Interface companies exploit excess capacity for consumers' benefit.

---

151 http://techcrunch.com/2015/03/03/in-the-age-of-disintermediation-the-battle-is-all-for-the-customer-interface/

- High-cost operations: Interface companies drive volume to low-cost, convenient suppliers.

- Increasing commoditization: Most treatments, including surgical procedures, have become routine and easy to barter.

- Volume-driven: Providers covet cash-paying customers and slash prices to attract them.

The changing colonoscopy market illuminates the disruptive threat of interfacing to routine care providers. Ten million Americans annually undergo colonoscopies at a cost approximating $10 billion. Colonoscopy prices can cost as much as $5,000 or as little as $500. Irving, Texas-based ColonosocopyAssist offers all-in, fixed-priced colonoscopies for $1,075. It provides services in 34 states without owning or managing any treatment facilities. Given that companies like ColonsocopyAssist are gaining market share, colonoscopy prices nationwide are falling. They should coalesce at or below $1,000 with procedures performed in convenient, low-cost settings.

These forays are just the beginning; I'll describe other interface companies in Chapter 7. Expect all-out assaults on routine care as interface companies aggregate users and providers. Some interfacing companies, like ColonsocopyAssist, will specialize while others will provide broader treatment menus. All will drive prices for routine care lower. Some interface companies, including SmartShopper and HealthEngine, offer payments to customers who agree to receive treatments at lower-cost venues. Imagine that business model's disruptive potential if it gains substantial market penetration.

Digital competition is winner-take-all. While hundreds of early-stage interface companies aspire to control customer demand for routine procedures, only a handful of Ubers and Lyfts will emerge. The winners will become powerful market drivers for transparent and value-based service delivery. Uber-like companies are coming to healthcare and customers will love them. When interfacing changes healthcare's supply and demand relationships (and it will), the change will happen fast. Be prepared.

Right Data. Right Time. Right Way

Technology is on the cusp of channeling diagnosis and treatment toward best outcomes at lowest costs. The emergence of unbelievably powerful cognitive computing platforms makes this possible. Like all technological advances, cognitive computing has great promise, disruptive application and the potential for misuse. Cognitive computing will deliver value when medicine harnesses its power to keep people healthy, intervene with precision and eliminate unnecessary costs.

Tech guru Michael Fertik, co-author of *The Reputation Economy* and founder of Reputation.com, uses the acronym "DAMM" (Decisions Almost Made by Machines) to describe how cognitive computing reshapes human decision-making. In Fertik's view, the convergence of the following three forces unleashes cognitive computing's power:

Big Search: In the DAMM world, the quantity of structured and unstructured data is swelling at an astonishing rate. A 2011 report from CSC, a global technology consulting company, estimates that the data universe in 2020 will be 35 zeta bytes (don't ask), an amount 44 times greater than in 2009. Search algorithms find targeted data/knowledge within massive data sets almost instantaneously.

Big Storage: For the first time in human history, it is cheaper to keep than delete data. Storing big data is essentially free. Nothing disappears and everything is searchable.

Big Analytics: The ecosystem's final piece is the emergence of powerful analytic platforms that collate, assess, interpret and visualize data. Big analytics brings meaning to unstructured big data, such as physician notes. It reassembles data/knowledge in ways that foster informed decision-making.

Powerful search engines curate data/knowledge. Big analytics employs choice architecture to evaluate and rank inputs. Results shape decision-making. For example, big analytics can assess thousands of job applicants using multiple sources (including social media) to narrow candidate selection. Aided by machines, managers make the final decisions. This is DAMM in action. In the future, every institution, person, service and product will receive machine-based performance scores. These scorecards will guide human human decision-making.

Big analytics is bringing equivalent scorecards to medicine. Machine-driven algorithms rank every clinician, institution and procedure. Customers increasingly make healthcare purchasing decisions based on these performance rankings. Companies that earn superior scores gain market share. The machine-driven selection process eliminates underperforming providers, usually without their knowledge. The emergence of big analytics offers enormous potential for improving organizational decision-making. No industry needs enhanced decision-making tools more than healthcare. Delivering the right care at the right time requires sophisticated care protocols informed by personalized health data from multiple sources.

Meaningful performance improvement begins with mission clarity and leadership. Data, metrics and solutions follow. Health companies that embrace value-based delivery can transform entrenched business practices. Properly focused, big analytics liberates companies. Powerful software drives performance improvement toward better outcomes and lower costs. MultiScale Health Networks and GaussSoft are two new companies that use big analytics to enhance decision-making and turbocharge performance.[152]

Launched in 2013, MultiScale Health Networks is a joint-venture with Providence Health & Services. According to its founder, Jim

---

152 Please note the author serves as an advisor to GaussSoft and MultiScale Health Networks

Harding, MultiScale is operating in "stealth mode" within Providence to deliver better outcomes. MultiScale is creating an Amazon-scale, big analytics application and data platform. It uses historical care data and retrospective analysis to guide prospective medical decision-making and optimize care efficiency. That giant sucking sound you don't hear is MultiScale's machine-based learning platform absorbing vast quantities of healthcare information and knowledge from all relevant data sources. MultiScale combines real-time, event-driven analytics with clinical expertise to deliver superior outcomes through enhanced workflow and process optimization.

Early successes include advances in neurology and cardiology as well as improved efficiency in both emergency and operating rooms. MultiScale designs effective, user-friendly point-of-care decision tools. In contrast to centralized EMR solutions, MultiScale's decentralized and distributive platform constantly improves its treatment algorithms as its knowledge universe expands. Healthcare delivery is personal, complex and idiosyncratic. It's breathtaking to consider how much better medical decision-making will become when medical professionals combine their expertise with transformative decision-support technology. MultiScale is leading the way. Harding believes the right time for the right data in healthcare delivery is right now.

While MultiScale uses big analytics to generate superior care outcomes, GaussSoft uses big analytics to increase organizational understanding of costs, resources and performance. Under fee-for-service reimbursement, costs are a secondary consideration. In essence, complex reimbursement formularies include expense allocations. Hospitals and doctors optimize treatment payment, not treatment efficiency. It hasn't paid to be cost-conscious. When measuring costs, almost all hospitals employ allocation methodologies that homogenize expenses and obscure precise performance measurement. Employing proven costing methodologies, notably time-driven activity-based costing (TDABC), has been too complex, too time-consuming and too expensive. Until now.

GaussSoft employs big analytics to implement TDABC through natural flow costing (NFC). GaussSoft's technology can measure millions of objects (products and services) at increasingly granular levels of analysis—as many levels as necessary to replicate actual expenditure patterns. By contrast, almost all other TDABC solutions account for a fraction of a million objects and only three or four levels of analysis. NFC uses existing data sources so implementation is faster and less expensive. To enhance its effectiveness, GaussSoft employs powerful data visualization tools to illuminate resource utilization, operating efficiency and relative profitability. Like MultiScale, GaussSoft is DAMM in action. Through big analytics, it enables front-line managers to make superior resource allocation decisions. The results: better care outcomes, higher quality, lower costs and greater profitability.

Righteous Analytics

For all its promise, machine-based learning is purely computational. Computers process 1s and 0s in search of statistically significant correlations. These correlations become the basis for probability-adjusted predictions that are increasingly accurate and insightful. However, correlation is not causation. Measurement has embedded error. Aided by machine-driven analytics, human judgment remains essential to advanced decision-making. The most important human inputs for computing platforms are organizational mission, vision, outcomes and objectives. This is not a new idea. In the 1500s, Martin Luther observed, "People must have righteous principals in the first, and then they will not fail to perform virtuous actions."

What is true for people is also true for organizations. The righteous first principles in healthcare are best outcomes, lowest costs, highest quality and customer-centric service. When their organizations embrace value-based care, big and righteous analytics will deliver the right data, at the right time and in the right way to healthcare decision-makers.

CHAPTER 7

IT'S THE CUSTOMER, STUPID!

We see our customers as invited guests to a party, and we are the hosts. It's our job every day to make every important aspect of the customer experience a little bit better.

JEFF BEZOS, CEO AMAZON.COM

A merica runs on value. It's in our DNA. Incumbent healthcare companies are largely tone deaf to consumers' needs. They execute transactions with limited patient involvement. Their mindset screams, "Care providers treat patients, not customers." Most healthcare executives don't even like the word "customer." Implicitly, they believe patients have little or no power. A payment system that rewards treatment volume reinforces this unbalanced relationship. It leaves little room for patient, dare we say customer, needs.

Power shifts when consumers make choices. Demand-driven change generates super-hero results. Suppliers bend to satisfy demanding customers. High-deductible health plans, more price and outcomes transparency and a surge in negative press are making ordinary Americans more aware of their healthcare purchasing power and more deliberate in their healthcare decisions.

Consider how other industries capitalize on customer engagement. Amazon has cut a swathe through industry after industry by focusing on low-cost, extreme convenience and maximizing customer value. Decry the loss of bookstores, but acknowledge that consumers purchase 40 percent of new books online through Amazon. Like heat-seeking missiles, customers seek Amazon's low prices and enjoy the convenience of one-click shopping.

Jeff Bezos, Amazon's founder and CEO, focuses relentlessly on discovering and delivering value to customers. Bezos crystalizes Amazon's vison succinctly, "We've had three big ideas at Amazon that we've stuck with... Put the customer first. Invent. And be patient. They're the reasons we're successful."

New-economy companies are leveraging technology, data and a Bezos-like emphasis on customers to amplify their value propositions, disrupt their industries and win market share. Netflix decimated Blockbuster by delivering low-cost DVDs with convenience. Now it's invented a new way to watch TV. The company produces high-quality programming (e.g. *House of Cards*), releases new episodes simultaneously and allows customers to binge-watch entire seasons. Why? The company's research indicated customers wanted this flexibility. Viewers are flocking to Netflix.

What do healthcare customers want? It's up to health companies to figure this out and deliver the goods.

Understanding the "Pictures in Customers' Heads"

The job to be done in almost all hospitals is driving treatment volume, particularly for high-paying, commercially insured patients. This business model optimizes revenue generation but neglects patients' real needs. It takes healthcare away from its healing traditions and its obligations under the Hippocratic Oath. Dr. David Feinberg discovered this medical-industrial- complex behavior at the UCLA Hospital System (now UCLA Health) when he became its CEO in 2007. Under Feinberg's leadership, UCLA transformed into a patient-centered organization. UCLA's story is a cautionary tale that depicts what can go wrong and right in healthcare delivery.

Feinberg inherited a $2.2 billion health system that was high-tech, highly ranked and arrogant. UCLA performed more organ transplants than any other U.S. hospital. It treated a million and a half patients per year and had Nobel Prize-winners on its staff. *U.S. News* ranked UCLA #1 in the West and #3 in the country. UCLA practiced amazing medicine but treated its patients terribly. The facilities were dirty and uncomfortable. Patients didn't know who was in charge of their care. There weren't enough wheelchairs or bedpans. Two out of three patients *would not* recommend UCLA to their family and friends.

Feinberg was stunned. He characterized UCLA's mission as, "Aren't you lucky you get to see us?" UCLA's rhetoric didn't mirror patients' experience. Feinberg halted all advertising and marketing campaigns. He needed to understand how an institution capable of performing miracles only ranked in the 38th percentile for referrals.

Feinberg knew he needed to experience UCLA through patients' eyes. He instituted mandatory rounds for himself and his leadership team. They visited patients, introduced themselves, asked patients about their care, offered to be helpful and left their cards.

On the ground level, UCLA was a mess. The hot food was never hot, the rooms were dirty, emergency visits for simple ailments took an average of 9 to 10 hours, and hospital workers never looked patients in the eye, introduced themselves, or explained what they were doing. In other words, UCLA was undermining its ability to deliver world-class care by failing to provide basic customer services.[153]

Feinberg's investigation into patient experiences revealed the truth: Negative "pictures" existed in patients' heads regarding UCLA's care quality, service delivery and customer experience. Until UCLA addressed its service issues and created "new pictures," the institution would continue to struggle. UCLA learned that conversations with patients and families are the best "technology" for achieving customer engagement, empathy and understanding. After months of investigation, observation and listening to patients, Feinberg instituted key, customer-focused changes. They included the following:

- Fast-tracking less-intensive ER patients to receive treatment in under 90 minutes;
- Having staff wear color-coded scrubs so patients could quickly identify their role;
- Creating lift teams to move heavy patients to increase efficiency and reduce harm;
- Teaching staff to make eye contact, identify themselves and explain their activities;
- Hiring professionals with interpersonal skills and a service orientation; and
- Making everyone responsible for facility cleanliness.

Feinberg realized quickly that patients in Southern California's competitive healthcare market had choices. UCLA needed to treat its patients as customers. UCLA needed to become *the* medical center of choice.

These customer-centric changes transformed UCLA. The organization's culture shifted from "you're lucky to see us" to "how can I help you?" Going further, Feinberg replicated Ritz Carlton's TalentPlus

---

153 https://www.youtube.com/watch?v=cZ5u7p-ZNuE

program to ensure new employees exhibited a service-orientation, empathy and patient-focus.

Today UCLA is the #1 academic medical center in the country and ranks in the 99th percentile for referrals. It is also the only academic medical center that has the word "kindness" in its mission statement.

Chasing Colonoscopies

Who knew a routine colonoscopy could illuminate the wild world of healthcare consumerism? Before getting to my story, let's examine the current state of colonoscopies in America.[154]

Colonoscopies are the most expensive way to detect colon cancer and prices vary widely. According to the 2012 report[155] by the International Federation of Health Plans, the average U.S. colonoscopy price was $1,195. The 25th percentile price was $536 and 95th percentile price was $2,627. Higher prices incorporate higher facility costs but do not improve outcomes. Procedures performed in hospitals and surgery centers are more expensive than those performed in doctors' offices.

Prior to 2000, colonoscopies were rare. That year, newscaster Katie Couric had a live colonoscopy on the *Today Show*. After her husband's death from colon cancer, Couric became a prominent advocate for colorectal screening.

Also in 2000, the American College of Gastroenterology announced that colonoscopies were the preferred strategy for preventing colon cancer. Heavy lobbying followed, and Congress directed Medicare to pay for regular colonoscopy screenings. Commercial insurers followed Medicare's lead and colonoscopies became standard preventive care for people over age 50.

Colonoscopy procedures are lucrative. Gastroenterologists are among America's highest paid physicians with average salaries in 2009 of $433,000.[156] Anesthesiologists also benefit financially from colonos-

---

154 Source: *The $2.7 Trillion Medical Bill*, Elisabeth Rosenthal, New York Times, June 1, 2013

155 http://static.squarespace.com/static/518a3cfee4b0a77d03a62c98/t/51dfd9f9e4b0d 1d8067dcde2/1373624825901/2012%20iFHP%20Price%20Report%20FINAL%20 April%203.pdf

156 *Ibid.*

copies even though a RAND study[157] found no medical justification for their high-cost services with healthy patients.

As preventive care, most insurers, including Medicare, cover the entire cost of colonoscopy procedures. Patients bear limited or no payment responsibility and have been indifferent to the procedure's wide price variation. That is changing.

An Anal Odyssey

In early November 2014, I had my annual medical check-up. My primary care physician noted I was overdue for a colonoscopy. He subsequently gave me an order for the procedure and a phone number to schedule it. Let's set the stage: My family has a history of colon cancer; secondly, my wife and I had just enrolled in a high-deductible health plan (HDHP) for 2015; and finally (as in *Dragnet*) I have changed participant names "to protect the innocent."

> **Stop #1 - Dominant University Hospital ("DUH"):** The next day I called DUH's GI clinic. Before scheduling the procedure, the receptionist spent 10 minutes recording my medical history. After a few minutes, I suggested she take necessary medical information from DUH's electronic medical record. She demurred insisting their doctors needed relevant information presented in a uniform way. I persisted, but she held all the cards. We finished the interview. Talk about patient (dis)empowerment!

> With my medical information recorded, we turned to scheduling. The first available appointment was St. Patrick's Day—almost five months away. If I had colon cancer, I didn't want to wait for leprechauns to learn about it. As important, I also wanted the procedure done in 2014 to avoid paying for the procedure under my HDHP. Hitting a brick wall, I became DUH's worst nightmare, a loyal customer seeking treatment outside their network.

---

157 http://www.rand.org/health/feature/anesthesia-costs.html

Stop #2 - Awesome Community Health Enterprise ("ACHE"): ACHE had a hospital near me, so I called general information to schedule a colonoscopy appointment. DUH's only consolation is that ACHE's customer service was even worse. It took five more calls to get to the right scheduling location, a GI practice associated with the hospital.

The office manager asserted they could complete the procedure in 2014, but not until I scheduled an evaluation exam with one of their specialists. Since the procedure was routine and I already had medical authorization, seeing the specialist was a waste of time. She insisted. I persisted, believing the only benefit was incremental income to the specialist. I finally said, "Thanks but no thanks." She scheduled the evaluation exam anyway. I know because I received a robo-call reminder the next week.

Stop #3 - Yelp and Dr. Avis Goodheart: Now what? The two biggest institutions near me couldn't meet my needs. I checked my health insurer's website for GI doctors, but found no useful information. Finally, I went to Yelp and found Dr. Avis Goodheart, a local gastroenterologist with three five-star ratings. The Yelp ratings didn't give me confidence. A June 2015 *U.S. News* commentary[158] observed that online physician ratings are highly unreliable.

Not knowing what else to do, I called her office. She came to the phone, agreed the procedure was routine (no preliminary exam needed) and offered me Thursday and Saturday dates in December. That's right, Saturdays! Her patients are often busy during the week and Saturday procedures make their lives easier. You could have knocked me over with a feather.

---

158 http://www.usnews.com/opinion/blogs/policy-dose/2015/06/12/online-doctor-ratings-are-garbage?utm_campaign=Brookings+Brief&utm_source=hs_cmail&utm_medium=email&utm_content=18313697&_hsenc=p2ANqtz-839Wa9iwQTgWxJzSnmHcc-Wg21RSSvysY9CWCjPVoilbZI-KHD0_LghV3hluD

The procedure went smoothly. Goodheart gave me photos of my clean colon and called me herself that afternoon to make sure I was recovering well. Shouldn't this be everyone's experience? It will be.

Somewhere in America

The Avis Goodhearts are out there. Imagine a group of consumer-oriented GI doctors delivering a seamless, personalized colonoscopy experience tailored to customers' needs, schedules and preferences. They'll rent procedure space at bargain rates from facility-heavy companies like DUH and ACHE. They'll answer all questions with a smile. They'll publish their prices and guarantee their work.

Imagine data companies crunching billions of medical records and customer surveys to align customers' medical needs with prospective doctors. ZocDoc and MD Insider are already doing this. Their recommendations will only get better. Imagine consumers discovering better, cheaper and more convenient colonoscopy centers. Katie Couric will become their champion.

Demanding consumers, customer-oriented providers and user-friendly information companies have enough market power to reconfigure healthcare's distorted supply-demand relationships. DUHs and ACHEs of the world beware:

> *2020 News Flash: Dr. Avis Goodheart, CEO of fast-growing Excel Colon Care, announces her company will offer $400 colonoscopies seven days a week at Walmart stores nationwide.*

Right Care. Right Time. Right Place.

Colonoscopies have become commodity care. They're routine, predictable and standardized. The following matrix identifies care delivery models based on their duration and uncertainty.

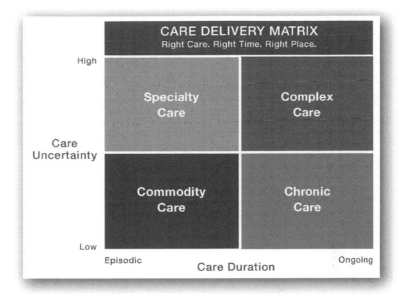

Each quadrant requires a different business model to compete in post-reform healthcare. One size will not fit all. Like colonoscopies, the majority of acute care treatments and procedures are routine and subject to commoditization. As products and services commoditize, consumer perceptions of quality shift from outcomes to speed, convenience and price. Health companies that understand commodity care will transform their operations to deliver better care at lower prices in customer-friendly venues. Organizations like DUH and ACHE that cannot schedule routine procedures quickly and/or require unnecessary preliminary exams must adapt or die. Winners differentiate. Value rules.

Second Opinion, Please!

A good friend (let's call him John Donne) in his mid-50s wrote me in 2015 describing his treatment for early-stage prostate cancer. Donne's journey starts terribly but ends well. Lessons abound. He titled his message "Cure vs. Treatment." Before sharing Donne's story, it's helpful to revisit the Hippocratic Oath (modern version[159]). Among its other covenants, the oath stresses the following:

- Holistic care: treat "sick human beings" not "fever charts" or "cancerous growths";

- Appropriate care: avoid "overtreatment" and "therapeutic nihilism";

- Collaboration: share knowledge and consult with other physicians;

- Self-awareness, empathy and humility: understand personal limitations; and

- Prevention: know prevention "is preferable to cure."

Consider the Hippocratic Oath while reading John's letter.

Dave,

Love your commentaries!

I was recently and awkwardly introduced to the dark side of healthcare. I just finished external beam radiation and brachytherapy for early prostate cancer.

What I came across was so evil and scary (across the board)—the level of greed and ethical corruption in conventional cancer care is unfathomable.

My local doc checked my PSA and referred me with a "just-over-the-threshold score" to a urologist within his system. When I asked for another opinion, there was an eight-week wait for an appointment.

---

159 Written in 1964 by Louis Lasagna, Academic Dean of the School of Medicine at Tufts University, and used in many medical schools today.

The local-yokel urologist did a biopsy, found two of 18 samples malignant and observed the following:

1) *Surgery was really my only option. He dismissed radiation by rolling his eyes. Seriously, no words, just an eyeroll. He said his new Da Vinci (branded robot) is the very coolest thing. He'd done almost a 100 procedures in his career, "which might as well be a million."*

2) *Questioned how much I valued my sexual function because "there are a lot of nerves that might accidently get severed"; and*

3) *I stood a really good chance of living 10 years longer.*

I just smiled and vowed never to see his face again. I know an "aw shucks" huckster when I see one.

I called my scientist brother. He referred me to a prostate cancer specialist, who stopped counting at 5,000 procedures. My good friend, a retired banker, had just done a nationwide search for a similar condition and recommended the same specialist.

The specialist concluded I had two options: surgery (not robotic, which is still experimental); or brachytherapy, the seed implants. I was not a good candidate for surgery, since the three tumors were in difficult places and would require retreatment within five years.

The specialist further noted that brachytherapy has a 97 percent cure rate with a 2 percent chance of incontinence and near-zero chance of impotence. He recommended five weeks of external beam radiation combined with brachytherapy. I just finished the treatments with no side effects.

I asked him why other docs prescribe high-risk treatments when less risky, more curative therapies exist. He said that each case is very different, depending on the patient's age, health and tumor characteristics.

He would not throw another physician under the bus. What I see, however, is a guy in a hospital system paying for his Da Vinci machine and his Mercedes. With his prescribed treatment, his health system could bill up to 20 procedures instead of just one or two. If side effects emerged from my bad decision (getting just one treatment opinion from the local yokel), so much the better for the health system.

I have never seen such a corruption of "sacrosanct trust." You can throw out the "Hypocritical Oath"!

The AMA won't adjudicate protocols because its statistical methodology allows for broad interpretations that keep the big health systems' "treatment machines" rolling.

That "doctors" are free to market their treatments as "best practice" is a sham. It's sad my local doctor could not warn me about the medical circus I was entering, since he participates in the same circus.

My father-in-law got caught in this mess a few years ago and died of liver cancer that started in his prostate. He trusted his local-yokel urologist to remove all of the cancerous tumors. The last two years of his life were unbearable due to chemo treatments. Still, his hospital billed his insurance early and often.

It is really sad that that a local yokel feels free to weigh my life and well-being against his need to pay for expensive equipment and "feed" his parent health system through misdiagnosis and overtreatment of well-insured individuals.

I know I am preaching to the choir, but this is a real conspiracy that touches average people and they suffer from it.

John

Where to begin? The Hippocratic Oath is a good place. Grounded in ancient Greek philosophy, it mandates patient-centered care, humility and consultation. Donne experienced none of these behaviors until he connected with the national specialist.

Donne is a highly educated and very capable professional with an expansive network. These attributes enabled him to resist and overcome health system pressure for expensive, inappropriate and likely harmful treatment. Good for him.

It's his last sentence, however, that haunts me. Don't all individuals, regardless of their circumstances, deserve meaningful second opinions when confronting scary medical diagnoses? The *revenue-first mindset* that governs U.S. medicine resists external interventions. It drives high volumes of profitable procedures through aligned facilities. As Donne's story demonstrates, patient needs are too often secondary considerations.

Emerging Market Solutions

Competitive markets respond to customer needs by developing solution-oriented products and services. There is a huge unmet need for meaningful second opinions. Grand Rounds and Pinnacle Care are industry leaders in providing independent second opinions. Two-thirds of Grand Rounds' case reviews recommend different treatment regimens. In 40 percent of Grand Rounds' reviews of prescribed surgeries, its experts recommend non-surgical therapies.[160] Pinnacle Care reports similar outcomes. It collected data about second opinions it performed from 2012–2014[161] and found that in a sampling of 1,000 cases with known outcomes: 41 percent led to a transfer of care to an expert provider; 34 percent resulted in a change of diagnoses and/or treatment; and 18 patients avoided unnecessary surgery.

Consider that 5 percent of all patients receive a misdiagnosis.[162] Pinnacle assists with research, care coordination, medical record con-

---

160 https://www.grandrounds.com/

161 https://www.pinnaclecare.com/second-look-can-save-your-life/

162 *Ibid.*

solidation and appointment scheduling. Its employees even attend second-opinion appointments with its customers[163] There's no mistaking that this is customer-driven service. Grand Rounds, Pinnacle and like-minded companies strive to deliver the appropriate amount of care to get the best outcomes. Their interests align with their customers' interests. The result is better, less harmful, more compassionate and more cost-effective care.

Currently, customers for second-opinion companies are wealthy individuals and self-insured employers. Companies pay small per-member-per-month fees to cover their employees. In consumer-driven reform, however, the market for independent second opinions will expand to counteract healthcare's information asymmetry (Donne's "local-yokel" problem). Enlightened payers and providers will offer independent second opinions to engaged customers and win their loyalty.

Celebrities who talk publically about their personal health decisions have inspired colonoscopies (Katie Couric); preventive double mastectomies (Angeline Jolie) and life-saving second opinions (Rita Wilson). Their candor is empowering consumers to ask questions and advocate for their own healthcare. Rita Wilson's initial tests did not detect her breast cancer. Her instincts and decision to get a second opinion led her to the surgery that saved her life.[164] She remains outspoken about the need to be vigilant and "arm yourself with information.[165]

No One is an Island

I chose my friend Donne's pseudonym purposefully. John Donne is the best-known of England's 17th century metaphysical poets. The following paragraph in Donne's eloquent *Meditation #17* (written in 1623) inspired the title for Ernest Hemingway's best-selling novel *For Whom the Bell Tolls* and Simon and Garfunkel's hit song "I am a Rock."

163 https://www.pinnaclecare.com/employees/

164 http://www.today.com/health/today-viewers-share-stories-how-second-opinions-save-lives-t15466

165 http://www.nydailynews.com/life-style/health/rita-wilson-breast-cancer-lesson-men-article-1.2188119

No man is an island, entire of itself; every man is a piece of the continent, a part of the main. If a clod be washed away by the sea, Europe is the less, as well as if a promontory were, as well as if a manor of thy friend's or of thine own were: any man's death diminishes me, because I am involved in mankind, and therefore never send to know for whom the bell tolls; it tolls for thee.

When American medicine misdiagnoses and overtreats, it diminishes consumers' confidence in the entire healthcare system. The American people deserve better. Independent, expert second opinions conducted in full consultation with patients, the customers, should be our standard of care. Consumer-driven reform demands better healthcare services and the market is responding.

We all are in this together.

Informed and Courageous

For too long, an autonomous physician culture, fee for service financial incentives and lack of outcomes transparency have limited patient participation in treatment decisions. Consumerism is pressuring healthcare providers to shift from this established mindset toward patient-centered care. While surrounding the patient with an integrated team of care providers and supporting that care delivery with technology is critical, it is even more important to give the patient a voice and a prominent role in the decision-making process.

Video Maven

"If necessary, would you like us to administer CPR?" First-year intern Angelo Volandes posed this question to a middle-aged Yale poetry professor with metastasizing brain cancer. The patient and her husband struggled to comprehend her end-of-life care alternatives. They heard Dr. Volandes' words but didn't understand their meaning. After a frustrating hour, Volandes suggested they tour the ICU. Seeing an intubated patient on a ventilator clarified their thinking. The distinguished professor died after a couple of good months in hospice—at home, comforted by her husband and surrounded by her cherished poetry books. While her story is sad, the professor was an informed patient who received the care she wanted. She achieved this positive outcome in partnership with her young doctor. Seeing the power of visual experience, Volandes took a year off from medicine to study filmmaking.

Fast-forward. Today, Angelo Volandes is an assistant professor at Harvard Medical School, an internist at Massachusetts General Hospital and CEO of Life Matters Media. The company produces simple, succinct films running six to seven minutes in length and designed to engender shared decision-making for life-threatening medical conditions (e.g. advanced dementia, heart disease, cancer). Each video is fact-based, non persuasive and nonjudgmental. Production teams include interventionists, cardiologists, oncologists, health literacy experts, ethicists and palliative care doctors.[166] Volandes has found that patients watching these videos better understand their own end-of-life care choices.[167] Interestingly, informed patients (like the Yale literature professor) generally make more conservative end-of-life care decisions, requesting "few or no life-prolonging procedures."[168]

Advancing Advanced Directives

Customer-focused providers like Volandes are changing healthcare by developing shared decision-making tools. Gundersen Lutheran Health System in LaCrosse, WI, has made end-of-life conversations a communitywide initiative. In the mid 1980s, the health system launched its Respecting Choices program[169] to bring hospital-based nurses, social workers and chaplains together to help patients plan and file advance directives with the hospital.

---

166 http://www.commonwealthfund.org/publications/newsletters/quality-matters/2012/june-july/qa

167 Jonathan Rauch, *How Not to Die,* TheAtlantic.com, Apr 24 2013; http://www.theatlantic.com/magazine/archive/2013/05/how-not-to-die/309277/2/

168 http://www.commonwealthfund.org/publications/newsletters/quality-matters/2012/june-july/qa

169 http://www.gundersenhealth.org/respecting-choices

Respecting Choices seeks to help LaCrosse residents make and document meaningful end-of-life decisions before a medical crisis occurs and they lose control of their care. In 2008, nearly all of the town's residents had created and filed an advance directive with Gundersen.[170] That year, LaCrosse boasted the nation's highest rate of completed advance directives.[171] While neither insurers nor Medicare reimbursed Gundersen for its advanced directives work,[172] the initiative empowered patients, improved their end-of-life care and lowered costs. A 2009 National Public Radio profile estimated that Gundersen Lutheran spent approximately $18,000 caring for patients in the last two years of life, compared to the national average of $26,000. End-of-life care at one New York City hospital exceeded a whopping $75,000.[173] Doing the right thing in healthcare is almost always cost-effective.

Let's Talk: Constructive End-of-Life Decision-Making

At Jeff Shields' memorial service, Genie Shields proclaimed that her husband's death has been a "gift," one that enriches all who receive it. When it became clear that lymphoma would take his life, Jeff Shields decided to spend his remaining time with family and friends at the Shields' rustic *Flying Bear* farm in southern Vermont. He loved *Flying Bear*. It was summertime. Jeff Shields "let go of the medical stuff," lived in the moment, took walks, wrote letters, played with his grandchildren, conversed with friends, penned a memoir and reveled in the farm's natural beauty and cycles of life. Looking back, Genie Shields reflects, "Jeff soared those last few weeks. As his world shrunk to just a hospital bed in the living room, the space around him just grew bigger and bigger." The concentration of Jeff Shields' generous spirit into that single spot radiated outward and infected all who came near with warmth, peace and equanimity.

My wife and I became close friends with the Shields in the mid-1990s. Jeff Shields was a leading healthcare attorney. I was a rising

---

170 http://www.npr.org/templates/story/story.php?storyId=120346411
171 *Ibid.*
172 In July 2015, CMS announced Medicare would begin paying for end of life counseling.
173

healthcare investment banker. We worked together on several trans-actions, played lousy golf and shared an interest in global affairs. As a former Peace Corps volunteer, I was still adjusting to Wall Street's "show-me-the-money" culture. The Shields became important role models. They were accomplished, highly principled and flat-out cool.

In 2004, Jeff Shields shocked many (including me) by shifting ca-reers and repurposing himself as an academic. Jeff Shields became Vermont Law School's new dean and he was great at it. He took stu-dents on weekly hikes, opined regularly on public radio, expanded the school's premier environmental curriculum, established a U.S.-China Partnership for Environmental Law, created distance learning and ac-celerated J.D. programs, undertook two major building projects and fought against the military's "Don't Ask, Don't Tell" policy. Cancer cut his tenure short. At his 2012 retirement, Jeff Shields observed the following:

> *I have loved this job. The opportunity to lead an institution with a mis-sion of public citizenship, public service and environmental advocacy has been exhilarating. The quality and values of our trustees, faculty, staff, students and alumni have lifted me every day since I started here.*

Jeff Shields' work wasn't done. Acclaimed author and surgeon Gawande featured Jeff Shields in a nationally broadcast *Frontline* documentary, "Being Mortal."[174] Camera crews trailed Jeff and Genie Shields during his final months. After his death, Gawande confided to Genie Shields that her husband was the program's "anchor." In a last noble act, Jeff Shields provides a compelling and very public example of dying well.

America's Evolving Conversation about Death

Next to a child's birth, a good death can be life's most powerful and human experience. People focus on what matters most. Important conversations occur. Human connection and relationships deepen. Life moves forward. Austrian poet and novelist Rainer Maria Rilke

---

174 http://www.pbs.org/wgbh/frontline/film/being-mortal/

hated how modern medicine strips dying of its "terrible intimacy."[175] He captures the tragedy of "medicalized" death in this passage, *"Love and Death are the great gifts that are given to us; mostly, they are passed unopened."*

Like Jeff and Genie Shields, more Americans are choosing to receive and open the gifts a good death offers. During the last decade, multiple organizations have emerged to advance American attitudes and behaviors regarding death. They're empowering people to undertake end-of-life care planning. They're urging Americans to talk, learn one another's stories and act purposefully. Let's visit some.

- Matt Holder and Alexandra Drane launched Engage with Grace in 2008 to stimulate conversations about end-of-life care. They want to ensure that people *"can end their lives in the same purposeful way they lived them."*

- At Death Cafe events, *"people drink tea, eat cake and discuss death. Death Cafes increase awareness of death to help people make the most of their (finite) lives."* It's catching on. Sponsors have hosted over 2,700 "death cafes" in 32 countries.

- Like Death Cafe, Death Over Dinner assembles people together to discuss end-of-life planning and share a meal. Since its 2013 founding, over 70,000 people in 20 countries have attended its dinners. [176]

- In 2010, journalist Ellen Goodman launched The Conversation Project "to help people talk about their wishes for end-of-life care." Still saddened and frustrated that she didn't know her mother's end-of-life preferences, Goodman believes "the conversation" should "begin at the kitchen table, not in the ICU." The Conversation Project has partnered with the Institute for

---

175 The Atlantic Monthly, *To Work is to Live Without Dying*, April 1996, pages 112-118
176 National Public Radio, *Let's Talk about Death Over Dinner*, Lesley McClurg, May 8, 2015

Health Improvement and the Screen Actors Guild to spread the word and get people talking.

Talking about death doesn't cause death. Instead, answering difficult questions about death creates a framework for end-of-life wellness. It enables individuals to design their end-of-life care plans well before they decline. This is as it should be. As the adage goes, "The best time to fix the roof is when the sun is shining."

Back from the Dead to Help the Dying

Dr. David Brown was the chairman of Cleveland Clinic's Anesthesiology Institute in 2011 when he began curative treatments for military-acquired hepatitis C. Five months into the seven-month regimen, everything went south. Hospital-acquired sepsis led to multiple organ failure and three-plus weeks in the clinic's ICU. Periodically conscious, Brown felt he was watching himself die. Brown's family sat vigil as the days turned into weeks. Twice they discussed do-not-resuscitate orders. Brown's care team put him on a ventilator. Pain and delusion were constant companions. Miraculously, with "a single heartbeat," Brown came back. He scrawled on his message board, "I've never felt so alive."

Brown's near-death experience catapulted him into a new career. He founded Curadux to help individuals and families navigate the complex and sometimes cruel medical world that treats advanced illness. According to Brown, "When patients lack capacity, the medical system imposes its will. If people don't want to become a burden, they have to think about death and plan ahead." Curadux recommends a five-step checklist for ensuring wise health-care decisions:

1. Assess: identify what matters to you most and clearly identify desired outcomes.

2. Explore: understand your medical condition and treatment options.

3. Decide: select treatment options that align with your values and goals.

4. Capture: formalize your decisions in written documents.

5. Share: communicate your decisions to family and professional advisors.

End-of-Life Wellness

A satirical 1997 headline from *The Onion* reads, *"World Death Rate Holding Steady at 100%."*[177] We all get older. We just die once. We don't get to practice. We want to get it right. Getting it right requires courage to do the following:

- Accept medical realities;

- Determine priorities for the time remaining; and

- Be proactive in communicating personal priorities.

Individuals weigh hopes (attending a wedding) and fears (not being a burden) in determining their priorities. When given the choice, most people care more about end-of-life quality than longevity. Key decisions are whether and when to receive palliative care, sometimes called "comfort care." Palliative care does not negate medical treatment but shifts focus to making patients more comfortable. Interestingly, several research studies have found patients receiving palliative and hospice care live longer than patients receiving standard care.[178]

How Doctors Die

177 *The Onion,* World Death Rate Holding Steady at 100 Percent, January 22, 1997
178 NPCO, Research Shows Patients May Live Longer with Hospice and Palliative Care, August 19, 2010

In 2011, Ken Murray wrote an influential essay observing that doctors with terminal conditions rarely pursue extraordinary treatment measures for themselves, but they do pursue extraordinary measures for their patients. Murray makes this startling observation:

> *What's unusual about doctors is not how much treatment they get compared to most Americans, but how little.*[179]

A 2014 Stanford Medicine study confirms Murray's observations. Almost 90 percent of physicians surveyed would choose do-not-resuscitate orders for themselves. This does not hold for patients. The study reported the following:

> *Doctors continue to practice aggressive treatment at the end-of-life, despite the fact that most Americans now say they would prefer to die at home without life-prolonging interventions.*[180]

Each patient is unique with individual opinions regarding their care. The healthcare system should honor these opinions. What doctors always have that patients often do not is a deep understanding of their prognosis and treatment alternatives. Applying advance care planning with shared medical decision-making grants patients this knowledge.

Final Words

Many believe that sudden death in old age, free of medical intervention, constitutes a good death. That type of death is quick and painless, but it also comes with no goodbyes and no important final conversations. The opportunity to end life on our own terms can become a profound gift for both the dying and their loved ones. Near the end of *"Being Mortal,"* Jeff Shields speaks to the *Frontline* cameras a final time and says the following:

---

179 Ken Murray, How Doctors Die, November 30, 2011

180 Stanford Medicine, *Most Physicians would Forgo Aggressive Treatment for Themselves at the End of Life*, May 28, 2014

These last couple weeks, I've been surrounded by family and friends. It's been terrific. Some of the best days of my life, I must say... so, I'm still a happy guy.

These were among Jeff Shields' very last words. He died later that day. "Death be not proud."[181] Jeff Shields' legacy is strong. His shining example of living and dying well endures.

U.S. healthcare does a grave injustice when it does not honor individual preferences during end-of-life care. It robs life of its dignity. It causes enormous emotional and financial harm. Fortunately, America does not need to choose between appropriate care and affordability. When American healthcare is morally responsive, its economics become self-sustaining.

Origins of Shared Medical Decision-Making (SDM)

The concept of shared decision-making began with Dr. John E. Wennberg and his research on outcomes variations. Wennberg studied non-medical influences on patient care and outcomes at both the Dartmouth Institute for Health Policy and Clinical Practice, home of the Dartmouth Atlas of Health Care, then later at Massachusetts General. Consistently, he found significant treatment variations based on doctors' own preferences and values. Wennberg concluded that informed patients participating in shared decision-making make better care choices and achieve better outcomes with less treatment variation.

In July 1989, Wennberg and Dr. Albert Mulley co-founded the Informed Medical Decisions Foundation to promote high quality medical decisions through collaboration between informed patients and their healthcare providers. The foundation's mission is "to advance evidence-based, shared decision-making through research, policy, clinical models and patient decision aids."[182] In 1997, the foundation partnered with newly formed Health Dialog[183] to advance SDM through care management protocols and video aids.

---

181 John Donne, Sonnet X, 1609
182 *Ibid.*
183 Health Dialog: Population Health Management Services is now a wholly owned sub-

The foundation develops content for the decision aids, validates their effectiveness and explores ways to introduce SDM into everyday clinical practice. Health Dialog distributes the aids through a licensing agreement with the foundation. Patients give the decision aids a 93 percent approval rating. Combining science with media enables providers to engage patients in SDM and achieve better outcomes with less utilization.

Wennberg once cited a study of prostate surgeries as his "most memorable experience in changing the hearts and minds to spread shared decision-making."[184] Group Health in Seattle and Kaiser Permanente in Denver both reported a direct relationship between shared decision-making and decline in unwanted prostate surgeries. Both healthcare organizations reduced unwanted and unnecessary surgical procedures.

Group Health has practiced patient-centered care since its creation in 1947. It's not surprising that a company that always asks, "What's best for our patients' health?" would embrace shared decision-making. In 2007, the state of Washington passed the nation's first legislation to recognize SDM as a higher standard of informed consent. The legislation also promoted certified decision aids by launching a demonstration project to encourage their use.

Group Health jumped at the opportunity and has distributed over 27,000 decision aids since then—more than any other healthcare organization. As of 2012, Group Health used 12 foundation/Health Dialog decision aids in six specialties: orthopedics, cardiology, urology, women's health, breast cancer and back care. Group Health trains its staff in SDM, monitors the effectiveness of decision aids and conducts aligned research.

In September 2012, Group Health physicians published an article in *Health Affairs* detailing an observational study of 9,515 candidates for knee and hip replacement. Their study evaluates how using SDM with decision aids influences health outcomes. The results confirm

---

sidiary of RiteAid Corporation. www.marketwatch.com/.../rite-aid-acquires-health-dialog-services- corporation-2014-04-01

184   www.informedmedicaldecisions.org/2014/03/21/shared-decision-making-champion-qa-john-e-wennberg-md-mph/

that informed patients, on average, choose less invasive therapies and incur lower care costs: 26 percent fewer hip replacements; 38 percent fewer knee replacements; and 12 to 21 percent lower costs.

Mayo Clinic's Shared Decision-Making National Resource Center embraces Dr. W. J. Mayo's commencement advice to the Rush Medical College class of 1910: "The best interest of the patient is the only interest to be considered..." The sentence included the requirement that "in order that the sick may have the benefit of advancing knowledge, union of forces is necessary."[185]

The "union of forces" brings together the physicians' clinical expertise with patients' personal knowledge of their conditions, circumstances and treatment goals. Mayo developed the Wiser Choices Program and the Knowledge and Evaluation Research (KER) Unit to help doctors effectively use decision aids in clinical settings. The goal of Wiser Choices is ensuring doctors have the right tools and resources to fully explain treatment options and consequences and help "patients make well-informed decisions that reflect their values and goals..."[186]

SDM is powerful medicine. By engaging patients in their care, it leads to better medical decision-making and gives patients the best chance of a successful outcome. Let's not overcomplicate this. Like advanced directives and informed second opinions, SDM is the right way to treat people.

Empowered Patients; Better Outcomes

Cancer Treatment Centers of America ("CTCA") also does an exceptional job of surrounding patients with meaningful, practical information and engendering informed decision-making. Richard J Stephenson founded CTCA in 1988, following the death of his mother, Mary Brown Stephenson, from cancer.[187] Stephenson and his family could not find a compassionate "whole-person" protocol for their

---

185 *Ibid.*

186 *Ibid.*

187 http://www.cancercenter.com/about-us/history/

mother. After her death, he honored her spirit by creating a new company dedicated to patient-centered cancer care.

That heritage and its cultural DNA, informed by voracious capture of patient insights, fuels a never-ending company-wide quest for improving patient experience. The company's business motto reads, "Patient Empowered Care®: You are at the center."[188] CTCA uses a team approach and makes sure the entire team participates in each appointment. This simple realignment means the oncologist, clinic nurse, dietician, naturopathic oncology provider and nurse care manager come together to answer patients' questions in a single visit. Patients report the approach is convenient (patients stay in one room while CTCA team members come to them during the appointment block), makes them feel more in control of their treatment and creates a less stressful treatment experience.[189]

In 2104, CTCA outscored its regional and national competition in every category on an independent, third-party survey of patients' perspectives on the quality of hospital care. Created by the Hospital Consumer Assessment of Healthcare Providers and Systems (HCAHPS), the annual survey was developed by the Department of Health and Human Services. It is the first national, standardized, publicly reported survey of its kind. CTCA excelled in all of the following categories:[190]

- Patients who gave their hospital a rating of 9 or 10 on a scale from 0 (lowest) to 10 (highest);

- Patients who reported, YES, they would definitely recommend the hospital;

- Patients who reported that their nurses ALWAYS communicated well;

---

188 http://www.cancercenter.com/ctca-difference/patient-empowered-care/
189 *Ibid.*
190 http://www.cancercenter.com/ctca-results/. For more information about HCAHPS and calculation of ratings, visit http://www.medicare.gov/hospitalcompare/about/HCAHPS-Star-Ratings.html

- Patients who reported they ALWAYS received help as soon as they wanted;

- Patients who reported that their doctors ALWAYS communicated well;

- Patients who reported that their room and bathroom were ALWAYS clean;

- Patients who reported that the area around their room was ALWAYS quiet at night;

- Patients who reported that their pain was ALWAYS controlled;

- Patients who reported that, YES, they were given information about what to do during their recovery at home; and

- Patients who STRONGLY AGREE that they understood their care when they left the hospital.

Cancer Treatment Centers of America makes patients the center of its clinical care paradigm. CTCA employees schedule convenient one-stop appointments, strive to keep halls quiet at night and ensure treatment protocols are fully understood. The company employs a holistic care model that incorporates naturopathic medicine, nutrition, pain management, mind-body medicine and spiritual support. Exceptional patient-satisfaction scores occur when providers prioritize customer service.

CTCA publically publishes its "Length of Life Results" annually in a report validated by Washington University. Its outcomes, on average, exceed national averages, particularly in the immediate years following diagnosis. Almost all CTCA patients are self-referred. Many come to CTCA after a bad care experience with other cancer centers. Engaged patients have better results. People who believe they will get better often do. Is it really surprising that patient-centered care generates superior results?

Engaging Productivity

In his book, *Practical Wisdom*, psychologist Barry Schwartz shares the story of "Luke, the wise janitor." No janitorial job description requires "patient engagement." He continues his story, explaining how one day Luke entered a hospital room where a father sat with his son. "The son," reveals Schwartz, "did not have a good prognosis and the father was upset."

The father began screaming at Luke for not cleaning the floor of his son's hospital room. Luke, in fact, had just cleaned the floor. Rather than argue, Luke mopped the floor again to restore calm and provide some comfort. For Luke, "It wasn't a big deal." Schwartz describes Luke's behavior as "practical wisdom" in action. While it's not in job descriptions, behavior like Luke's makes the world a better place. In hospitals, practical wisdom aids healing.

Aristotle defined practical wisdom as a combination of moral will and moral skill. Together, these attributes guide humans to consider a particular set of circumstances and do the right thing. Luke knew his encounter with an emotional father required kindness and empathy. Luke's story shows how impossible it is to write rules intricate enough to govern all behavior. Putting customers first is a way for providers to overcome compliance-heavy, activity-centric operating environments. Motivating employees to create better customer experiences is a win-win-win: better for patients; better for employees and correlated with better across-the-board performance.

Daniel Pink, author of *Drive*,[191] examines what motivates professionals to achieve higher performance. His work builds on Schwartz's theories of practical wisdom and illustrates why carrots and sticks aren't sufficient to motivate professional behavior. Pink cites an MIT study that found financial rewards for cognitive tasks were counterproductive.

Participants receiving the top-level rewards demonstrated the worst performance on a battery of word puzzles, spatial puzzles and physical

---

191   Daniel Pink, *Drive: The Surprising Truth About What Motivates Us*, 2009

challenges. Researchers speculated that perhaps even the top-tier reward amount was too low in the MIT study to motivate participants. So, they took their test on the road to India. Same findings. Higher incentives led to worse performance. Pink argues that professionals require "Autonomy, Mastery and Purposeful work" (AMP) to operate at high-performance levels. Sharp Healthcare illustrates how to make this happen.

Sharp Tactics

In 2001, Sharp HealthCare in San Diego launched The Sharp Experience to engage its employees in patient care and service improvement. It's the industry's most advanced effort to improve productivity through workforce engagement. The Experience includes:

- An annual two-day All-Staff Assembly for all Sharp employees and constituents (over 22,000) at the San Diego Convention Center;

- Topic-specific improvement teams;

- Quarterly employee forums;

- Performance reviews with behavior standards (Employees routinely ask, "May I help you? 'I have the time.'");

- Employee recognition ceremonies; and

- Shared performance reports.

The list goes on. Since initiating The Experience, Sharp has won a Baldrige National Quality award, turbocharged patient satisfaction scores, reduced employee turnover by 50 percent and improved its Moody's bond rating from Baa1 to Aa3. More practical wisdom in action. Aristotle would be proud.

I attended Sharp's 2014 All-Staff Assembly. It was part state of the union, part revival, part vaudeville and part pep rally. The theme was "Live Big. It's Your Legacy." It explored individual and collective identity. Outside the hall, exhibits invited participants to document their personal legacies, share their stories, and contemplate their remaining "jelly beans" (days on the planet).

Inside the hall, program activities coalesced individual participants within a collective whole to celebrate and advance Sharp's health and wellness mission. Master of Ceremonies (and CEO) Mike Murphy announced a new 7th "pillar of excellence" (Safety) and recognized individual, team and division accomplishments in the other six pillars (Quality; Service; People; Financial; Growth and Community). Sharp's award-winning film team released four compelling videos documenting how Sharp improves lives. Not a dry eye in the house. Elsewhere the Sharp Choir sang. Senior leaders put on campy renditions of 70s' game shows. Featured speakers testified on end-of-life care. Everybody danced. It's not accidental. Sharp's genius is recognizing that custodians and kitchen staff are as important to organizational productivity and customer experience as nurses and doctors.

Managerial science lags other sciences by 50 to 70 years. Most healthcare companies employ time and engineering science to enhance productivity. It's not enough. As Pink observed, human beings require autonomy, connectivity and purposeful work to operate at the highest performance levels. Our biology confirms this. At the dawn of life, single-cell organisms monopolized our planet. Over time, cells combined and specialized to form more complex species, culminating in human beings.

The Sharp Experience illuminates how biology works within high-performance cultures. Individuals combine and specialize to act with a single purpose. In essence, the organization and its people become a single, high-functioning organism. Sitting in the audience, I felt both the collective energy, and my connection to healthcare's larger purpose: to provide better, more affordable and more convenient healthcare for all Americans. That is my Sharp experience.

Engaging Technology

While human connection is essential for effective care delivery, technology can enhance patient experience by offering greater convenience, rich data analytics, personalized platforms, greater efficiency and lower costs.

Technologically savvy healthcare businesses will increasingly optimize patient care by using connectivity to learn what patients are doing, what they want and how they feel about their experiences with the provider. New platforms like the Apple watch and personal health monitoring and tracking devices are also connecting patients to providers in groundbreaking ways.

Susannah Fox, chief technology officer for the Department of Health and Human Services (HHS), served previously as an associate director of the Internet Project at the Pew Research Center. In that capacity, she designed research to understand the impact of technology and social media on healthcare and the consumer's healthcare experiences.[192] Even a snapshot of the statistics from Pew's Health Fact Sheet highlight the impact the Internet has on how consumers gather, discuss and manage healthcare information:[193]

- Ninety percent of U.S. adults own a cell phone;

- Fifty-eight percent of U.S. adults own a smartphone;

- Thirty-one percent of cell phone owners and 52 percent of smartphone owners have used their phone to look up health or medical information;

- Seven in 10 U.S. adults say they track at least one health indicator;

---

192 http://www.hhs.gov/about/leadership/susannah-fox/index.html
193 http://www.pewinternet.org/fact-sheets/health-fact-sheet/

- Forty-six percent of people who use fitness trackers say that this activity has changed their overall approach to maintaining their health or the health of someone for whom they provide care;

- Forty percent of people who use trackers say it has led them to ask a doctor new questions or to get a second opinion from another doctor; and

- Thirty-four percent of people who use trackers say it has affected a decision about how to treat an illness or condition.

In its Health Fact Sheet, Pew also reports that 19 percent of smartphone owners had downloaded an app specifically to track or manage their health. There are countless apps designed to monitor personal health activities and move that data from patients to physicians. Imagine, if you will, that you are a diabetes patient who is supposed to walk two miles a day. Doctor's orders. Today, you walked only one mile and instantly your doctor's office reached out to you to ask why you skipped half of your prescribed daily exercise.

The Z's Have It

Other innovative companies are augmenting engagement by bringing doctors to patients. Three of them have a "Z" in their name.

Zipnosis delivers online healthcare 12 hours a day, responding to patients within one hour for $25. It focuses on select conditions that can be "safely and accurately diagnosed without a physical examination."[194] Patients complete a five-minute interview. The content and number of questions refine with each answer, like face-to-face sessions with doctors. Board-certified clinicians review patient questionnaires and respond during virtual office hours from 8:00 a.m. to 8:00 p.m. They prescribe treatment and, if necessary, medi-

---

194 https://zipnosis.com/faq

cation. The service is free if clinicians determine a customer's condition isn't suited to online treatment or Zipnosis clinicians fail to respond to patient questionnaires within 60 minutes (during regular business hours). Users can complete the diagnostic questionnaire 24/7. Zipnosis is fast, efficient, effective, cheap and convenient. Who wouldn't use that kind of service?

ZocDoc schedules medical appointments based on specialty, services provider, office location, availability, educational background or insurance network. It's free to patients; providers pay a subscription fee to list their practice and open appointments. Users book appointments online. The service launched in New York City in 2007. At the time, ZocDoc served 700,000 people per month.[195] Their service now covers 40 percent of the U.S. population across more than 2,000 cities. ZocDoc has a Spanish-language version and provides online check-in services.[196] ZocDoc is growing fast, attracting venture capital ($95 million as of June 2013) and poised (like Uber) to link customers with suppliers.[197]

ZoomCare's patient experience matches its tagline, "Healthcare on Demand." Based in Portland, OR, ZoomCare is a network of freestanding clinics in the Pacific Northwest. They're neighborhood-based, designed for walk-in patients and provide transparent pricing for all services. Insured patients pay slightly more to cover claims-processing costs. ZoomCare approaches care delivery very differently from traditional health systems. The company has a customized operating system that integrates the patient portal, analytics tools and financial software.[198] ZoomCare keeps costs low by using physician assistants and nurse practitioners. The company relies on evidence-based practices to ensure continuity of care across its clinics. Its sophisticated yet simple patient portal makes finding a clinic, selecting a provider

195 https://en.wikipedia.org/wiki/ZocDoc
196 *ibid*
197 *ibid*
198 http://www.mckesson.com/blog/zooming-in-on-neighborhood-healthcare/

and scheduling appointments as easy as Open Table makes restaurant reservations.[199]

These businesses are based on interfacing—a concept I introduced in Chapter 6. They connect patients to healthcare opportunities much like Uber, Facebook, Kayak, and VBRO connect consumers to rides, retailers, airfare and lodging. They share a "resell mindset," technology's twist on traditional supply and demand economics, and capitalize on familiar technology models to turn unsold/empty space (cancelled or open appointments) into revenue. They connect buyers with sellers and in the process, provide consumers with considerably more convenience, choice and control of their healthcare. The-doctor-will-see-you-now mentality simply can't compete.

It's the Customer Stupid!

Amazon's Bezos knows that successful companies NEVER stop giving customers high-value products and services. Everything else (growth, profitability, recognition) follows from that core truth. At UCLA, Feinberg's patient-centric strategies have not only improved patient-experience scores dramatically, but also have paid big financial dividends. Patient-centric care drove the financial improvement, not revenue cycle optimization. Feinberg observed, "I really believe that the reason our financial performance at UCLA has been so outstanding is that we haven't focused on financial performance. But rather we've focused on taking care of patients."[200]

American healthcare consumers are awakening to their collective power. If health companies don't respond to consumers' needs, they'll find other companies who will. This is no time to play defense. Health companies must engage their customers, understand the pictures in their heads and tailor their services accordingly. Knowing and acknowledging what customers think, good and bad, is essential to earning their trust. Transparency, shared decision-making, patient-centric

---

199 http://www.opb.org/news/article/zoomcare-putting-price-tag-health-care/

200 https://www.youtube.com/watch?v=55cKZwCBSiE discussing "Prescription for Excellence: Leadership lessons for creating a world-class customer experience from UCLA Health System"

care, better listening, meaningful second opinions, engaged employees and engaging technology are all in the toolkit. Take this advice to the bank. In post-reform healthcare, winning health companies will ALWAYS align service delivery with customer wants, needs and desires.

SECTION III: Adapt

AMAZONING HEALTHCARE

We always over-estimate the change that will occur in the next two years and under-estimate the change that will occur in the next ten. Don't let yourself be lulled into inaction.
BILL GATES, *THE ROAD AHEAD*

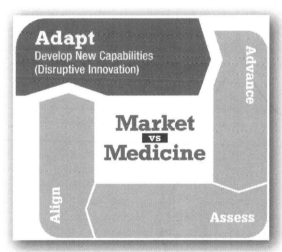

- Chapter 8: Advantage Care Management
- Chapter 9: The Clinic Connection
- Chapter 10: What Would Einstein Do?
- Chapter 11: Banner Days

Disruption is scary. Incumbents (think Kodak) often don't re-alize the market threat from disruptive innovation (digital imaging) until it's too late. In many ways, healthcare's disrup-tive challenge is more complex than Kodak's. No one ever said Kodak wasn't expert at making film. Healthcare organizations simultane-ously must improve their current operations (sustaining innovation) while adapting to value-based payment and retail-oriented competi-tors (disruptive innovation).

I first encountered disruptive innovation guru, Harvard Professor Clayton Christensen, at Merrill Lynch in the early 2000s. Merrill had hired Christensen to advise it on responding to the competitive threat posed by online brokerages. Christensen convinced Merrill to disrupt itself by offering a low-fee online-brokerage alternative. Christensen's core thesis is that incumbent businesses place too much emphasis on customers' current needs and fail to appreciate how new technologies will reshape market demand for their prod-ucts and services.

Section III, *Adapt,* explores how disruptive innovations in pay-ments and services will challenge the fundamental sustainability of current business models.

- Chapter 8, ***Advantage Care Management,*** chronicles how emerg-ing care management companies are developing the capabili-ties required to manage the health of large populations under risk-based payment models.

- Chapter 9, ***The Clinic Connection,*** explores the emergence of retail delivery models that meet consumer price and service demands more cost-effectively than established business mod-els that emphasize revenue optimization.

- Chapter 10, ***What Would Einstein Do?,*** shifts the focus back to incumbents and suggests strategies for governance, operations and change management that can enhance organizational competitiveness in post-reform healthcare.

- Chapter 11, **Banner Days,** examines how Banner Health has constantly reinvented itself since its formation in 1999. In the process, Banner has emerged as a leading and innovative health company, one capable of delivering consistent high-quality care, managing the health of large populations and restructuring academic medicine.

Disruption is the appropriate mindset for healthcare executives leading industry transformation. Unlike traditional disruption theory, however, healthcare disruption will not result from technological breakthroughs. It will emerge through service innovation rather than product innovation. Healthcare disruption will occur as payment programs (risk-based, outcomes-focused, bundled, transparent) reformulate and as retail competitors deliver better healthcare services at lower prices in more customer-friendly venues. In this sense, an Amazon-like focus on meeting customer needs will differentiate winning companies in healthcare.

Amazoning Healthcare

When Aaron Martin led Amazon's foray into self-publishing, his worldview was both simple and devastating. The only irreplaceable components of the "book business" were the authors and the readers. Amazon's technology could diminish and even replace publishers, distributors and book stores systematically by attacking each of these vulnerable supply-chain components.

Martin left Amazon in January 2014 to lead strategy and innovation at Providence Health & Services, one of the nation's largest healthcare systems. Martin believes the same forces that disrupted book publishing, distribution and sales are now attacking healthcare. His job, in essence, is to prepare Providence for the industry's pending disruption. In Martin's mind, the analogs for "authors and readers" in healthcare are "care providers and patients." The intermediate supply-chain components are vulnerable (see chart below). These include hospitals, insurance companies, brokers, device manufacturers and pharmaceutical suppliers.

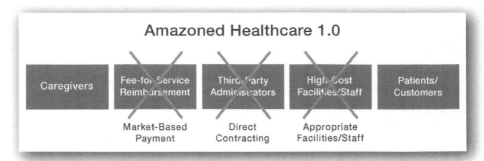

Independent companies are well-positioned to exploit and disintermediate inefficient components embedded within America's high-cost delivery system. They will employ the following tactics:

- Market-based payments for routine treatments;

- Direct negotiation/contracting between doctors and patients; and

- Appropriate, lower-cost facilities and staffing levels.

In "Amazoned" healthcare, value-based care delivery wins. The market will guide purchasers toward higher-quality, lower-cost providers with great service. No organizations understand this transformative opportunity better than emerging care management companies, nimble urgent/emergency care companies and uber-retailers (think Walgreens). They are jumping into healthcare with both feet.

For the first time in modern history, incumbent health companies confront existential challenges, unrelenting competition and widespread societal frustration with the status quo. Unlike before, playing defense and settling for incremental improvement are not winning strategies. Expect many established companies to lose their independence or cease operations altogether. Winning companies will adapt to marketplace demands for better, more affordable and convenient healthcare services. Outcomes matter. Customers Count. Value Rules!

CHAPTER 8

ADVANTAGE CARE MANAGEMENT

You treat a disease, you win, you lose. You treat a person,
I guarantee you, you'll win, no matter what the outcome.
                                                    PATCH ADAMS

My wife, Terri, and I are the proud "parents" of Baxter and Bailey, brother and sister Norwegian Forest cats. Norwegian Forest cats are big with striking green eyes, double fur coats, tufted ears and toes and lion-like manes. They're Norway's official cat and the only cat breed that climbs head-first down trees.

Baxter and Bailey's medical home is Blum Animal Hospital in Chicago where they receive care under the watchful eye of Dr. Rob Dann (a.k.a. the world's greatest vet). Blum is a busy, friendly place that treats all manner of pets and owners. The staff members know Baxter and Bailey by name and coo every time their pictures appear on computerized medical records. Blum sends us regular reminders for vaccinations and primary care visits. All prices are transparent. The vets and staff members fully consult with us before administering any treatments.

When Baxter was a year old, he suffered a stroke that paralyzed his back legs. We rushed him to the Animal Veterinary Emergency and Specialty Center where they diagnosed him with hypertrophic cardio-myopathy (enlarged heart) and a spinal cord thromboembolism. His prognosis wasn't good. With appropriate care and medication, they thought he could walk again and might live another 18 months. Dr. Michael Luethy, a certified animal cardiologist treated Baxter in consultation with a certified neurologist. Dr. Dann coordinated all care discussions. The vets and specialists worked together with a unified medical record and agreed-upon diagnostic tests.

The story has a very happy ending. Baxter returned home, became accustomed to taking three medication pills every day and slowly regained his mobility. Eleven years later, he moves well, takes just one pill a day and is incredibly obnoxious at meal time. Baxter sees his cardiologist for a checkup once a year, and we now expect him to live a full lifespan. Dr. Leuthy calls Baxter his "miracle cat." His recovery is testimony to Baxter's strong desire to get better, his body's self-healing capabilities, a nurturing living environment and the coordinated care he received from skilled professionals.

The logic, efficiency and effectiveness of Baxter's and Bailey's care model is compelling. In most respects, our cats receive better primary and specialty care services than Terri and I do. Veterinary care is consumer-oriented and market-driven. As opposed to healthcare for humans, the pricing of animal healthcare is transparent and reasonable. Service is great, hours are convenient and veterinarians earn our trust. Trust is essential for tough end-of-life medical decision-making, where veterinary care providers guide us with compassion, empathy and honesty. Wouldn't it be wonderful if care management services for people, particularly those with chronic disease, were as customer-centric and effective?

Market-driven reform by consumer-focused companies will transform primary healthcare by promoting health, diagnosing disease earlier, managing chronic conditions effectively and meeting customers' needs.

The Care Management Conundrum

Across the healthcare landscape, there is abundant care activity but limited care coordination. Better care management is U.S. healthcare's most vital need and least developed capability. American healthcare's biggest failing is how it treats those at the margins of life, burdened by disease and buffeted by incessant treatment interventions. Failure to coordinate care delivery is an indictment on American healthcare. By contrast, effective care management is logical, efficient and compassionate.

In American healthcare, treating patients on a volume basis is the rule, not the exception. Payers and providers work in concert to push as much volume through the system as they can justify. This is Job 1 in almost every doctor's office and hospital throughout the land. The real job-to-be-done, however, is getting care providers and patients to work together to achieve better outcomes and better overall health. Get this mission right and care management emerges as naturally as breathing.

Among its many provisions, the Affordable Care Act's most disruptive was eliminating exemptions for prior conditions from health insurance policies. The inability to exclude covering sick people now requires health companies to develop the following capabilities to manage the care of large populations:

Earlier Diagnosis and Treatment of At-Risk Patients: Five percent of the population consume half of healthcare services. Healthcare's heaviest users are old, frail and/or very sick. Care management for this population is improving but will always be expensive. Identifying at-risk patients before they require extensive medical intervention is key to both better community health and keeping healthcare costs under control. These ticking-time-bomb patients represent about a quarter of the U.S. population. Their lifestyle choices, social behaviors and stress-filled lives place them on a path toward significant and debilitating chronic disease. Earlier diagnosis and proactive intervention dramatically improves well-being at significantly lower costs.

Effective Patient Engagement: U.S. healthcare fails to proactively manage care for large populations. The system's costs swell because too many patients lack the tools, knowledge and confidence to manage their medical conditions. Care management companies have lacked the business models, expertise and funding to find and treat at-risk patients before they require hospitalization. This is changing. Patient engagement is essential to high-quality disease management. Care providers cannot do it alone. Together, aligned patients and care providers are an unstoppable force.

Community-Based Advocacy and Support: Great care management makes it easier for individuals to make smarter lifestyle choices. This does not occur in isolation. Better health requires a team. At-risk patients need coaches and care providers as much or more than specialists to live better, longer and more fulfilling lives. Building healthier communities that reduce isolation, promote wellness, reduce stress and encourage engagement is everyone's responsibility.

Comprehensive Behavioral Health: Clinical and observational data demonstrate poor behavioral health is a major catalyst for chronic disease, poor health outcomes and high health-care expenditures. Many patients turn to ER care when they don't receive front-end counseling or medication to manage their mental health. In Reinventing American Health Care,[201] Dr. Ezekiel Emanuel names depression as a root cause of poor preventive health. More investment in mental health is vital to effective care management.

Care management companies that develop these capabilities will experience expansive demand for their services and dominate in post-reform healthcare.

Care Management Catalysts

Without market demand for services, promising care-management companies wither and die. American healthcare under-invests in care management because the system pays expansively for specialty care, not for primary care services. Facility and service-line investment flows from reimbursement with predictable results: too many hospitals and ambulatory centers; not enough community clinics and behavioral health centers. Governments and corporations are the primary funders of medical expenditures. They have been passive enablers of runaway healthcare spending that is inefficient and unsustainable.

The tide is turning. Governments and businesses are increasingly demanding greater value for their healthcare purchasing. Expanding Medicare Advantage and more aggressive employer approaches to managing employee wellness illustrate how governmental and private payers become catalysts for expanding U.S. healthcare's care management capabilities.

---

201   Ezekiel J. Emanuel, *Reinventing American Health Care: How the Affordable Care Act Will Improve our Terribly Complex, Blatantly Unjust, Outrageously Expensive, Grossly Inefficient, Error Prone System*; Public Affairs, 2014

Expanding Medicare Advantage

Medicare has offered beneficiaries the opportunity to purchase health insurance from private health plans, mostly HMOs, since the Nixon administration. With much fanfare, the George W. Bush Administration passed the Medicare Modernization Act (MMA) in 2003. MMA introduced a new drug benefit to Medicare beneficiaries. It rebranded Medicare's private health-plan purchasing program as Medicare Advantage and included incentives to increase its attractiveness to beneficiaries.

Medicare Advantage plans bundle all services (physician, hospitalization, diagnostics, pharmacy, etc.) into one comprehensive plan with a fixed, or capitated, monthly payment. Plan sponsors can tailor benefit packages to make them more attractive. Beneficiaries have flocked to Medicare Advantage plans even as CMS has reduced their subsidy levels. Since 2005, enrollment in Medicare Advantage plans has more than tripled from 5.4 million enrollees to over 17 million enrollees in 2015.[202] Plans include HMOs, PPOs, private fee-for-service plans, special-needs plans and Medicare medical savings account plans.[203] The plans limit out-of-pocket costs to $6,700 annually. Medicare assigns ratings (one to five stars) to Medicare Advantage plans.

With adjustments and caveats, Medicare Advantage shifts enrollees' healthcare cost risk to the private plan sponsors. This risk transfer encourages better care management through enhanced primary and disease management services. Village Practice Management's agreement with Aetna enables Dr. Clive Fields, whom we first met in the Introduction, and his Houston-based team to coordinate care delivery for covered members with complex conditions. The result is healthier patients, fewer ER visits and lower total care costs. Win. Win. Win.

---

202 http://www.modernhealthcare.com/article/20150319/BLOG/150319868/why-providers-should-care-more-about-medicare-advantage

203 http://www.medicare.gov/sign-up-change-plans/medicare-health-plans/medicare-advantage-plans/medicare-advantage-plans.html

Value-Based Purchasing by State Governments

Recognizing population health's inherent benefits, state governments are shifting increasing percentages of their low-income residents into Medicaid managed care programs.[204] Although coverage gaps exist, the range of services available to participants under Medicaid managed care programs is more coordinated and comprehensive, including behavioral health, chronic disease management, substance abuse and even housing support services. Each state program is unique and a laboratory for experimenting with different approaches to service provision, payment, monitoring and assessment. Successful approaches replicate and amplify. This reflects a natural and elegant evolutionary process.

In the same way, the 17 state-run healthcare exchanges are real-life "laboratories" for the federally-run exchanges that operate in 34 states. No state exchange has flexed its market muscle more than California's. As an active purchaser of healthcare services, Covered California has achieved robust enrollment, moderate premium growth, high customer satisfaction and improving quality scores.[205]

With over 1.5 million members, Covered California is the nation's largest state-run exchange. It's also the most active in screening participating health plans and shaping benefit design. During its first two years of operation, Covered California rejected several health plans that met ACA participation requirements. Peter Lee, Covered California's Executive Director, describes their approach as follows:

> *Not letting [health] plans define what's right for consumers, but defining it on behalf of consumers ... is a better model for the market. We want to make sure every consumer has good choice but not infinite choice.*

---

204 The most common definition of population health is "the health outcomes of a group of individuals, including the distribution of such outcomes within the group." Source http://ajph.aphapublications.org/doi/abs/10.2105/AJPH.93.3.380

205 http://www.npr.org/sections/health-shots/2016/02/11/466187414/will-healthcare-gov-get-a-california-style-makeover

Limiting choice seems counter-intuitive and perhaps un-American, but behavioral science has proven otherwise. People have a limited capacity to process choices and shut down when overwhelmed.

A famous grocery store experiment illustrates the "too much choice" conundrum.[206] Researchers found that large-jam (24 jars) promotions attracted more customers than small-jam (6 jars) promotions, but generated substantially fewer purchases. Sixty percent of customers tasted jams from larger displays while only 40 percent tasted jams from smaller displays. On average, customers sampled two jams from each display. Primed by a $1 coupon, however, 30 percent of small-display viewers bought jam while only 3 percent of large-display viewers did so.

In a corollary to health plan selection, vast investment menus embedded within company IRA programs diminish rather than stimulate employee participation. Participation increases when employers limit and shape investment choices. Behavioral finance predicts these results. Too much choice overwhelms prospective buyers and dilutes sales.

Beyond limiting plan choices, Covered California actively manages health plan design and administration in the following ways:

- It negotiates premiums down and mandates adherence to defined quality goals;

- It mandates participation in health-disparity workgroups, collection of health status data and monitoring of preventive health service use;

- It standardizes co-pays and deductibles (e.g. for lab tests and doctors' visits); and

- It caps monthly drug costs at $250 for gold, silver and platinum plans and $500 for bronze plans.

206 http://www.nytimes.com/2010/02/27/your-money/27shortcuts.html?_r=1

Health plans appreciate the clarity of Covered California's plan design. They understand the "ground rules." Standardization levels the playing field and facilitates the entry of new plans into the marketplace. Companies compete on price, network configuration and customer service.

Health plans also appreciate that Covered California provides access to new members. Unlike many state exchanges, Covered California aggressively markets its program to California citizens and small business. Seeing value, Californians are enrolling in record numbers. Increasing customer demand for their products increases heath plans' willingness to engage with Covered California on program design and pricing.

Covered California is now considering the adoption of quality and cost performance standards for hospitals and doctors.[207] New provisions would require health plans to identify and expel under-performing providers. While these proposals are controversial, Peter Lee is crystal-clear on Covered California's outcomes-based goals as evidenced by his following statement:

We are now shifting our attention to changing the underlying delivery system to make it more cost-effective and higher quality. We don't want to throw anyone out, but we don't want to pay for bad quality care either.

Lee's statement reflects the power of market-based forces to propel American healthcare toward better care outcomes, lower costs and greater customer convenience. Winning health companies will differentiate on these performance criteria. Enhanced care management services will be their "secret sauce."

Employer-Sponsored Care Management
Like Medicare Advantage, employers are using capitated payments to lower coverage costs and improve their workers' health, wellness and

---

207 http://www.npr.org/sections/health-shots/2016/03/18/470851581/california-insurance-marketplace-aims-to-kick-out-poor-performing-hospitals

productivity. In these direct-contracting programs, self-insured companies contract directly with a network of healthcare providers.

Airplane manufacturer Boeing launched a two-year, winner-take-all competition in 2015 between the University of Washington Medicine and Providence Health & Services to manage the health and wellness needs of its 157,000 Seattle-based employees. After the test period, Boeing will evaluate quality metrics, patient engagement, patient satisfaction, savings and other predetermined metrics. Whichever contracted provider performed better, earns the direct-contract option for Boeing employees.

Alan May, a vice president for human resources at Boeing, explained the company's objective as follows: "Boeing is seeking to test its ability to establish direct contracts with providers that can deliver savings as well as gains in quality, access and patient experience."[208] The competing plans know they'll need to meet Boeing's quality goals and reduce Boeing's healthcare costs by up to 25 percent in order to win the competition. Boeing's approach encapsulates the *market mindset vs. regulatory mindset* discussed in chapter 5 and demonstrates how motivated employers can improve healthcare outcomes and lower costs.

Intel Corporation eliminated its private insurance carrier and contracted with Presbyterian Healthcare Services in Albuquerque to manage care for its 54,000 New Mexico employees and dependents.[209] Intel projected that the arrangement, designed with financial incentives tied to performance targets, could save the company between $8 million and $10 million through 2017.[210] Like Boeing's direct-contract experiment, the Intel contract incentivizes Presbyterian to keep costs low, outcomes high and be fiscally accountable for coordinating employee care. To better manage primary and preventive care for the workforce, Presbyterian operates a clinic on-site at Intel's manufacturing facility in Rio Rancho, New Mexico. The close proximity between patient and provider gives Intel's leadership more direct insight and oversight as the program proceeds.

---

208 *Ibid.*

209 http://www.modernhealthcare.com/article/20130713/MAGAZINE/307139976/slimming-options

210 *Ibid.*

As governments and employers make healthcare companies more accountable for improving the health and wellness of large populations, these companies are developing care management capabilities that transfer resources from acute care to primary care, behavioral health, chronic disease management and health promotion. The result is better healthcare at lower costs. Market-driven demand creates super-hero results. Health companies that deliver better care management are up-ending entrenched, activity-based care models with high costs and sub-par outcomes.

Meet the Disruptors

Direct care programs by governments and self-insured employers are expanding as purchasers of healthcare services seek more value for their money. Disruption is also coming from within the industry, as traditional players reinvent themselves to meet market demands for higher-value healthcare services.

Asset-Light Health Companies

Asset-light health companies represent one class of disrupters. These companies refrain from heavy facility investments and concentrate on effective care management. They use their healthcare facilities more intensely and, when necessary, rent facilities in overbuilt markets at favorable prices. Asset-light health companies deliver primary and specialty care services, manage care risk for large populations, provide Internet-based home care services and support shared decision-making—all without the overhead of hospitals and other high-cost acute-care facilities. Their business models align with better care at lower costs. They truly put patients first.

Notable asset-light companies include the following: Dean Clinic[211] in Madison, Wisconsin; GroupHealth[212] in metropolitan-Seattle;

---

211 http://www.deancare.com/
212 http://www.ghc.org/

Health Partners[213] in the Twin Cities; HealthCare Partners[214] in southern California; and Kaiser Permanente[215] throughout California. While these organizations have existed for decades, they're now poised to exploit marketplace demands for more efficient and cost-effective care delivery. Asset-light models, equipped to treat patients as people rather than revenue sources, deliver value-based care.

Asset-light health companies combine insurance capabilities with targeted treatment expertise. The approach lends itself to direct contracting with employers that desire superior care management services. It also offers flexible treatment options for customers.

Dean Clinic, for example, offers extended hours, a full service on-site pharmacy and an optical store. Their clinic locations also provide a full range of therapy services, including occupational therapy, physical therapy and speech therapy. Health Partners in the Twin Cities operates a large primary care and specialty care network of physicians and clinics. It also makes healthcare easier for consumers through Virtuwell, an online clinic that provides diagnosis and treatment 24/7 within thirty minutes for $45.

Asset-light models promote shared decision-making. Health company interests align with patient interests. Members become educated healthcare consumers. They build trusted relationships with care providers that promote earlier diagnoses, chronic disease management and effective behavioral health interventions. Members are healthier, require fewer acute treatments and generate lower total-care costs. Moreover, informed patients are more engaged in their care and achieve better health outcomes. As Group Health discovered with knee and hip replacement surgeries, informed patients often select less intensive and more conservative treatment regimens.[216]

In contrast to most healthcare providers, Job 1 at asset-light health companies centers on providing appropriate care to informed customers in multiple, convenient settings. These companies are

---

213 https://www.healthpartners.com/public/

214 http://www.healthcarepartners.com/Default.aspx

215 https://healthy.kaiserpermanente.org

216 http://content.healthaffairs.org/content/31/9/2094.abstract

well-positioned to take market share from incumbent providers operating centralized, high-cost, activity-centric business models.

Asset-Light and Ready: DuPage Medical Group (DMG)[217]

DuPage Medical Group, the largest independent physician group in Metropolitan-Chicago, illustrates how value-based care provision is transforming and improving U.S. healthcare. DMG is an asset-light company that delivers high-quality, efficient, patient-centric care. Their physician-led business model is well-positioned for taking health insurance risk and managing the care of large populations.

Moreover, DMG is poised for growth. In December 2015, DMG entered a strategic partnership with Summit Partners, which acquired a minority stake in DMG's practice management company, DMG Practice Management Solutions/MPAS (Midwest Physician Administrative Services). The $250 million recapitalization is a combination of debt and equity. This transaction was notable for two reasons:

- Unlike many medical groups that have sold to health systems or insurance companies, DMG believes it will be more competitive as an independent, physician-based company.

- As growth equity investors, Summit believes that DMG's business model and orientation offer enough potential upside for their participation as a minority owner.

The DMG-Summit partnership heralds a new chapter in post-reform healthcare. Asset-light health companies like DMG are winning marketshare by delivering better outcomes, lower costs, greater convenience and superior customer experience. Their ability to attract private equity capital drives growth and accelerates market evolution toward value-based care. DMG currently employs more than 500 physicians in over 60 locations. The company provides primary, specialty

---

217 *Asset-Light and Ready: Physician Groups Embrace Accountable Care,* Carsten Beith and David Johnson, May 2016

and ancillary healthcare services to nearly 400,000 patients/customers. DMG generates annual revenues in excess of $600 million.

DMG formed in the early 1960s with an innovative physician group practice model that delivered centralized, personalized, leading-edge primary and specialty care along with related medical services. In the early 1990s, DMG merged into MedPartners, the nation's largest physician management company. After MedPartners' 1999 divestiture of its physician practice business, DMG combined with two other physician groups to operate as an independent entity in the Metropolitan-Chicago market.

Most physician groups employ business models that distribute all profits to physician partners at year-end without any retained earnings. In contrast, DMG's efficient operating model enables it to compensate its physicians well, generate substantial retained earnings and fund targeted strategic investment in facilities and ancillary services. These investments generate incremental earnings for DMG's physician partners. Today, almost 50 percent of DMG's revenues is non-physician generated. This business model has fueled DMG's rapid growth.

DMG believes physician independence and physician managerial control are competitive advantages. Customers follow their physicians. Accordingly, the company separates business and clinical decision-making. Physicians occupy a majority of seats on the company's corporate board. DMG's growth-oriented culture fosters innovation in the follow ways:

- DMG operates facilities and diagnostic services that are more convenient, efficient and cost-effective. For example, its ambulatory center conducts over 20,000 annual surgeries, more than double the level of typical ambulatory centers. Efficiency dramatically lowers per-unit surgical costs and boosts profitability.

- DMG's Management Services Organization (MSO) has advanced administrative capabilities that enable the company to manage risks, optimize physician productivity and reduce overhead.

- DMG's BreakThrough Care Centers manage care for fragile Medicare patients. Co-ordinated teams consisting of primary care physicians, micro-specialists, extenders, pharmacists, social workers and health coaches tailor care plans to individual needs. Their goal is to improve customer well-being and eliminate unnecessary acute interventions. For example, BreakThrough hospitalists approve and guide emergency care at local hospitals.

- DMG has engaged with Blue Cross Blue Shield of Illinois to access member cost and quality data. DMG bolsters its care management capabilities through deeper understanding of patient risk stratification, outcome variation and facility costs. This helps DMG physicians deliver the right care at the right time in the right place.

- DMG assumes payment risk in all its contracts. It adjusts transaction structures to meet customer and market needs. DMG welcomes the opportunity to take full-capitated risk with Medicare Advantage patients. Many providers aspire to offer superior care management, but few achieve that goal. As DMG CEO Mike Kasper observes, "I've never met a provider who didn't think they can manage risk. Few ultimately can."

Kasper's growth strategy is to "monetize DMG's efficiency." He wants DMG to double operations in 3-5 years through internal growth, acquisition and expansion into new geographies. Requiring a strategic investor that could provide capital, advice and complementary professional services, DMG turned to Summit Partners.

Summit Partners is a growth equity firm with a long-term partnership-oriented investment perspective. In the healthcare sector, they focus on growth-oriented health companies promoting "value not volume." They welcome minority-ownership in well-run companies. Summit is a minority investor in more than 70 percent of the companies in its healthcare portfolio.

Summit understands the potential embedded in physician-led care management companies. Managing Director Darren Black describes Summit's healthcare investment philosophy this way, "We help physician groups that want a growth partner. We work side-by-side with them to build value right out of the gate and over the long-run." Summit's positive experience as investors in HealthCare Partners has encouraged the firm to explore similar physician group investment opportunities. In DMG, Summit identified a rare combination of advanced care management and practice management capabilities.

Based on their work with HealthCare Partners, Summit believes physician groups are best positioned to manage care within integrated delivery networks. Such companies keep their patients healthy through pro-active, prevention-focused care delivery. Engaged care teams working in concert with informed, engaged patients produce superior outcomes at lower costs. As Darren Black observes, "Historically, care is delivered at the most expensive place possible. We want to change that idea and make sure care is delivered efficiently with better outcomes."

Everybody wins.
Summit Partners provides far more than a "monetization opportunity" for DMG's physician shareholders. Summit will help DMG identify and evaluate growth opportunities in new markets. DMG will rely on Summit to value potential acquisitions and conduct due diligence. Summit also will provide ongoing perspective on risk management, capital formation and market evolution.

The combination of high-performing physician groups with savvy private equity investors has enormous potential to disrupt entrenched and inefficient healthcare business models. Disciplined growth capital enables integrated physician groups to expand value-based service provision to new markets. As risk-based payment expands, expect asset-light health companies to gain market share.

Enhanced Primary Care
The best outcomes in healthcare occur when individuals and their primary care providers proactively treat disease or avoid it altogether. Not everyone is lucky enough to have unimpeachable health. Delaying necessary care to save money accelerates the advance of chronic disease

with catastrophic health and cost consequences. Engaging customers through enhanced primary care is the best way to avoid, diagnose and manage chronic disease.

Enhanced primary care emphasizes the front-end of the care cycle through real engagement, frequent dialogue and shared decision-making. Providers work with customers to give them the knowledge, tools and confidence to manage their healthcare needs. If customers need specialty care, enhanced primary-care care providers are there to coordinate specialty care intervention and patient recovery.

Powerful new primary care companies are emerging to fill America's care management void. They employ team-based approaches to deliver customer-centric care in convenient locations. They're community-based and target specific customer groups. Like asset-light health companies, their business models lend themselves to managing the care of distinct populations. Many operate successful Medicare Avantage programs. They avoid unnecessary specialty care by emphasizing wellness, preventive care and disease management.

Let's revisit Houston, Dr. Clive Fields and Village Family Practice Management ("VFP") to see enhanced primary-care services in action. VFP is among a vanguard of health companies rediscovering the power of relationship-based care delivery. After Houston, we'll profile several up-and-coming enhanced primary-care companies. They represent bottom-up, consumer-focused, market-driven healthcare reform. They are rebels with a cause. They exist to provide better, more affordable and more convenient healthcare for everyone they touch.

VillageMD (VMD)

When insurance executive Tim Barry was expanding Universal American's Medicare Advantage business from $250 million to $2.8 billion in annual premium revenues, he scoured the country for superior primary-care practices to manage enrollees' care. None was better than Fields' primary care physician group, Village Family Practice (VFP). The group had 55 percent fewer hospital admissions, 45 percent fewer readmissions and 50 percent lower costs. Fast-forward a few years, Barry and Fields have joined together with uber-insurance executive

Paul Martino to create Chicago-based VillageMD in 2014. Their goal is to take VFP's superior care-management model nationwide.

Fields identifies the following four core strategies for achieving superior care management:

1. Manage enough primary care physicians in any population to significantly improve health and healthcare economics;

2. Practice value-based medicine;

3. Provide coordinated, primary care in a data-driven model; and

4. Structure payment incentives to reward better outcomes.

Fields describes the medical and financial benefits of coordinating care delivery through enhanced primary care services in the following way:

> *An Accountable Care Organization ("ACO") structure ties it all together. Primary care is the lowest-paid specialty in medicine. Where a specialist might average $450,000 a year, primary care docs make $140,000. The ACO incentivizes providers to keep patients healthy and minimize acute care. That's a more favorable model for primary care clinicians who rely more on cognitive, diagnostic skills than an orthopedic surgeon, for example, who relies on procedural skills.*

VillageMD compensates its physicians very well for practicing smart, outcomes-based medicine. They travel to patients whose medical conditions or personal situations make office visits impossible. "People are more honest, more responsive and more comfortable in their homes. You can see their economic situation, their support network. You get more insight into their care and compliance," notes Fields.

In Houston, VFP makes 100 to 150 home visits a year to its most fragile patients to coordinate their care. By regularly monitoring patients, VFP care providers ensure drug compliance, eliminate fragmented interventions and proactively treat chronic illness. Their customers are safer, healthier and happier.

VFP's performance speaks for itself. Its Houston patients' average length of stay in rehabilitation facilities is 17 days, compared with the market average of 41 days. The average Medicare hospitalization is $16,000. Fewer hospitalizations and readmissions saves insurers millions of dollars. VFP receives premium rates from Medicare Advantage plans, such as Aetna, who benefit from VFP's ability to reduce acute-care treatment costs.

"We're seeing large contracts with huge increases," reports Fields. "The insurer can pay a primary care doctor 20 percent more and decrease total care costs. The insurance companies know that paying our primary care doctors more keeps their enrollees healthier. Reduced acute spending offsets higher primary care payment several times over."

Jessica Elin, a researcher for *Market vs. Medicine*, accompanied Fields on visits to two of his Houston patients. Both were elderly, homebound and dependent on others for their care. When Fields began visiting the first patient, that patient was using ambulance services to transport him to and from dialysis treatments three times a week. He was too weak to get himself in and out of the bed or a car. His wife wasn't strong or sturdy enough to assist him.

Fields's goal was simple: coordinate therapy and medical care to the point where the patient could lift himself out of bed and travel to and from dialysis in a car. He jokingly observed that Aetna could have saved money by buying the family a durable car rather than paying regularly for ambulance service. Fields also noticed the patient couldn't afford to refill necessary medication and was low on medical gloves necessary for daily hygiene. Within two minutes, Fields found the drug at an affordable price at a nearby pharmacy using his GoodRx[218] app and made a note to bring a box of gloves on their next visit. "I buy 100 gloves for $6. The patient pays $9.95 for a dozen. It's ridiculous that a lack of affordable access to these types of low-cost medical products compromises patients' health."

---

218 http://www.goodrx.com/

The second patient, also a retired professional, lived alone but received 24/7 care from family members. He suffered from multiple, advanced non-curable chronic conditions. Fields' primary goal was to "keep him as comfortable as possible in his own home for as long as possible." Fields also wanted to avoid unnecessary medical interventions, particularly disruptive ER visits. On this particular visit, Fields' "treatments" included replacing batteries in the smoke detector to allay the patient's concerns about his house burning down. Given the patient's heart condition and high blood pressure, reducing his stress level was essential.

After the visit, Fields commented candidly, "He's not going to get better. He's not a candidate for rehab. If he goes to the ER, he'll end up in the hospital with expensive tests and recommendations for rehab services that won't do anything for him."

Fields' care extended to one of the second patient's care providers. Fields engaged that patient's niece in a conversation about health and wellness. She remarked to Fields that she never wanted to take as many pills as her uncle, so she had just joined a gym. Fields inquired about her workout with real interest and enthusiasm. Most people need a coach as much as a doctor. Fields is both.

The VMD model also provides practical, patient-centered care in office visits. Fields opens his practice on Saturdays. "Doctors don't make money by seeing patients on Saturdays. We make money by participating in savings generated through great primary care and avoiding unnecessary ER visits." Jessica got to see this first-hand. The Saturday she visited, Fields saw a patient who needed an immediate ultrasound diagnostic test. His nurse called a few walk-in imaging centers and found one (within 10 minutes of the office) that could perform the procedure right away. Coordinating that appointment took 5 minutes and cost thousands than an ER-administered ultrasound test. As the primary care doctor accountable for that patient's annual medical costs, VFP seeks out such opportunities to reduce total care costs.

In VillageMD's business model, primary care physicians manage their members' healthcare service delivery. "Doctors are the only power base that has not had chance to run healthcare," observes Fields. He notes that doctors are at precipice of opportunity to "grab the golden glove" and be responsible for driving better health outcomes. "No more excuses of 'insurance doesn't reimburse enough,' 'patients don't' listen,' 'hospitals charge too much.' We [primary care physicians] need to figure out how to manage and treat patients differently." That's how VillageMD will advance primary care services.

VillageMD trains physicians to manage patient populations with data to drive better outcomes. For example, Fields uses service-oriented benchmarks to measure how timely and efficiently they see patients. "91 percent of our patients check in and out within 60 minutes. We also measure how long it takes to answer calls, average hold times and numbers of dropped calls."

For Fields, primary care medicine should be patient-centered. His father made house calls in the 1950s, "because that's how you took care of your patients." He talks and thinks passionately about how VillageMD can benefit patients and doctors. "We're concierge medicine without the concierge or the cost." He travels extensively to primary care practices around the country, proudly demonstrating how the VillageMD approach can be adapted to their local market while keeping their practice independent. VillageMD employs a full-time marketing person to talk to and recruit primary care doctors to join their company.

Despite initial success, Fields is also realistic. "We're dealing with people's lives, not widgets. There is no way to know for sure if our business model will work. We need to spend more time perfecting the model; take more time to understand the best metrics for measuring and assessing population health and determining best practices. We need to know when our patients visit the ER, so we can make sure they get the right post-ER care."

Since its inception, VillageMD has more than tripled in size and created a path-breaking partnership, called Primaria, with Community Health Network (CHN) in Indianapolis. Launched in October 2015, Primaria employs VillageMD's practice model to provide patient-centric, value-based care for CHN and independent providers in central Indiana. Services include data management, medication management and behavioral health programs. Community's CEO Bryan Mills believes Primaria will "improve patient outcomes and drive down healthcare costs." Primaria is powerful medicine for addressing America's sick-care delivery model.

ChenMed

ChenMed was founded by Dr. James Chen, a Taiwanese immigrant, who opened his first primary care clinic in Miami in 1990. He sought to improve outcomes and reduce medical costs for healthcare's most expensive patients: senior citizens living with at least five or more chronic conditions. He designed his clinics and care delivery to specifically keep these patients healthy and avoid unnecessary treatment. ChenMed manages care for over 31,000 people nationwide. Like VMD, ChenMed is growing fast.

Chen tweaked the model in 2003 after his own cancer diagnosis showed him how challenging it was to get good coordinated care.[219] By 2005, Chen had arrived at his current approach: "collaboration, coordination and focus on the patient experience starting with the doctor-patient relationship."[220] The clinics still primarily focus on elderly patients covered by Medicare and Medicare Advantage plans.[221]

Most services are on-site, including as many as 14 specialists at some locations, depending upon patient needs. Clinics dispense medication and perform a range of diagnostic testing. ChenMed contracts with on-site translation services in up to 200 languages and hires bilingual staff — doctors and assistants — as warranted by location and patient population. ChenMed (JenCare Neighborhood Medical Centers outside of Florida) operates approximately 60 multi-passenger vans to transport patients to the company's 36 medical centers serving seniors in 25 cities nationwide.[222] ChenMed also gives each patient a Life Card

219 https://innovations.ahrq.gov/profiles/physician-led-clinics-offer-integrated-coordinated-care-high-risk-seniors-under-capitated
220 *Ibid.*
221 http://www.marketwatch.com/story/bringing-better-health-care-to-seniors-florida-based-medical-practice-creates-38-fewer-hospital-days-for-seniors-2013-06-03
222 https://innovations.ahrq.gov/profiles/physician-led-clinics-offer-integrated-coordi-

to facilitate electronic check in at appointments. The card centralizes insurance data, personal and emergency contact information, even the patient's most recent EKG results.[223]

ChenMed engineers care delivery to increase the time doctors spend talking to and helping patients. It works. In September 2014, ChenMed's population of Medicare patients spent 40 percent fewer days in hospitals than the national average.[224]

Oak Street Health

Headquartered in Chicago, Oak Street Health Partners operates neighborhood-based clinics delivering value-based care to a targeted patient group comprised primarily of Medicare and Medicaid patients. They also deliver medical and dental services.

Founder Mike Pykosz graduated from Harvard Law and worked at the Boston Consulting Group before returning home to Chicago.[225] With enthusiastic investor backing, he opened four primary care clinics designed specifically to succeed under the population health paradigm.

Pykosz identified Medicare and dual-eligible patients (those enrolled in both Medicare and Medicaid) living in low-income, underserved neighborhoods. Too often, these older, poorer clients fall victim to expensive, fragmented care delivery that compromises their health. Oak Street believes it can be profitable by coordinating care for these medically-fragile clients.

Pykosz focused first on engagement. Oak Street incorporated community centers into each of its clinics. This added social incentives for visiting clinics. Second, Oak Street created treatment panels, or teams, comprised of geriatric specialists, primary care doctors, nurses and medical assistants. Each panel sees only 500 patients. It takes a team to

nated-care-high-risk-seniors-under-capitated

223 Ibid.

224 http://www.economist.com/news/united-states/21618901-hints-how-provide-better-health-care-less-money-problem-solvers

225 http://www.hhnmag.com/Magazine/2014/Oct/cov-risk-accountable%20care-population-health

provide comprehensive care services to dual-eligible customers. The cap on the number of patients gives each panel more scheduling flexibility and longer and more meaningful appointments.

What's good for Chicago's patients is even better for Chicago. Oak Street Health actively revitalizes the communities it serves. It hires neighborhood residents and often turns vacant buildings into thriving clinics. Best of all, it upgrades care and provides hope to fragile, disadvantaged citizens.

One Medical Group

Founded in 2005 by entrepreneur Dr. Tom X. Lee, One Medical Group is concierge medicine without high annual fees. One Medical's membership-based model embraces customer service and availability with medical offices that are more hotel-style than clinical, bringing hospitality to healthcare but making it affordable. At One Medical, patients pay an annual membership fee of $199.[226] The fee supports the unbillable time and attention patients want and need from care providers to manage their health services.

Venture capital quickly bought into Lee's vision. Just two years after opening a solo practice in San Francisco, Lee secured millions of expansion dollars from Benchmark Capital. It was the firm's first investment in healthcare.[227] One Medical currently has physicians in Boston, Chicago, Los Angeles, Phoenix, New York, the San Francisco Bay Area and Washington, D.C. Lee is looking to scale the model and draw physicians back to primary care. Attracting young, healthy patients is essential to the company's business model. One Medical Group has 24/7 phone support, a mobile app, and it encourages patients to email their doctors with any follow-up questions.

While they have different cultures, target markets and business models, these relationship-based primary-care companies share the following traits that enhance patient engagement, achieve better outcomes and reduce total care costs:

226 http://www.onemedical.com/nyc/membership/
227 http://www.nytimes.com/2011/02/01/health/01medical.html?pagewanted=1&_r=5&ref=science

- Team-based care models that engage with customers and provide comprehensive services;

- Intense customer focus that looks for and addresses root causes of illness;

- Coordinated care delivery that emphasizes wellness and prevention; and

- Avoidance of unnecessary testing, treatments and acute interventions.

These emerging care-management companies are attacking the fragmentation and inefficiency at the core of American healthcare delivery. Incumbent providers that persist in activity-based treatment models will lose patient volume as these companies expand. Enlightened health companies see the writing on the wall. They're moving to disrupt entrenched practices that fragment care delivery. They're building alternative care delivery models that enhance patient engagement and advance care management. They're disrupting themselves.

Self-Disruption

Innovative health companies are responding to pressure from disrupters by building their own care management capabilities to coordinate care delivery for employees and other at-risk lives. Moving beyond treatment-centric business models, their care management initiatives emphasize prevention, monitoring, early detection and proactive medical interventions.

Mercy Health and Pharos Innovations

Headquartered in Cincinnati, Mercy Health now manages healthcare services for multiple populations throughout Ohio. To improve care coordination and avoid costly losses, Mercy has engaged

Pharos Innovations to assist the health system with customer engagement and treatment adherence. Early results are promising. Patient engagement and compliance are up. Total care costs are down. The challenge is scaling this program successfully throughout Mercy's expansive network.

Headquartered in Northfield, Illinois, Pharos has focused on patient engagement since 1996. Johns Hopkins-trained physician Dr. Randall Williams founded the company to validate his belief that "engaging patients in their daily self-care is the optimal path to reducing medical costs."[228] Between 1996 and 2004, the company developed and validated a sophisticated customer engagement model, intermixing technology with people-guided interactions. Since its commercial launch in 2004, Pharos has partnered with Medicare, Medicaid, the Veterans Administration, ACOs, large and small hospital groups and numerous commercial payers to lower costs through better patient engagement.[229]

Tel-Assurance is Pharos Innovations' proprietary, real-time, remote monitoring technology platform. The device-free system collects patient data daily. To promote treatment compliance, the system sends alerts and action items to care managers. Because data is collected in real time, care coordinators can intervene quickly when needed. The interaction helps Pharos' clients reduce more dangerous, costly clinical events among their patient populations. Pharos reports close to a 100-percent prescription-refill rate and daily patient engagement, an 85-percent retained-appointment rate and a 60 percent reduction in all-cause hospital admissions.[230]

Park Nicollet Health System

Park Nicollet Health System in Minneapolis (now part of Health Partners), participated in a CMS Physician Group Practice Demonstration involving Pharos.[231] Park Nicollet's goal was to increase its shared savings

228 http://www.pharosinnovations.com/about-us-2/
229 *Ibid.*
230 http://www.pharosinnovations.com/
231 http://www.pharosinnovations.com/resource-center/case-studies/

by better managing patients' chronic disease. Pharos' Tel-Assurance was chosen as the patient-engagement platform.

Park Nicollet's managers identified their rising-risk patients and assigned teams of centrally located care coordinators to groups of between 250 and 300 patients. The coordinators relied on Tel-Assurance data to monitor compliance and alert them to clinical changes warranting physician follow-up. CMS, Park Nicollet and 650 patients all experienced better health status:[232]

- 59 percent reduction in all-cause hospitalizations for enrolled patients;

- $2.6 million annual cost reduction for Medicare;

- 21 percent reduction in hospital admissions per 1,000 patients; and

- 30-day admission rates below 5 percent.

Northwell Health and CareConnect

Northwell Health (formerly North Shore-LIJ Health System) is a large health system in New York City and Long Island that is making a bold move into care management through its health insurance subsidiary, CareConnect. With 2,700 staff physicians, thousands of affiliated doctors, laboratories and services ranging from diagnostics to hospice care, Northwell created a provider-owned insurance network to expand its customer service platform.[233]

CareConnect is an exclusive provider organization (EPO)—a provider-sponsored managed care plan which covers services within the plan's network. CareConnect emerged from Northwell's employee health insurance program, which managed healthcare services for enrolled members by using an EPO model.

---

232 *Ibid.*

233

When CareConnect opened in 2014 to non-employee subscribers, it retained the positive attributes of its employee insurance program. By limiting care to Northwell's providers, CareConnect is able to offer competitive premiums. Working exclusively with Northwell providers also enables CareConnect to deliver services above and beyond those of traditional insurance companies.

CareConnect emphasizes human connection. It schedules appointments for members across an entire care event. For example, patients who need imaging services, lab work and surgery as part of their treatment protocol work directly with a CareConnect representative to schedule everything at one time. In 2014, CareConnect fielded 100,000 incoming calls. Humans, not auto routers, answered each one within an average of 6 seconds.[234]

CareConnect had 15,000 members when it launched in 2014. CareConnect's CEO, Alan Murray, expects to have 100,000 members by 2018. It's an aggressive plan centered on giving customers what they want and reducing demand for acute services.

Care Management Rising

The force of value-driven care is irresistible. Government, corporate and individual demands for better care management are reshaping traditional supply and demand relationships. Companies of all shapes and sizes are experimenting with business models that deliver better, more affordable and convenient healthcare. The competitive process will determine ultimate winners and losers based on their individual and collective abilities to deliver the best outcomes at the lowest prices. In the process, winning companies will earn consumers' trust by squaring their actions and rhetoric.

---

234 http://www.healthcaredive.com/news/customer-service-key-for-north-shore-lij-health-plan-success/405181/

CHAPTER 9

THE CLINIC CONNECTION

*People have to follow their hearts, and if their
hearts lead them to Walmart, so be it.*

JAMES MAYNARD KEENAN

Rick Kimball knows value when he sees it. As head of Goldman Sachs' and Morgan Stanley's healthcare practices, Kimball led initial public offerings totaling more than $3 billion and advised on many of the industry's most important mergers and acquisitions. When his daughter twisted her ankle in 2015, Kimball witnessed the pitfalls of current medical practices and experienced the promise of disruptive new care delivery companies.

This prototypical American medical saga unfolded as follows. Twelve-year old Eliza Kimball shrieked in pain as she fell awkwardly off a foam roller in her Manhattan apartment. Her foot immediately began to swell. Fearing a broken ankle, her mother and a friend debated what to do. They settled on a belt-and-suspenders approach: an initial visit to a nearby CityMD Clinic followed by a consult with their pediatrician.

Rick Kimball arrived at CityMD as Eliza checked in. The facility was spotless, modern and super efficient. Even without an appointment, the CityMD providers were able to treat Eliza right away. They examined her injured foot, took X-rays and fitted her with a walking boot. On the way out, CityMD gave team Kimball a CD with the X-rays of both feet. The entire care episode took less than an hour. Rick Kimball's $75 co-pay covered its cost.

The next day, the CityMD physician called with good news. They'd sent the radiology images to an orthopedic specialist who concluded Eliza's ankle was not broken. Having compared the X-rays of Eliza's injured foot with her healthy foot, the specialist noted that Eliza's good foot contained a cyst that could become problematic. Team Kimball was grateful for the notice and agreed to monitor the cyst's growth.

That same day, Rick Kimball took Eliza to their fancy Upper-East Side pediatrician. They sat in a cramped waiting room filled with sick kids for an hour before being ushered to a treatment room. After a 30-minute wait, their pediatrician breezed in, did a quick examination and insisted Eliza immediately see a pediatric orthopedic surgeon for a second opinion. Total exam time was under 10 minutes. Total wait time exceeded 90 minutes.

The Kimballs then visited the specialist in his Park Avenue office. They sat alone in a "crusty" waiting room for over 30 minutes before seeing the doctor. After reviewing the X-rays, the specialist agreed that Eliza's ankle was not broken. He didn't notice the cyst on her other foot. Rick Kimball's health plan didn't cover second opinions, so he paid the specialist's $600 fee and marveled at the difference between CityMD and traditional medicine. CityMD is customer-focused and uses technology to enhance the speed, accuracy and convenience for routine procedures. In contrast, traditional medicine is slow, inefficient, expensive and haphazard.

As Eliza's story indicates, our expectations for healthcare service delivery within large health systems are very low. We tolerate inconvenience, excessive diagnostics and high costs while receiving mediocre care. The equation changes when consumers make purchasing decisions and providers reconfigure business models to satisfy demanding customers. We shouldn't be surprised by the terrific, affordable care Eliza received at CityMD. Instead, we should expect that superior healthcare services will become routine. Market-based healthcare reform is working nonstop to make this happen.

As Healthcare Goes Retail[235]

If you think healthcare is a tough business, consider the retail industry. In the last 50 years, retailing has experienced shopping malls, strip malls, mass retailers, big box retailers, club stores, specialty stores, value players and e-commerce. By the year 2000, seven of the largest eight retailers in 1980 had either filed for bankruptcy, been acquired or ceased to become relevant. Technology and changing consumer attitudes drove each transition in retail sales as consumers experienced greater choice, lower prices and more convenience.

Consumerism has the force and precision of heat-seeking missiles. Customers flocked to Walmart because it offered more selection, greater convenience and lower prices than local mom and pop retailers. Amazon threatens Walmart because it offers even more selection, even greater convenience and even lower prices. Consumerism is an intricate, never-ending dance between companies and their customers.

---

235 http://dupress.com/articles/retail-transformation-choice-experience-trust/

Businesses exist only to find and keep customers. Success requires constant engagement, constant adjustment and a consistent ability to give customers what they want, where they want it and at competitive prices.

Retailing is being turned upside down once again by big technology, changing customer preferences and intense competition from new entrants. A June 2015 Deloitte University Press report titled "The Retail Transformation" identifies the following four pressures challenging retailers:

1. Lowered barriers to market entry are bringing in many new small players and fragmenting the retail landscape;

2. Online marketplaces are transcending geographic proximity and expanding market demand for highly specific offerings. Small niche players can reach consumers regardless of physical location;

3. Technologies such as on-demand fulfillment are changing how and where retailers hold inventory; and

4. New retail models are arising out of new technologies and new ways to connect with consumers.

The Deloitte report concludes that the "retailers most likely to survive the current shift are those that can provide a tremendous variety of offerings while maintaining, or reviving, the personal touch of the mom-and-pop corner store."

Now for the bad news. The same shifts disrupting the retailing industry are coming to healthcare. Retail-clinic companies are establishing footholds in markets throughout the country. Like CityMD, they employ technology to enhance the customer experience, increase efficiency and lower prices. Their convenient locations and nimble business models support high-tech service delivery with a personal touch.

Convenient walk-in urgent care clinics fill the gap between expensive ERs and waiting days or weeks to see a primary care physician.

These companies—CityMD,[236] ZoomCare[237] (profiled in Chapter 7) and MedSpring[238]—appeal to young, tech-savvy urban professionals. They also attract patients who need immediate service and prefer these upscale clinic settings over traditional doctor's offices. Most of these new retail companies began as innovative start-ups. Others, such as MedSpring (owned by dialysis giant Fresenius) represent diversification strategies for their corporate parents.

New concierge practices offer private care, personal relationships and on-demand availability at an affordable price point. OneMedical (profiled in Chapter 8) currently charges a $200 annual membership fee. Patients can see a primary care physician without advance appointments. They enjoy appointments averaging two-to-three times longer than typical 15-minute primary care appointments. Members can communicate with their primary care physician 24/7 via email and mobile platforms.

MedLion, also a subscription-based practice, offers doctor visits for $10, labs and imaging services for up to 50 percent less than traditional providers and helps patients find affordable specialists when necessary.[239] MedLion is currently in 10 states along the East Coast with plans to expand into the Midwest.

Qliance Health in Washington manages the health of approximately 35,000 patients. Its primary care physicians earn a flat monthly fee, paid upfront. Qliance doesn't hassle with co-payments, co-insurance or deductibles. Half of its patient population is on Medicaid. Demographics vary widely across age, health and financial circumstances. Still, Qliance claims to average approximately 20 percent savings, compared with traditional fee-for-service providers.[240] Qliance's affordable-care-with-better-outcomes approach has attracted investments from business gurus Bezos and Michael Dell.[241]

---

236   http://www.citymd.com/

237   https://www.zoomcare.com/

238   http://medspring.com/

239   http://medlion.com/

240   http://time.com/3643841/medicine-gets-personal/

241   *Ibid.*

These concierge and retail clinics are ideally situated to become interface companies, liaisons between patients and providers offering affordable, bundled care. They help consumers select and manage specialty care when needed. From banking to law to airlines to insurance, small nimble companies find and exploit opportunities to deliver value to demanding customers. Retail clinics fit that pattern, but they're not alone. Like banks, law firms and airlines, big-market retailers are consolidating to cut costs, increase scale and accommodate demanding customers. CVS Health, Walgreens and Walmart also believe healthcare is a target-rich environment.

The Big Disrupters: CVS, Walgreens and Walmart

When CVS Caremark announced it would stop selling tobacco products by October 1, 2014,[242] the decision grabbed international headlines.[243] Praise and doubt ensued. The American Pharmacist Association, which had been calling for a ban on all tobacco sales since 2010, applauded the decision, as did President Obama. Wall Street, however, was bearish. Analysts estimated that dropping tobacco could cost CVS $2 billion in annual revenues or about 3 percent of overall sales.[244]

To emphasize its new commitment to health, CVS Caremark changed its name to CVS Health. CVS's future is not in groceries and incidentals. It aims to be a health and wellness company offering convenient, low-cost primary care and disease management services.

In addition to 7,700 stores, CVS has over 900 walk-in clinics. Pharmacy services account for over half of overall corporate revenues. The decision to cease tobacco sales and launch smoking cessation programs through its MinuteClinics[245] expands the company's

---

242 http://www.usatoday.com/story/news/nation/2014/09/03/cvs-steps-selling-tobacco-changes-name/14967821/

243 http://www.bbc.com/news/world-us-canada-26051519

244 http://www.usatoday.com/story/news/nation/2014/02/05/cvs-will-no-longer-sell-tobacco-products/5207853/

245 http://www.sustainablebrands.com/news_and_views/behavior_change/mike_hower/cvs_health_finds_financial_incentives_help_people_quit_smo

commitment to its pharmaceutical and clinic-care businesses.[246] Wall Street read the tea leaves wrong. Despite ending tobacco sales, CVS Health's revenues have increased. Increases in pharmacy and clinic sales more than offset declines in front-of-store sales.[247] CVS has spoken. It's in healthcare to stay and playing to win.

If you don't think that big retailers like CVS will be managing the health of millions of Americans over the coming decade, what are you smoking?

What do CVS, Walmart and Walgreens have in common? The three Fortune 500 giants are publically traded and practice disciplined investment growth. They attract customers through quality products, lower prices and convenience. They understand consumers. They're very efficient. They know how to exploit competitive strengths. For example, Walgreens and CVS stores are within five miles of 75 percent of U.S. residents. This offers a level of customer access unavailable to incumbent health companies.

In response to the pressures confronting all retailers, CVS, Walgreens and Walmart are investing in healthcare services to increase revenues, attract customers, increase brand loyalty and provide needed services. Individually and collectively, they bring the following powerful capabilities to support their healthcare business strategies:

Exceptional Supply-Chain Management

Walmart achieves "everyday low prices" by employing state-of-the-art supply chain management. In 1992, Walmart launched Retail Link to integrate its supply chain and collaborate with vendors on inventory levels and sales. In 1995, Walmart launched its Collaborative Planning, Forecasting, and Replenishment (CPFR) program. In the 2000s, Walmart implemented RFID tagging and reduced inventory by improving product flow. Today, Walmart sells products made in

---

246 http://www.slate.com/blogs/moneybox/2014/09/03/cvs_stops_selling_cigarettes it_wants_to_be_taken_seriously_as_a_healthcare.html

247 http://time.com/3557120/cvs-revenues-increase-after-cigarette-ban/

70 countries through 11,000 stores in 27 countries.[248] The company thrives on razor-thin margins from high-volume sales.

CVS relies on Descartes System Group Inc.'s 20/20 Visibility technology to provide vendors and suppliers with order and inventory data across its massive supply chain. Stakeholders track deliveries, manage inventories and assess supplier performance. Reducing unnecessary inventory saves CVS millions of dollars.[249]

Like CVS, Walgreens is transitioning from a drug store selling groceries to a more holistic health and wellness business model. In 2012, Walgreens purchased 45 percent of Alliance Boots, the largest pharmacy chain in Europe, and in 2013, the combined company signed a drug distribution deal with Amerisource Bergen. These transactions position Walgreens to negotiate more favorable prices for generic drugs through bulk purchases. Walgreens' former CEO, Greg Wasson, notes, "Alliance Boots and AmerisourceBergen are experts in pharmaceutical supply chain distribution. We are very good at it, but the combination of what they both do to improve our supply chain, take that off of our hands, and improve our service levels is really the opportunity that we are excited about."[250]

National Platforms, Tailored Strategies

Walgreens, Walmart, and CVS have large pharmacy platforms that advance medication compliance and support primary care delivery (e.g. infusion services). At the same time, their in-store offerings make it easy to meet total care-management needs.

Big retailers benefit most when customers come to their stores. Health clinics can break-even and increase store profits through incremental sales. The clinic's nurses can direct customers to purchase monitoring and exercise equipment. The clinic's dieticians can

---

248 http://www.scdigest.com/ASSETS/ON_TARGET/12-07-27-1.php

249 http://www.inboundlogistics.com/cms/article/winning-supply-chain-strategies-adversity-breeds-creativity/

250 http://www.babson.edu/executive-education/thought-leadership/retailing/Documents/walgreens-strategic-evolution.pdf

suggest healthy diet plans with foods from the grocery aisles. Store design makes incidental purchases easy.

Ben Wanamaker, Walmart's senior manager of strategy and operations for health services, formerly served as Executive Director of the healthcare program at the Clayton Christensen Institute for Disruptive Innovation.[251] In response to customers' dissatisfaction with banks, Walmart began offering targeted financial services (e.g. check cashing, wire transfers, bill payment and prepaid debit cards) at below-market prices in 2007. The retailer now operates more than 1,000 Money Centers.

As in financial services, Walmart is well-positioned to become a trusted and logical source for healthcare services. Let's hope it succeeds. Walmart's rural client base disproportionately suffers from chronic disease. Improving care access, knowledge distribution and ongoing monitoring are vital for improving health status in rural America.

Transparent/Competitive Prices

Walmart successfully pioneered $4 generic prescriptions.[252] Now Walmart is offering $40 primary care check-ups, about half the standard industry cost. Walmart employees and family members with Walmart insurance pay only $4 for their check-ups. Similarly, a pregnancy test costs only $3 and a cholesterol test costs just $8. "It was very important that we establish a [low] retail price for healthcare products because price leadership matters to us," said Jennifer LaPerre, a Walmart Senior Director responsible for health and wellness.[253] Likewise, CVS and Walgreens clinics post prices for all services. There are no surprises and no sticker shock.

Resourceful and Customer-Centric

Walgreens, Walmart and CVS offer sophisticated rewards programs to entice customers and influence behaviors. For example, United

251 http://www.christenseninstitute.org/our-team/ben-wanamaker/

252 http://blogs.wsj.com/corporate-intelligence/2014/10/17/Walmarts-new-everyday-low-price-a-40-doctor-visit/

253 *Ibid.*

Healthcare subscribers (in Illinois and Arizona) who complete certain healthy activities within United's Health4Me™ mobile app earn points in Walgreens' Balance® Rewards program. Participants can redeem their points toward purchases at Walgreens. By encouraging micro-habits, such as tracking steps with a Fitbit, the program helps customers lead healthier lives while helping health plans reach higher levels of patient engagement. According to Dr. Vidya Raman-Tangella, head of UnitedHealthcare's Innovation Center of Excellence, "We have seen that rewarding healthy behavior can help people make sustained, positive behavior change. Our collaboration with Walgreens will play an important role in encouraging consumers to take a more active role in their overall health and well-being."[254]

Adaptable and Market-Focused

In 2011, Walmart circulated a Request for Information (RFI) seeking strategic partners to "expand access to high quality health services by becoming the largest provider of primary healthcare service in the nation."[255] Public opinion challenged Walmart's ambitious agenda. Walmart demurred but continued its solicitation process.

Walmart never lost sight of its objective. Three years later, it partnered with QuadMed to roll out its in-store Care Clinics nationwide.[256] Walmart selected QuadMed for its expertise in establishing and running employer-based clinics. Walmart is intent on becoming a dominant primary care provider across America. Walmart tests and adjusts its service offerings in multiple markets. When necessary, Walmart partners with other companies to advance its capabilities. Walmart builds on success and learns from failure. Walmart believes it can underprice and out-deliver America's current primary care providers.

---

254 http://news.walgreens.com/press-releases/general-news/select-unitedhealthcare-plan-participants-will-soon-have-access-to-walgreens-balance-rewards-for-healthy-choices.htm

255 http://www.futureofcapitalism.com/2011/11/walmart-health-care#

256 http://www.bizjournals.com/milwaukee/print-edition/2014/11/21/quadmed-clinic-launch-for-Walmart-could-be-game.html

Major acquisitions by CVS (Target Clinics) and Walgreens (Rite-Aid) underscore their commitment to operating retail clinics across America. Each is experimenting with store designs, service offerings and reward programs to attract and keep new customers.

Strong Brands; Precision Marketing

In January 2011, Walgreens embarked on a very public campaign to promote healthier foods and lifestyles. With the support of First Lady Michelle Obama, the company announced a five-year plan to decrease prices on fruits and vegetables; reduce salts, fats and sugars in thousands of its store-branded packaged foods; make healthy food options more available in underserved urban markets; and work with suppliers to achieve similar objectives. Walgreens announced new standards for healthy foods along with bright green "Great for You" labeling. In the same way that Starbucks has become synonymous with environmental sustainability, Walgreens' goal is to make its brand synonymous with healthy eating.

To further spread the word, Walgreens advertised its re-worked private brands through blogs, social media and online partners (www.parentask.com) rather than the usual print ads and in-store signage.[257] Two years later, customers could find renovated stores with freshly prepared healthy food choices "at the Corner of Happy & Healthy."[258]

Not to be outdone, CVS launched a new tag line, "Health is Everything," with its 2014 name change to CVS Health and supported it with an all-encompassing branding campaign (digital, print, television, outdoor and experimental ads) developed by advertising giant BBDO. Along with the new branding and to burnish its health-oriented image, CVS launched its "OneGoodReason" nationwide smoking cessation program, expanded its Minute Clinic locations and launched programs to encourage customers to take their medications regularly.

---

257 http://www.nytimes.com/2011/02/11/business/media/11adco.html
258 http://www.bizjournals.com/chicago/news/2013/01/24/walgreens-makes-a-convincing-case-for.html

"For our patients and customers, health is everything, and CVS Health is changing the way healthcare is delivered to increase access, lower costs and improve quality," said Larry J. Merlo, president and CEO of CVS Health, in a statement. "As a pharmacy innovation company at the forefront of a changing healthcare landscape, we are delivering breakthrough products and services, from advising on prescriptions to helping manage chronic and specialty conditions."[259]

CVS, Walgreens and Walmart are betting their future on health and wellness. Would you bet against them? Jeff Kang, Walgreen's former Senior Vice President for Health and Wellness, said it best, "There's magic in the clinic. It happens when pharmacists and nurse practitioners work in collaboration with customers and primary care physicians to manage their healthcare needs whenever, wherever and however it's convenient."

The Provider Response?

Most health systems and some insurers are responding to increasing clinic competition by establishing their own retail clinics in convenient locations. In Chicago, Northwestern Memorial Healthcare has rebranded as Northwestern Medicine. It is building regional hubs for primary care physicians, complete with marble floors and other expensive appointments. These Taj Mahal-like facilities extend the powerful Northwestern brand and reinforce its commitment to regional healthcare delivery. Other Chicago-based health systems are pursuing similar strategies to expand their regional presence. This retail strategy is necessary, but it carries greater market risk than expansion strategies being pursued by retail clinic companies.

Northwestern and other hospital-based services currently benefit from higher reimbursement payments for treatments offered in their clinics. When patients receive treatments at provider-based clinics, governmental and commercial payers reimburse the clinics at higher hospital rates for equivalent treatments. For example, a colonoscopy can cost five-to-ten times more in a hospital-based clinic than in

---

259 http://www.adweek.com/news/advertising-branding/cvs-rebrands-first-ads-bbdo-159874

a non-hospital clinic. The economic sustainability of provider-based clinics is dependent upon receiving these higher payments for routine services.

As the market moves toward greater pricing transparency and customer-based purchasing, it will become more difficult for provider-based clinics to justify their higher fee schedules. Creative retail companies with better information and tools are establishing customer-friendly, value-based purchasing models for routine services. The wider the gap between reimbursed prices and market prices, the greater the opportunity for disruptive technologies to redirect customers to lower-priced treatment alternatives.

After Northwestern acquired my dermatologist's practice, she told me a number of her patients were upset that their bills increased even though they were getting the same services. She had always been part of Northwestern's network and still received the same salary, so she didn't understand why her treatment charges were increasing. I told her there were four potential answers: First, Northwestern could be recouping the cost of acquiring the practice. Second, it could be adding a substantial "facility fee" to cover its overhead costs. Third, it could be optimizing its revenue under its current reimbursement agreements with health insurers. Or fourth, a combination of any or all of the above.

My answer increased her understanding but didn't alleviate her concerns. She responded, "I only care about giving my patients the best care. I don't want to think about the economics." Unfortunately, her patients' co-pays and deductibles are increasing (including mine) to the point where some are considering other alternatives. It's a trickle of patients now, but it could become a flood as more convenient, lower-priced, user-friendly alternatives emerge for the same procedures.

Implications

Expect continued growth and refinement of disruptive retail clinics. Nimble start-ups and uber-retailers will offer new services, expand capabilities and perhaps even perform small procedures. They will become hubs for chronic disease management and platforms for home-based services and telemedicine.

As the retail clinic market matures, supply and demand relationships will shift. Value-oriented clinics will gain market share. Eliza Kimball will get all the care she needs at CityMD. Her parents won't invest time and money in traditional treatment channels. Higher-cost and less-coordinated provider-based clinics will lose market share. Their ability to rely on preferential reimbursement payments for economic sustainability will diminish. In fact, Congress seems intent on reducing the ability of health systems to receive preferential payments in clinic settings. Despite fierce opposition from the American Hospital Association, the 2015 budget eliminates preferential reimbursement in ambulatory facilities built or acquired after November 2, 2015. The bill passed with overwhelming House and Senate support.

The societal message to health systems is clear: Make your retail clinics competitive or customers will find routine treatment elsewhere. Even more troubling for traditional providers is the increased willingness of consumers to shop for routine services in response to behavioral incentives built into high-deductible health plans (HDHPs).

It's well-documented that the expansion of HDHPs is making consumers more price-conscious when making medical decisions. For example, I now know each routine 15-minute dermatology check-up costs me $175. Less documented is the effect HDHPs have on the timing of medical expenditures. Unlike ancient times (two years ago) when Americans used excess flexible-spending money to buy glasses in December, HDHP customers manage their deductible spending throughout the year.

Ambulatory centers now experience an uptick in cash payments at year-end for routine procedures, mostly from patients with HDHPs. Subscribers want to avoid making the high-deductible payments unless they get really sick. While under the deductible limit, many customers choose to pay cash and receive discounts rather than run treatments through their insurance providers. It makes sense. The more that people spend their own money for healthcare services, the more carefully they spend it.

The Retail Message

Like rock 'n roll, retail healthcare is here to stay. The more it establishes itself, the more customers will demand convenient, transparent, low-cost and user-friendly healthcare services in retail locations. As the Deloitte University Press study on retail transformation observed, every paradigm shift in retailing "increases consumer choice while reducing consumers' total cost in terms of money, time and opportunity."[260] This is wonderful news for everyone except incumbent health companies. They must adapt to this overwhelming consumer preference for competitive retail services or lose market relevance.

Consolation, technological advances and changing consumer preferences pose fundamental challenges to incumbent retailers as well as incumbent health companies. The strategic decisions of CVS, Walgreens and Walmart to aggressively pursue retail healthcare reflect these changing market dynamics. The Deloitte report offers the following advice to incumbent retailers on how best to navigate a turbulent marketplace:

> *Amid all this change, the retail value chain is unbundling, and even remapping. Design, sales, and support are less strongly linked, with small, niche entrants drawing from a range of flexible options to execute these activities. To compete effectively, traditional retailers should reimagine how they create and capture value, thinking past omni-channel positioning to examine, and find the best uses for their assets. Digital marketplaces with on-demand fulfillment can be incredibly well-suited to providing low prices and extensive choice. Brick-and-mortar assets can serve as a stage for customized consumer experiences that go far beyond ambience to surprise and educate the consumer. Done right, these experiences can become so valuable that they inspire consumers to choose to pay for them themselves.*

> *Another opportunity for many large retailers is to become industry infrastructure providers. Because sourcing and procurement, inventory management, store operations, marketing, and fulfillment become more*

---

260 http://dupress.com/articles/retail-transformation-choice-experience-trust/

efficient as they scale, established retailers can extend these capabilities to support smaller, more fragmented niche players. Traditional retailers can also move to transform into consumer agents—new entities that use deep understanding of consumers to help them navigate product choices.[261]

While there is a lot of industry-speak incorporated into this summary, its conclusion is clear: the current business paradigm for incumbent retailers is unsustainable. Winners will reevaluate their competitive positioning and pursue strategies that connect with customers by improving their customer experience. This will require introspection, out-of-the-box thinking, courage, experimentation, commitment and an increased willingness to take risk.

What is true in retailing is even more true in healthcare. Unfortunately, healthcare must travel farther to embrace and excel in consumer-oriented business environments. Entrenched, counter-productive cultures won't concede to enlightenment overnight. Antibodies will attack constructive initiatives. During this transformational period, health company leadership and governance are more important than ever. It's time for healthcare companies to enter the retail arena and prepare for battle. As Theodore Roosevelt observed over a century ago, "In any moment of decision, the best thing you can do is the right thing. The worst thing you can do is nothing."[262]

Health companies can only move forward by embracing value, consumerism and high purpose. It's the American way.

261 ibid
262 http://www.goodreads.com/author/quotes/44567.Theodore_Roosevelt

CHAPTER 10

HEALTHCARE'S IDENTITY CRISIS: WHAT WOULD EINSTEIN DO?

The definition of insanity is doing the same thing over and over and expecting different results.
ALBERT EINSTEIN

I n the fall of 2013, the board of Minneapolis-based Fairview Health Services hired me to advise them on a potential merger with South Dakota-based Sanford Health. The transaction was in trouble and the board wanted an independent advisor to help guide its deliberations. Fairview is a $3.5-billion-revenue health system with a statewide delivery network. It's aligned with the University of Minnesota Medical Center and has very strong academic and community-based medical services. Sanford is a well-endowed, largely rural health system serving nine states with $3 billion in annual revenues. It had expanded rapidly, invested significantly in applied research and wanted to extend its Minnesota presence.

The merger was logical beyond belief. The Twin Cities area is the commercial center for the upper Midwest and also the Dakotas and Montana. The geographic region of the Fairview and Sanford facilities replicates the broadcast maps for the Minnesota (baseball) Twins and (football) Vikings. The University of Minnesota's brand strength is legendary. This is Lake Woebegone country. Everyone from Duluth to Sioux City to Billings loves and respects the Gophers. A Fairview-Sanford merger would have created a powerful specialty-care feeder network for the University of Minnesota Physicians (UMP) and the University of Minnesota Medical Center (UMMC). Large teams from both organizations along with their advisors began assembling a plan for combining the companies.

Ironically, the Fairview's academic constituents, who had the most to gain from a merger with Sanford, objected to it the strongest. Issues related to control, trust and leadership surfaced repeatedly. During due diligence, the university itself made a proposal to acquire Fairview, further complicating the negotiating dynamics. Not surprisingly, the negotiations became very public and political. In response to a negative review from Minnesota's State Attorney General, Sanford withdrew from the discussions before a preliminary proposal had even emerged from the work teams.

How could such a promising combination collapse so quickly? The answers lie within a complex maze encompassing process, governance, leadership and identity. Even though I'd served as Fairview's investment banker for over a decade, I never appreciated the differing academic and community physicians' worldviews. Mythology played a role. Academic physicians seemed to believe that if community physicians were any good, they'd be academic physicians. Community physicians seemed to believe that academic physicians wouldn't last a week in the real world. Despite practicing within one system since Fairview's 1997 acquisition of UMMC, academic and community physicians competed for patients and pursued strategies that benefited one group at the expense of the other.

Fairview is a complex organization that exists within a progressive marketplace that embraces value-based delivery. In the 1970s, University of Minnesota physician Paul Ellwood worked with the Nixon Administration to pass legislation that created health maintenance organizations (HMOs). As I mentioned in Chapter 8, Health Partners, a major Twin Cities healthcare provider, operates with an asset-light business model that positions it well for direct-care contracting with employers and managing patient populations. Large, enlightened employers are demanding more value from both healthcare insurers and providers. Nimble companies like Zipnosis—the online healthcare provider I described in Chapter 7—are developing consumer-friendly platforms that deliver care services conveniently at very low (and transparent) prices.

Market pressures bring healthcare's inherent contradictions to the surface. It's impossible to optimize revenues without compromising patient care. It's impossible to be a low-cost provider and train doctors. It's impossible to be customer-centric within enormous, centralized medical centers. It's impossible to please specialists while putting patients' interests first. Rhetoric and reality do not align. The center cannot hold. Established roles and operating models no longer work. Health companies like Fairview are at the vanguard of an industrywide identity crisis as incumbents cope with unfamiliar and unfriendly market dynamics.

Healthcare's dynamism is creating unprecedented strategic opportunities for aligning new business models with customers' needs. It's no longer a one-size-fits-all health company marketplace. Each company must select and execute strategies that position it best for post-reform success. The stakes are high. Many companies will fail.

Strategic decisions are complex and multi-faceted. Tactical considerations include geography, competition and sources of competitive advantage. Organizational leadership and governance have never been more important. Whether they realize it or not, the bridge is already burning for incumbent health companies. Business as usual is not a viable strategy.

At the Dilemma's Horns

Like the late Yogi Berra, Albert Einstein had many quotable observations. Here's one of his most famous: "The definition of insanity is doing the same thing over and over and expecting different results." The American healthcare system already wastes a trillion dollars annually and delivers mediocre results. As Steve Jobs might say, it's time for America's health companies to "think different."

First things first. Fairview and other incumbent health companies confront strategic dilemmas. By definition, dilemmas have no inherent solutions. They require organizations to manage through the tensions created by opposing values: e.g. between mission and margin; between scale and complexity; between institutional control and community value. In his book *No Problem*,[263] Alex Lowy characterizes dilemmas as follows:

> *Dilemmas direct you to the heart of the issue. Dilemmas take courage. Dilemmas involve trade-offs and accommodation. Dilemmas are transformational; when you recognize and acknowledge an essential conflict, you open yourself to the possibility of needing to modify, resolve or redefine the terms of engagement.*

In Fairview's case, the company must align its community and academic medical practices in ways that create value and meet customers' needs. Fairview's managers need to retool their research and education activities to advance population health and build healthier communities. They must reconfigure their facilities to lower costs, increase convenience and reduce care variation. These are not easy challenges.

---

263 Alex Lowy, No Problem, AuthorHouse™, 2007

It's entirely appropriate to ask, "What would Einstein do?" Here are some suggestions from the great man himself:

We cannot solve our problems with the same thinking we used when we created them.

To raise questions, new possibilities, to regard old problems from a new angle, requires creative imagination and marks real advance in science.

You have to learn the rules of the game. And then you have to play better than anyone else.

Once we accept our limits, we can go beyond them.

Strive not to be a success, but rather to be of value.

Einstein's observations go to the heart of the issue. Resolving Fairview-like strategic dilemmas requires strategic clarity regarding organizational purpose and priorities. It takes astute leaders exploiting disruptive tensions to align historic operating profiles with today's operating realities. In post-reform healthcare, most high-cost business models aren't sustainable.

Embracing value-based care delivery is essential for success. Easier said than done. The dilemma lies in transforming current organizational cultures and business models into high-performing, value-driven, customer-centric care companies. It's adapt-or-die time for incumbent health companies. The competition has sharp horns and relentless energy.

To Fairview's credit, the organization is tackling its dilemma head on. In October 2015, Fairview announced its intention to merge its operations with the University of Minnesota Physicians (UMP) to create a unified care delivery system: University of Minnesota Health. Fairview and UMP will cease to exist. The goal is to create a world-class integrated medical company that delivers high-value, coordinated care; extends specialty care to rural communities; elevates the university's medical school; improves community wellness throughout the state and advances path-breaking medical research. As Einstein might observe, it's time for Fairview and UMP to play the new game better than anyone else.

Time for Existential Questions

Admiral James Stockdale was Ross Perot's running mate on the 1992 independent ticket. His opening statement at the vice presidential debate was: "Who am I? Why am I here?"[264] That line generated a huge laugh and immediate connection with the large viewing audience. Unfortunately, that opening quip was the high point of the admiral's debate. It went downhill from there. However, Stockdale's two questions synthesize a basic truth: businesses (and politicians) must offer value to customers (and constituents) to win.

As healthcare's supply and demand relationships normalize, health companies must adapt their business models to provide value to customers. Like Stockdale making his case to voters, incumbent health companies must ask themselves tough questions. Unlike Stockdale, who wasn't prepared for the national stage, winning health companies will meet and exceed customer demands. Here are several existential questions health companies should consider when designing their post-reform strategies:

- What businesses are we in?

- What are our competitive advantages?

- Which risks should we own; which should we shift to others?

- Is our leadership and governance up for the challenge?

- Who are our customers?

- How well are we meeting their needs?

264 http://www.nytimes.com/1992/10/14/us/the-1992-campaign-james-stockdale-reluctant-politician-tempers-professional-edge.html

- Are we too dependent on fee-for-service reimbursement payments?

- How strong is our brand? What does it say about us?

- Do our operations square with our rhetoric? Do we both speak and live the truth?

Answering these questions and executing strategies that deliver real value to customers will differentiate winning health companies. No company is good at everything. Each company needs to determine where it excels and execute better than ever to thrive in the post-reform marketplace. Before delving into specific business strategies, let's turn our attention to governance.

Governance Matters[265]

Nonprofit health systems have not required high-powered governance to thrive within healthcare's highly-regulated, reimbursement-oriented operating paradigm. Relative to other industries, healthcare has not experienced significant disruption and operates largely as it did 50 years ago. Doctors administer care in centralized settings and third-party payers, notably governments and insurance companies, reimburse providers for the care they deliver. Very few large hospitals have closed. Community-based governance models have supported organizational success during this prolonged period of stable operations.

Nonprofit health-system boards tend to be large and philanthropically focused. They often lack critical expertise, suffer from uneven attendance, distribute governance responsibilities broadly and even cede responsibility for organizational strategy to management. More than ever before, organizational leadership will determine which health systems develop the expertise and capabilities necessary to maintain organizational competitiveness. To win, health systems must pair managerial talent with effective board governance to ensure

265   Dr. John Koster and David Johnson, *Dynamic Tension: Rethinking Health System Governance,* January 4, 2016

superior performance, appropriate resource utilization and proper strategic positioning. The risks associated with not upgrading organizational governance are dangerously high.

Unlike their for-profit counterparts, nonprofit boards must satisfy multiple constituencies in defining their purpose and operating orientation. Lacking the clarity of advancing shareholders' interests, nonprofit boards instead strive to advance community benefit, which has multiple and sometimes conflicting interpretations. In seeking to exercise their governance responsibilities, nonprofit boards often over-emphasize organizational interests and/or tolerate underperformance.

This mission ambiguity argues for greater rigor in defining organizational vision, performance standards and strategic imperatives. The best strategies often require organizations to *stop providing* long-offered services. These cancelling decisions almost always generate opposition and can become difficult for community-based nonprofit boards to execute.

Modernizing health system governance requires clarity and commitment in the following five areas: 1. Board Character; 2. Board Composition; 3. Board Orientation; 4. Board-CEO Dynamics; and 5. Board Management.

Board Character
Boards govern, they don't manage. Their responsibilities require profound respect, loyalty and care for the organization. Board members must have enough distance from operations to see the bigger picture and provide insightful strategic guidance. With rare exceptions, board members should attend all meetings. They should come prepared and participate actively. Boards exercise enterprise-wide responsibility. They should operate as a unified body with no representational seats, conflicts of interest or reserve powers. Board members must trust one another and the governance process. Individual members must be able to speak freely and openly share concerns. Interactions must be honest, deliberative and respectful. Health systems should compensate board members to recognize their time commitment and increase performance accountability.

Board Composition

Smaller boards are better. According to a 2014 survey by Spencer Stuart, an executive search and leadership consulting firm, the average board size for S&P 500 companies is 11. Only 17 percent of S&P 500 companies have more than 13 members. Smaller boards enable members to know one another well and engage fully in the governance process. It is essential to recruit board members with relevant competencies. Which competencies health system boards require should be a topic of frequent debate. For example, health systems may consider having members with expertise in consumerism and technology. Board members with career experience in disrupted industries can offer valuable insights into strategic repositioning, new business development and competitive pressures.

Board Orientation

Importantly, boards own organizational strategy. Boards should devote at least 50 percent of their time to understanding, discussing and guiding both short-term (the next year) and longer-term (5 to 10 years) strategy. It is essential for boards to regularly examine the three-to-five biggest threats confronting the organization. Beyond strategy, boards should develop a meaningful information architecture with metrics that summarize organizational performance and highlight troublesome issues. There should be no more subcommittees than necessary (e.g. audit, compensation, human resources). Content experts from the board should chair subcommittees staffed with other board members. In-depth oversight should occur in committees with results reported to the full board by committee chairs.

Board-CEO Dynamics

The board's most important responsibilities are hiring, evaluating and guiding the organization's CEO. The CEO selection process should incorporate strategy, capabilities assessment, organizational culture and succession planning to identify candidates that fit. Once selected, they must work with new CEOs to ensure their success. The old expression "It's lonely at the top" rings true. CEOs often cannot share their deepest concerns with their leadership teams. For this reason, it makes sense to have board members provide perspective and give both personal and professional advice. The best boards provide a safe conduit for CEOs to unburden themselves and debate sensitive topics. They also hold executive sessions at each meeting, so members can discuss topics, observations and concerns without the CEO in attendance. Typically, board chairs share insights from executive sessions with CEOs to preserve trust and guide decision-making.

Beyond the CEO, board members should develop relationships with the organization's senior management team. As part of professional development and evaluation, CEOs should provide opportunities for senior leaders to interact with the board. This is particularly important when undertaking succession planning.

Board Management

Effective board chairs are essential for successful board operations. In addition to setting meeting agendas, board chairs police deliberations (no wild goose chases), keep the dialogue moving, encourage participation and bring issues to resolution. To optimize the board's contributions, board chairs should develop a feel for the board's calendar and work plan. Once a year, the board chair should canvas all board members individually to learn about their assessment of the board's performance, solicit suggestions for improving board deliberations and to discover any hidden concerns. Annual board surveys can aid in the review process. Finally, boards must have guidelines and mechanisms for replacing board members at appropriate times. Year-end conversations create opportunities for these dialogues.

Reconfiguring board governance is a daunting endeavor. It requires moving long-time supporters off the board. CEOs may resist more rigorous oversight and perceived loss of control. Orthodox thinking clouds awareness and obscures realistic market assessments. Honest discussion regarding organizational capabilities and competitiveness can be excruciating. It may seem both easier and safer to maintain the status quo and muddle through.

And yet... the threat posed by value-based service demands is existential for many, perhaps most, health systems. They lack the culture, capacity and capabilities to transform in ways that meet customer demands for better healthcare and accommodate substantial financial risk. Health systems cannot dodge the approaching tornado. Better to address industry disruption with wide-open eyes and strong leadership supported by equally strong governance.

Business Model Segmentation

The care-delivery matrix diagram below segments care delivery by outcome uncertainty and care duration. As discussed in Chapter 7, each of these care quadrants represents a separate business with different labor, facility and supply requirements. Healthcare providers cannot excel in each business area. Companies need to assess their relative strengths and weaknesses to determine where and how to compete in a value-based marketplace.

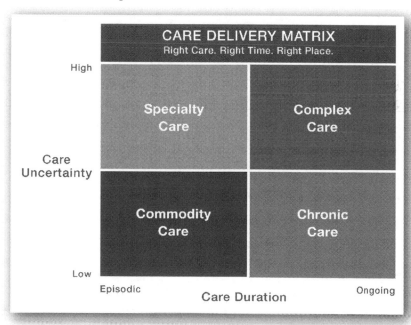

Most care today is commodity and non-acute chronic care. Knee replacement surgery was once specialty care and is now routine. As outcomes become more certain, perceptions of quality shift to price, convenience and customer experience. Enlightened health companies recognize that they must standardize care protocols, reduce performance variation and understand their true operating costs to deliver value-based care: right care, right time, right place, right price. To compete in post-reform healthcare, companies must play to their strengths and execute flawlessly.

Complexity's Challenge to Integrated Health Delivery

As with all companies, health systems grow organically and through acquisition by pursuing horizontal and/or vertical strategies. All growth strategies fall within this four-corner matrix:

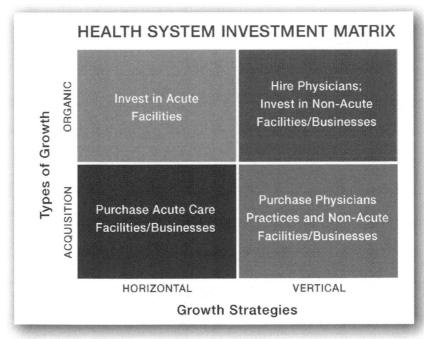

Historically, health systems have largely pursued horizontal growth by building or acquiring acute care facilities. As reform marches forward, many health systems are growing vertically by expanding their care continuum to become integrated delivery systems (IDSs), capable of managing care for distinct populations. Growth creates economies of scale by spreading fixed costs over larger operating platforms, eliminating duplicative functions and increasing negotiating leverage. Growth also increases organizational complexity by blending cultures, introducing new business and/or regulatory risks and requiring more expansive oversight.

As companies grow, diseconomies of complexity offset and sometimes overwhelm beneficial economies of scale. Vertical growth is more complex than horizontal growth. It's clear that IDSs have more operating complexity than hospital management companies. Accordingly, it's probable that health systems developing IDSs will experience greater diseconomies of complexity.

IDSs represent a major business-model shift for treatment-focused health systems accustomed to fee-for-service payments. The following chart displays the shift in risk that accompanies the IDS business model:

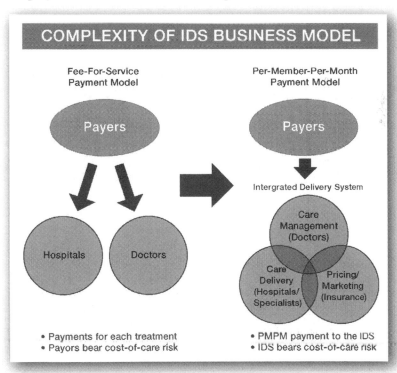

Given its inherent complexity, vertical integration creates several potential sources of conflict and energy drain. They include the following:

- **Culture clashes:** Operators and suppliers see the world differently. They aren't inclined to solve one another's problems;

- **Embedded problems don't disappear:** Vertical integration cannot create demand for faltering businesses. Customers gravitate to lower-cost, higher-value products and services;

- **Mushy transfer pricing:** Absent real market competition, internal service pricing and cost allocations become political exercises;

- **Favoritism for internal suppliers:** Operators cannot seek higher-value external alternatives;

- **Too much refereeing:** Disputes between operating divisions expand and intensify. Senior managers expend too much energy resolving disputes. Solutions are often sub-optimal; and

- **Lost focus:** Companies lose competitive advantage. Diseconomies of complexity overwhelm the benefits of vertically-integrated operations.

Humana's Cautionary Tale

As young lawyers, David Jones and Wendell Cherry started a nursing home company on the advice of one of their real estate clients. Each invested $1,000. Their first facility opened in 1962 on Liverpool Lane in Louisville. They named their company Extendicare in 1968. By the early 1970s, Jones and Cherry were operating the country's largest long-term care company. In 1972, they sold their nursing homes and set their sights on hospitals. Extendicare applied large-scale management practices to hospital operations as demand for hospitals exploded. Extendicare became Humana in 1974. Within a decade, Humana was the nation's largest hospital company.

First with Extendicare and then Humana, Jones and Cherry used horizontal integration and the economies of scale to build efficient, nationwide delivery platforms.[266] Humana's movement into health insurance was almost accidental. An Arizona hospital lost a regional HMO contract. Hospitals need patients to survive. Humana responded by creating a health insurance plan in Arizona to channel patients to its hospital.

Like General Motors, IBM and Pepsi before it, Humana decided it could become more profitable by owning its suppliers. Aligning all elements of a company's supply chain is the essence of *vertical integration*. While simple in concept, executing vertical integration is hard. It fails more often than it succeeds.

Humana's vision was elegant. The company offered low-cost health insurance to expand market presence and increase patient volume for its efficient hospital network. Health plan subscribers using in-network facilities and physicians avoided co-pays and deductibles. Humana also built primary care centers with salaried physicians to steer specialty-care volume to in-network providers. However, Humana encountered significant challenges pursuing integrated delivery:

- The health plan sent subscribers to lower-cost, out-of-network providers;

- Primary care physicians competing with Humana's primary care centers did not refer patients to Humana's hospitals;

- Competing health plans reduced referrals to Humana's hospitals;

- Hospital occupancy declined;

---

266 For a more complete discussion of Humana's early history and its experiment with vertical integration, see *Market Driven Health Care* by Regina Herzlinger, pp. 140-145, 1997

- As its insured physician network expanded, Humana's delivery efficiency declined;

- Employed-physician productivity declined;

- Hospital costs spiked; and

- Employee moral within Humana's hospitals plummeted.

Humana admitted defeat, spun off its hospitals and sold its primary care centers. By 1994, the once-proud hospital company was now exclusively a health insurance provider. Humana's failure to master integrated delivery serves as a warning to industry incumbents dancing with strategies that combine insurance, risk management and care delivery. Complexity is a demon that can destroy organizational dreams and devour organizational resources. This is particularly true in academic medicine. As the Fairview case study at the beginning of the chapter illustrates, advancing academic medicine's clinical, research and educational missions within competitive markets is an exceptionally difficult task.

The Academic Question

Medicine is the single profession that combines education, basic research and business operations under one umbrella organization. Architecture schools don't design buildings. Business schools don't manage corporations. Public policy schools don't run governments. Why do we run hospitals from medical schools? Coordinating medical education, medical research and clinical care delivery within one academic framework led management guru Peter Drucker to describe academic medical centers (AMCs) as "the most complex organizations ever created."[267] Reform-based pressures to reduce cost and improve care expose all health systems to increased financial

---

267 http://www.creative-healthcare.com/blog/2014/11/

pressure. AMCs manage additional pressure to sustain educational and research missions.

Academic medicine is vital to American healthcare. The U.S. has approximately 400 AMCs, including 130 with direct ties to medical schools. AMCs have diverse operating profiles that reflect their individual histories and market circumstances. Together, they provide 20 percent of the country's patient care and 40 percent of its charity care. AMCs operate 60 percent of the nation's Level 1 trauma centers, treating the most difficult cases. They annually graduate 17,000 doctors and train over 30,000 medical residents while conducting the majority of NIH-funded (National Institutes of Health) research. AMCs have overlapping missions, multiple revenue sources and intricate subsidy arrangements. To fund medical education and research, AMCs receive public and private funding, clinical-care subsidies and philanthropy.

The AMC's decentralized governance model grants department chairs significant autonomy to manage their specialties (e.g. cardiology). This leads to breakthrough innovations but complicates care coordination. The academic model becomes even more complex when AMCs affiliate with networks of community hospitals and physicians. Typical physician debates over protocols, costs, referrals and capital investment often intensify. Despite the complexity, AMCs are major enterprises. They have iconic brands and enjoy widespread public support. Underlying the AMC's current business model, however, are tough operating realities:

- A high percentage (e.g. 60 to 80 percent) of an AMC's care could be provided in lower-cost community hospitals.

- PwC (formerly Price Waterhouse Coopers) research finds only 22 percent of consumers are willing to pay more for AMC care.[268]

---

268 http://www.pwc.com/us/en/health-industries/health-services/aco-accountable-care-organizations.jhtml

- According to the Dartmouth Atlas, AMCs are often the most aggressive providers of high-cost, end-of-life care. Within the overall AMC category, faculty medical practices (e.g. UCLA) generally have higher end-of-life care costs than group practices (e.g. Mayo Clinic).

- Few AMCs rank among the Joint Commission's top quality performers.

- AMCs confront significant state and federal funding cutbacks for Medicare, Medicaid, indigent care and medical education. The Affordable Care Act's funding for new Medicaid patients will partially offset these cutbacks.

- Despite an infusion of stimulus funding, NIH research funding has plateaued and is likely to decline.

Sub-titled "Strategies to Avoid a Margin Meltdown," a 2012 PwC Health Research Institute report highlighted AMCs' revenue, quality and governance challenges. It concluded, "up to 10 percent of traditional AMC revenues are at risk." For AMCs with tight operating margins, this could be catastrophic. PwC recommended improving clinical outcomes, integrating into larger care networks, expanding telemedicine, becoming an information hub and enhancing translational research.

1999 Revisited: Managed Care and Academic Medicine

The mid-1990s managed-care movement slowed medical inflation by shifting treatment risk to hospitals and doctors through capitated payments. Medical expenditures held steady at 13.6 percent of GNP between 1992 and 1999. Operating losses on managed care contracts along with Medicare budget cuts hit health systems hard and led to significant industry consolidation. Like today, many questioned the AMCs' sustainability and advocated reform. In November 1999, Dr.

Steven Schroeder, then CEO of the Robert Wood Johnson Foundation, delivered a remarkable lecture on academic medicine and the public interest.[269] In the following words, he emphasized the need for fundamental rethinking of the academic mission in healthcare:

A time of stress and fundamental change is precisely the time to reexamine mission, purpose and focus.

Schroeder worried that market-based strategies to increase revenues were separating AMCs from their public trust responsibilities:

...in responding to the exigencies of the marketplace, the risk is that we protect form over function. The danger is that we ultimately risk academic medicine's special standing as a public trust. Academic medicine is an enormous public resource. How can it live up to the unique opportunities and responsibilities it has been entrusted with to improve the health of the public?

A survey following Schroeder's lecture revealed that almost 60 percent of AMC deans believed their institutions would decline in size by 2009. That clearly hasn't happened. Academic medicine has prospered in the new millennium as U.S. healthcare expenditure has ballooned to 18 percent of GNP. According to the Institute of Medicine, Americans are living shorter lives in poorer health than citizens in 16 advanced economies. Clearly, the current model requires improvement. Particularly given today's challenging funding environment, Schroeder's core question still resonates, "How can AMCs meet their unique responsibilities to improve the public's health?" Here are some suggestions:

- **Mission:** expand the "heal, teach and discover" missions to include health promotion and disease prevention.

---

269 http://www.milbank.org/uploads/documents/ebert/index.html

- **Business Model:** Partners' CFO Peter Markell believes AMCs will evolve into two independent business models: 1) *population health* for most care (e.g. 80 percent) where AMC networks deliver consistent, high-quality episodic care in low-cost, convenient settings; and 2) *referral centers* for complex cases. The ability to charge premium prices for referral care will depend upon outcomes, reputation and the level of regional and national competition.

- **Networks:** Align with large care networks to distribute population health services and expand the referral base for complex cases. Reducing total cost-of-care episodes requires coordination along the full primary-tertiary continuum.

- **Direct Contracting:** Develop population health expertise by actively managing their employees' health. Given their strong brands, AMCs are well positioned to contract directly with governments and private employers for both specialized care and population health services.

- **Consumerism:** Employ technology, shared decision-making, social media and transparency to engage customers and win their loyalty.

- **Facilities:** Become more distributed and less acute-care centric. AMC campuses must adjust their facility mix to deliver community-based population health services and national and regional referrals.

- **Education:** Build more alignment and fusion between health schools (medicine, nursing, dentistry, pharmacy, public health, administration) to deliver appropriate care efficiently and manage the health of large populations.

- **Research:** Undertake more research into behavioral strategies and technologies that promote wellness, prevent illness and tailor treatments to individuals. Expect more collaboration across academic disciplines (e.g. agriculture, business and health schools researching the links between food production, diet and disease).

In an ancient fable, a frog carries a scorpion across a river on its back. At the deepest point, the scorpion stings the frog. With its last gasp, the frog pleads, "Why?" Just before drowning, the scorpion replies, "It's my nature." In the long run, perpetuating expensive, acute-care-centric operating paradigms will be self-defeating for all health systems. The existential question for AMCs is whether they can adapt their business, teaching and research models to address public demands for better health services within today's stringent funding environment. AMCs that change their nature and embrace value-based business models will redefine academic medicine, justify the public's trust and thrive for decades.

Leading Organizational Change

Entrenched cultures, complex business models, changing competitive dynamics, asset-heavy operations and heavy regulation make sustaining innovation difficult for incumbent health companies, much less adapting to the disruptive innovation embedded in new value-based payment systems. Where incumbents stumble, new entrants with new capabilities and nimbler operations will emerge to capture market share. Leadership and organizational change will determine which incumbents remain competitive and which falter.

In 1996, Harvard Business School professor John Kotter published *Leading Change*.[270] Originally conceived as the next installment in a series of research projects, *Leading Change* became a seminal work on organizational transformation. Like his television namesake, John Kotter returned home. In 2012, Kotter re-issued *Leading Change* with a new preface. Why? The speed and complexity

---

270 John Kotter, *Leading Change*, Harvard Business Review Press, 2012

of market forces today requires even more agile and change-friend-ly organizations.

Kotter's key insight is that management is not leadership. Management makes systems work. Leadership builds new systems and transforms old ones. Too often, complacency stymies organizational change. Only effective leadership can overcome it. *Leading Change* offers an eight-stage, sequential process for guiding organizational transformation. It's clear, logical and incisive. Missing steps can and usually do cause failure. Here are the eight steps:

1. Create Urgency
2. Build Guiding Coalitions
3. Vision and Strategy
4. Communicate Change
5. Empower Employees
6. Short-term Wins
7. Consolidate Gains
8. Anchor Change in Culture

Placement of "Vision and Strategy" third is illuminating. Far too many CEOs crystalize their vision before doing the hard work of creating a sense of organizational urgency and building strong coalitions to sustain change strategies. In Fairview's proposed merger with Sanford, senior management created the necessary urgency but failed to build a sufficiently strong guiding coalition to overcome internal opposition. A strong vision alone is never enough. Interestingly, the best visions and strategies emerge from defining urgency; overcoming complacency and building powerful change coalitions.

Rhetoric exhorting transformation overwhelms healthcare; yet, there are few examples among health systems of true organizational change. Structural impediments slow progress. Fee-for-service reimbursement still accounts for over 90 percent of provider revenues. If we're being honest, however, structural explanations are insufficient. There's too much management in healthcare and not enough leadership.

Health system executives know their organizations need to deliver transparent, outcomes-driven, customer-friendly care. In *Leading Change*, Kotter provides a roadmap for the bumpy but ultimately rewarding journey. In post-reform healthcare, health companies will win when their customers are healthier, happier and spending less on healthcare services.

Aspirational Marketing and the Power of "Why"

Health companies are awakening to the market reality that consumerism is redefining healthcare delivery. Winning companies in all industries connect with customers, gain their trust and earn their business, over and over again. This will happen in healthcare. Alison Lewis, Johnson & Johnson's Chief Marketing Officer, observes that "brand love leads to loyalty beyond reason." True "brand love" overcomes price disparities, inconvenience and logic. Customers not only buy products they believe in; they buy products that support their own beliefs. Emotional connection drives consumer decision-making.

The question, of course, is how do companies establish durable brand love? This question is vital for health companies, since they historically have executed transactions with limited input from customers.

Start with "Why"

Conventional marketing begins with "what" products companies sell, explains "how" those products differentiate and ends with logic-based pitches for "why" customers should buy them. Rational appeals highlighting product features and competitive prices rarely generate breakout sales. It's too easy for customers to find the same or better value elsewhere.

Simon Sinek, the author of *Start with Why*, describes conventional marketing as "outside in." Everyone knows *what* they do. Some know *how* they do it. Very few know *why* they do what they do. By contrast, Sinek's "golden circle" has the "why" at its center. Human beings are hard-wired to respond to appeals grounded in purpose, trust and belief. The "why" gets us up in the morning and motivates us to act. In a widely-viewed Ted Talk, Sinek uses Apple to highlight the power of "inside-out" appeals. In reality, Apple is one electronics manufacturer among many competing for global market share. Conventional marketing would showcase images of Apple's computers (their "what") and highlight their elegant design, integrated operating system and ease of use (their "how") before making the "why" sales pitch. Pretty boring.

Apple is anything but a conventional company. Apple's marketing starts with "why" and works outward. Apple's iconic founder, Steve Jobs, wanted to "make a dent in the universe." Apple challenges the status quo and "thinks different." Apple demonstrates this through its computers' elegant designs, integrated operating system and ease of use. Same "how", different context. Customers flock to buy Apple products.

In Sinek's words, people don't buy Apple for *what* Apple does. They buy Apple for *why* Apple does what it does. By using Apple products, customers align with Apple's values and project those values to the world. In so doing, customers begin to see themselves as they would like others to see them. Like all positive relationships, brand love increases self-esteem, confidence and interconnectedness. It satisfies deeply human needs.

Even as he was turning Apple around in 1997, Steve Jobs intuitively understood the importance of customer perspective, self-image and experience. In response to a hostile question that year, Jobs described Apple's creative process as "starting with the customer experience and working backward to the technology. You can't start with the technology and try to figure out where you're going to sell it."[271]

Health company advertising often starts with breakthrough technology and/or stories of miracle cures. They feature the what and not the why. All health systems have great doctors, grateful patients and believe in quality. That's not enough to differentiate and build true brand love. Consumerism is forcing health companies to appreciate customers' actual experience—to feel their fears, frustration and

---

271 https://www.youtube.com/watch?v=FF-tKLISfPE

confusion. Patients/customers want care providers on their side, looking out for their interests and making their healthcare journey easier. The unfortunate truth is that health systems often fail at this human level. Care is impersonal and systematic. Patient experience is an afterthought. Even quality is inconsistent.

Introspection can lead to redefining the organizational "why." It's never been more important. Health companies can't say they put patients first and act otherwise. Hypocrisy crucifies brand loyalty. Ask Volkswagen. In this sense, "why" marketing mirrors John Powers' three marketing commandments: 1) Be interesting; 2) Speak the truth; and 3) Live the truth. Powers' caveat is that if organizations can't live their truth, they should change what they're doing so they can.[272] Winning health companies will live their truth.

Answering "Why"

Consumerism gives health companies the opportunity to rewrite their patient/customer relationships. If undertaken with wisdom, empathy and humility, brand-building can establish trust, win "loyalty beyond reason" and make everything better for patients, care providers, employees and communities. Johnson and Johnson uses the following quote to communicate its commitment to customers, "Consumers are our invited guests. It's our job to make every experience a little better." Imagine how great American healthcare could be if health systems adopted this philosophy. Brand love isn't clever. It reflects deep trust between companies and customers built over years of interactive, mutually beneficial experiences. To paraphrase Scottish theologian William Barclay, "There are two great days in an organization's life—the day it's created and the day it discovers why." For health companies, discovering and acting upon the "why" is the foundation for building "brand love" and winning in post-reform healthcare.

---

272 Jonah Sachs, *Winning the Story Wars*, A Creation Myth for Marketers, 2012

"Why" in Action: Shared Accountability at Intermountain Healthcare

In 2014, Intermountain Healthcare changed its mission statement from "Excellence in the provision of healthcare services to the Intermountain West" to "Helping people live the healthiest lives possible." A commentary accompanying the mission change announcement demonstrates the power of emphasizing "why":

> *We are now focusing even more strongly on prevention and wellness, shared-decision making with our patients, and on using our resources and technology to help patients enjoy their lives without needing our hospitals and clinics, if possible. Our new Mission reflects that expanded role—it describes "why we exist.* [273]

Wow! Who wouldn't want to receive healthcare services from companies that live this mission? Of course, rhetoric is cheap. Intermountain's challenge is to put its lofty ambitions into practices that improve people's lives. That's not easy. The "sickcare" business in America is lucrative. This makes Intermountain's decision to embrace wellness even more impressive.

For calendar year 2016, Intermountain has launched a "shared accountability" insurance product through its health insurance company, SelectHealth. SelectHealth Share operates on the premise that providers, insurers, employers and employees must collaborate to create affordable healthcare that delivers necessary medical services, promotes wellbeing and engages all participants. To participate, employers, employees, providers and SelectHealth agree in writing to comply with provisions that support "predictable premiums, greater affordability and healthier lives." Specifically, participants stipulate to do the following:[274]

---

273 https://intermountainhealthcare.org/blogs/2014/11/intermountain-healthcare-announces-a-new-mission-vision-and-values-statement/

274 https://selecthealthshare.org

Employers

- Agree that SelectHealth will be the company's sole carrier
- Offer high deductible health plans and subsidized health savings accounts
- Contribute at least 70 percent of the premium cost
- Create a healthy work environment
- Meet 50 percent to 70 percent employee participation over three years in key "employee engagement" metrics (see below)

Employees

- Establish health savings accounts
- Select and engage with primary care physicians
- Complete annual health assessments
- Participate in digital coaching
- Engage in at least two physical-activity campaigns annually
- Participate in management programs for chronic diseases
- Complete preventive screenings

SelectHealth

- Support employer and employee engagement with meaningful financial incentives
- Employ evidenced-based medicine
- Practice shared medical decision-making
- Develop reports and metrics to track progress and increase adherence
- Develop online tools to support quality and cost transparency
- Implement population health and wellness programs
- Implement efficient and effective prescription drug programs

Providers

- Comply with evidenced-based standards and business best practices
- Provide complete, timely and accurate documentation
- Participate in compliance training

- Participate in emergency call coverage
- Keep patients, where possible, in the SelectHealth care network
- Provide equal access for all patients
- Accept accountability for quality, cost and patient engagement
- Share performance data
- Disclose all conflicts of interest

SelectHealth Share excludes no one, but participation requires commitment and accountability. This can be particularly difficult for physicians and subscribers who cherish independence. The offsetting benefits, however, are wonderful—healthier workplaces, communities and individuals. Everyone wants this.

The Moral of "Why" Stories

As with Apple, people will flock to SelectHealth Share not for *what* it does, but for *why* it does it. Customers align with Intermountain's values because they make them feel better about themselves. These values burnish the image customers wish to project to others. Shared values create powerful company-consumer connection. It's *brand love* in the making. Bert Zimmerli, Intermountain's avuncular Chief Financial Officer, repeatedly makes the statement that, "Healthcare is personal. It touches our teams, family and friends." Zimmerli personifies an Intermountain culture that truly cares about its community and its customers. No organization is perfect. Intermountain makes its share of mistakes. Here's the difference: Intermountain lives its values. Nothing is more important in winning customers' trust.

Apple and Intermountain illustrate a simple truth. Companies experience the benefits of brand love when customers believe that company is "in their corner" and "on their side." Here's the catch. All companies, including health companies, actually have to be on their customers' side to earn brand love. They can't just say it. They have to live it.

Market Evolution

Almost every healthcare transformation discussion includes Kodak's cautionary tale—how the once iconic company fails to embrace digital imaging, capsizes and drowns. The story's moral is to embrace disruption, reinvent care delivery and thrive in the post-reform marketplace. Easier said than done. These transformation discussions almost never discuss how Kodak's chief rival, Fujifilm, navigated the same disruptive market environment, adapted and emerged more successful than ever. Today Fujifilm is a diversified company and more profitable than ever. Film accounts for less than 1 percent of revenues. In early 2012 as Kodak confronted bankruptcy, Fujifilm's CEO Shigetaka Komori described Fujifilm's response to the disruptive threat posed by digital imaging as follows:

> *As time passes, the facts show that when a company loses its core business, some companies are able to adapt and overcome the situation, while others are not. Fujifilm was able to overcome by diversifying.*

Leadership, culture and execution (not money, brand or market position) were the key attributes that enabled Fujifilm to succeed where Kodak could not.

In *The Origin of Wealth*, Eric Beinhocker applies evolutionary theory to explain market function, organizational competitiveness and wealth creation. In Beinhocker's view, economies are complex adaptive systems that incorporate *physical technologies* (inventions), *social technologies* (organizational structures) and *business designs* to create more productive and wealthier societies. The core evolutionary formula (*differentiation, selection and amplification*) describes the three-stage process through which new products emerge, demonstrate their superiority and win market share. Relentless market repositioning creates winners and losers as customers purchase preferred products and services. The fittest companies survive by adapting to shifting consumer preferences.

It's a widespread misconception that evolution results in survival of the fittest. Evolution actually causes elimination of the weakest. In business, companies that collaborate, pursue competitive advantage and keep customers' interests first are most likely to survive. Strong companies that fail to adapt lose competiveness and market relevance. Differentiation, selection and amplification unfold as industries transition. Disruption is the marketplace application of these forces on industry incumbents. IBM survived the transition from mainframe to desktop computing by reinventing itself as a services company. Digital Equipment Corporation's (DEC's) inability to manage the transition from mini to desktop computers led to its bankruptcy.

Health Systems' "Kodak Moment"[275]

Like Kodak and Fujifilm in the late 1990s, health systems know that attractive fee-for-service payment will not continue indefinitely. Value-based payment and competitors are emerging to displace health companies overly dependent on traditional operating models. Despite this looming and disruptive threat, most health systems are not preparing to compete in market environments where the criteria for success are price, outcomes, convenience and customer experience.

Let's make the Kodak-Fuji metaphor plain. Fee-for-service payment is film. Value-based payment is digital imaging. Health companies should answer the following questions honestly to assess whether they're adapting to new market realities:

- Is the health company's outpatient strategy focused on insanely convenient, low-cost and connected customer service or on provider-based reimbursement, raising prices and closing offices at 5 p.m.?

- Is the health company replicating high-end services in saturated markets or consolidating services into centers of excellence that have scale, better outcomes and lower costs?

275 David Johnson and Gaurov Dyal Market Corner Commentary, *Fujifilm's Moment*, December 8, 2015

- Does the health company have a digital strategy? Has it embraced telemedicine and virtual clinics? Is the company increasing customer convenience or adhering to centralized, inconvenient delivery models?

- As consumers experience higher out-of-pocket payments, does the health company view price transparency as a competitive advantage or a threat?

- Do the health company's service offerings create or diminish value for the communities they serve? Are disease management, wellness and post-acute care areas of key focus? Is the health company willing to cannibalize its acute operations to develop better community-wide health outcomes?

- Is the health company willing to partner with innovative companies that provide competitive advantage or does the health company believe these companies threaten its core businesses?

- Are the health company's decisions driven by a short-term profitability or longer-term investments that improve customers' health and well-being?

- Does the health company's leadership and culture more resemble Kodak's or Fuji's? Can it make effective resource allocation decisions?

Healthcare has some well-honed maneuvers: doubling down on activity-based payment while giving lip service to value-based delivery and pushing up rates to drive cost and premium increases. While this old healthcare playbook still has force, its magic is evaporating. Continuing to follow it carries embedded danger. The wider the gap is between artificial supply-driven prices and competitive prices, the greater the opportunity for competitors with higher-value services to steal away customers. American healthcare needs a new playbook.

Health companies need to face the tough questions of figuring out who they are and who they want to be in the new healthcare order. Winning companies reconfigure operations to deliver tangible value to customers. Service and convenience matter; almost everybody wins when health companies deliver better care at lower prices in customer-friendly venues.

Some grizzled incumbents will fade away—addition by subtraction. Winning health companies employ market mindsets to create value for customers. Outcomes improve. Prices decrease. Service and convenience matter.

Darwinian Logic

Like film manufacturing in the late 1990s, healthcare delivery is at a significant inflection point. A constellation of politics, economic pressures and technological advances imperils current health company operating models. Value-based healthcare is good for consumers and good for the country. As evolution teaches, the fittest health companies will embrace this reality, adapt operations and thrive in the new marketplace. In his seminal work, *On the Origin of Species*, evolutionary theorist Charles Darwin made this somewhat surprising observation about species survival:

> *It is not the strongest of the species that survives, nor the most intelligent that survives. It is the one that is the most adaptable to change.*

What is true in nature is also true in markets. Winning health companies adapt their business models to meet customer demands by delivering better care at lower prices in customer-friendly venues. They earn continued existence by following evolution's three-stage adaptive process:

- *differentiating* their services in ways that customers value;
- customers *selecting* those services by purchasing them; and
- *amplifying* their presence by increasing market share.

By nature, complex adaptive systems advance civilization. Incumbent health companies confront an unprecedented existential challenge. What would Einstein do? The only alternative is to dig deep, accept the daunting realities and fight to establish winning positions in post-reform healthcare. For those pursuing better, affordable healthcare for all Americans, Winston Churchill has the best advice, "Never, ever ever ever ever give up."

CHAPTER 11

BANNER DAYS – BRINGING IT ALL TOGETHER

We exist to make a difference in people's lives through excellent patient care.
BANNER HEALTH'S MISSION STATEMENT

On a beautiful summer day in 1998, the leadership teams for Lutheran Health Systems (LHS) and Samaritan Health System (Samaritan) met over lunch outdoors in Minneapolis to discuss a combination of LHS' and Samaritan's metro-Phoenix hospitals. I attended as LHS' investment banker and advisor. After introductions, Samaritan's CEO, Jim Crews, proposed integrating LHS' two hospitals in Mesa, the fast-growing area east of Phoenix, into Samaritan's delivery network. Samaritan's four-hospital system was Arizona's largest. Adding LHS' two Mesa hospitals would give Samaritan a 33 percent market share in metropolitan Phoenix.

Lutheran Health Systems was a largely rural health system with a strong balance sheet headquartered in Fargo, North Dakota. The system operated 28 hospitals, 30 nursing homes and other health services in 14 Midwestern and Western states. LHS' enigmatic leader, Steve Orr, was a former management consultant with a corporate orientation. He is the only individual I've known to be both chairman and CEO for a nonprofit health system. Orr treated rating-agency meetings like investor road shows and was instrumental in launching the first nonprofit healthcare investor conference.

From Samaritan's perspective, the merger was essential. To raise cash, Samaritan had just sold a major hospital in the Phoenix area, two smaller ones outside Phoenix and half of its share in a regional health plan. Samaritan had tried to merge with Tucson Medical Center and sell to Catholic Healthcare West. In each case, discussions terminated over issues related to organizational fit and control. The organization was exploring proposals from for-profit health systems Tenet Healthcare and Columbia (now HCA). Crews was determined to find a merger partner and structure that would enhance Samaritan's ability to serve metro-Phoenix's healthcare needs.

Midway through the lunch, Orr asked me to walk with him. He wanted to know if I thought a partial merger of LHS' Arizona facilities made sense. I told him that I didn't believe it did. What made sense, if anything, was a total merger of both companies. He agreed as long as he could become the combined organization's CEO. We returned to the table and redirected the negotiations. In September 1999, LHS acquired

Samaritan Health System and became Banner Health System, a company with annual revenues of $1.6 billion and over 22,000 employees.

Today, Banner Health is among the nation's leading and most innovative health companies. It operates 29 hospitals, more than 200 physician clinics and two large medical groups in seven states. With over $7 billion in annual revenues, Banner employs 48,000 people, provides 43 percent of the Phoenix-area hospital admissions and is Arizona's largest private employer. Banner has a strong iconic brand along with high customer and employee satisfaction. Banner operates as a *"clinical outcomes company,"* doing whatever it takes to consistently deliver high-quality clinical outcomes. Notable clinical achievements and activities include the following:

- Among the nation's highest ICU survival rates;

- Standard protocols applied systemwide through physician-led clinical consensus groups;

- Operating one of the nation's largest simulation and training centers; and

- Partnering with world-renowned University of Texas MD Anderson Cancer Center on cancer care.

Banner's integrated delivery system includes the Banner Health Network (BHN), which manages the health and wellness of nearly a half-million members in public and private health plans. BHN has become a national leader in provider-owned accountable care organizations. With the 2015 acquisition of the University of Arizona Health Network and 30-year affiliation with the university's College of Medicine, Banner now seeks to reinvent academic healthcare.

Banner's business model emphasizes leadership development and values new perspectives. Unlike most health companies, it often hires from outside healthcare to meet customers' needs. Banner is well-managed, consistently profitable and growth oriented. Above all,

Banner prioritizes patient care and customer satisfaction across all of its service centers.

As Banner came together in 1999, no one predicted it would become a leading health company. Combining a largely rural health system with a struggling regional system hardly seemed like a recipe for success. Banner's emergence into national prominence reflects vision, leadership, governance and execution excellence. Most importantly, Banner epitomizes organizational adaptability and the corresponding ability to shift business models in response to customer demands and market forces.

In the Beginning

Orr became Banner's first board chairman and CEO. Crews became president of Banner's Arizona operations but would soon leave the company. Samaritan's Board Chairman Wilford Cardon became the vice-chairman of Banner's board. Through Orr and Cardon's combined effort, the new Banner board had only 15 members. They included seven members from each legacy company and one independent member. Orr and Cardon insisted on a single, forward-looking governance model with no representational seats and no reserve powers. According to Cardon, "Legacy board members burned their canoes at the river, left previous loyalties behind and committed 100 percent to Banner's success."

It was a small board, particularly by nonprofit standards. Banner selected members with board experience and modestly compensated them for their time and commitment. From its beginning, Banner's board has met quarterly to address strategic, big-picture topics. Ironically for Orr, these characteristics enabled Banner to navigate its first real governance test, a dispute with him over Banner's leadership structure.

Less than a year after assuming the chairman and CEO role, Orr announced his intention to leave the CEO role in three years but remain as a compensated, non-executive board chairman. Orr's plan was to recruit and train the future CEO before relinquishing control to him or her. After conducting its due diligence, the board's search committee concluded that Orr's proposal would limit their ability to attract strong CEO candidates. Living up to its "Banner first" dictate, the board refused to accept Orr's proposal and insisted on his departure from the company.

"Orr would have brought in a lackey," said Cardon, "and that's not the kind of CEO we had in mind. We knew we would get a better candidate if the former CEO did not remain as chairman. No one would want to come in as CEO and be under the thumb of the old CEO. I knew then that our governance was in great shape." Surviving its first crisis so soon after its launch, the Banner board unified to a degree that individual members did not exhibit any legacy-oriented behaviors. There was no time to celebrate. The company was losing money, the management team was in disarray and Banner needed a new CEO.

Finding Fine

Peter Fine became Banner's president and CEO on November 13, 2000. Fine almost missed his initial interview. Of the 10 candidates, he interviewed last, so he could attend his son's Friday night football game outside Milwaukee. He took the first direct flight to Phoenix the next morning. Fellow passengers included dozens of rowdy green-and-yellow-clad Green Bay Packer fans traveling for Sunday's game with the Arizona Cardinals. Packer fans tend to be big people. Their extra weight (Go Packers!) forced the plane to land mid-journey and refuel. Fine tried but could not reach the board to inform them of his delay. Tired of waiting, several board members were preparing to leave when Fine arrived.

"We were in the room waiting for Peter," recalls Cardon. "One of our Type A personalities announced, 'Nobody stands me up. Nobody comes late for an interview to be CEO. I'm not staying. I'm going to give him 5 to 10 minutes.' That's when Peter walked in. The interview went forward. Later, all the Type A personality could say was, 'Damn... he hit a home run.' I worked with Peter as board chairman for three years. Hiring Peter was the best decision our board ever made."

Fine believes his game plan won him the job. Before his second board interview, he met with four key organizational leaders for two hours each. Those conversations gave him insight into how Banner could move forward. "They enabled me to create a game plan for the organization. I gained credibility in the second and last interviews with that game plan. Clearly, the plan and my knowledge of the company impressed the selection committee. I believe that's why they offered me the job."

The board embraced Fine's vision for Banner. Fine wanted to tackle antiquated business practices and improve clinical delivery. His strategies for Banner emerged from a deep understanding of healthcare's calcified traditions and his own frustrating patient experiences. "I had been a patient too many times. I understood great clinical care. I wanted to make it happen at Banner."

As Fine assumed control, he needed freedom to reconfigure the company without undue Board interference. "If we were going to earn the board's trust," he said, "the leadership team needed to be totally transparent." At his first board meeting as Banner's CEO, Fine suggested the board include an executive session at each meeting to discuss his performance and other topical issues among themselves.

Fine's request that the board meet in executive session without him increased his credibility and the board's trust in his leadership. Fine believed that the board's role is to provide oversight and objective counsel to management. He wanted full transparency and honest dialogue. The board agreed. For his part, Fine also holds the Banner board accountable for their performance. On one occasion when he felt the board had overstepped its bounds, Fine challenged them. Fine observes, "CEOs usually aren't that direct but directness is a strong personality trait of mine. In that session, the board agreed it had exceeded its authority and some members apologized. I was stunned." Honest debate and jostling between management and governance creates a healthy, dynamic tension between CEOs and their boards. It leads to better decision-making.

Banner's success reflects a strong, respectful relationship between management and governance. Banner's incisive leadership is a differentiating competitive advantage that propels the organization forward.

20/20 Vision

Fine got to work quickly, accomplishing a great deal of change in a short period. "You can compare what he did to other leaders of major organizations who have successfully sought to make changes within their first 100 days," said Ron Bunnell, Banner's first Chief Financial Officer and now its Chief Administrative Officer. The company was dysfunctional. A typical new CEO uses the first year to assess people, products and facilities. Their intent is to avoid disruption. "I took a different path," Fine recalls. "I told people their lives would get disrupted."

Fine and the Banner leadership team have created a culture of constant improvement. Fine believes that "everything we do can be done better, we just haven't found the way." To that end, Banner has "reinvented" itself three times: with Fine's arrival in 2000, again in 2009 and most recently in 2015. Three words guide Banner's leadership philosophy—accountability, discipline and transparency.

As Bunnell recalls, "From the first day, Peter had a sheet of paper with guiding principles, now affectionately called 'Peterisms.'" These were nine principles Fine had developed to guide the organization, its culture and its behaviors. Here they are:

1. **Misery is Optional** – We choose the attitude we bring to work. Personal and professional challenges are always going to come up.

2. **Plan the Work, Work the Plan** – Having a plan keeps you focused on the most important items that must be achieved. A plan helps you to keep the distractions at bay.

3. **3Es (Energy, Excitement and Enthusiasm)** – It's up to you to set the bar for your team. Bring the energy. Show enthusiasm. Create the excitement for your team. You have a big impact on your team's mindset and engagement.

4. **Tune Out the Static** – Don't let other people put their monkey on your back. Stay focused on your plan and find ways to filter out the noise that can distract you.

5. **Visibility Breeds Credibility. Credibility Breeds Trust:** If you are a desk jockey and enjoy spending more time in a spreadsheet then getting out and meeting people...you will not be successful as a leader as Banner. You must be out among your team members so they know you care about them. Be in their space, watch them, listen to them, ask questions. Engage them where they are. Don't hide in your office.

6. **Disruption Creates Opportunities:** Disruption can be seen as an unfortunate event or it can be seen as an opportunity to innovate and get ahead. As a leader, see this as an area of strength for you to develop.

7. **Beware of Eeyores**: Eeyore was the donkey character from Winnie the Pooh. Eeyore would always dwell in misery. Employees who go around in constant gloom-and-doom mode and exhibit negative behaviors are like a cancer on your team. If left ignored, they will slowly destroy your team around you. Deal with eeyores by coaching them back up or removing them from the organization. Don't ignore them.

8. **Have Passion for Complexity and High Tolerance for Ambiguity**: Healthcare is very complex and we are continuously evolving and improving. The future is not dictated and absolutely clear. However, we set a vision and strategy and move forward with our best information and adjust to what comes along the way. As a leader, you must embrace this and lead your teams through it. If you are uncomfortable with leading through ambiguity and complexity, you are going to have a challenging time in your role at Banner.

9. **Lead, Follow or Get Out of the Way:** If you are not leading or following, you are in the way of others who are.

Peterisms became mantras and strategies that reinforced Fine's vision and helped guide execution. "Peter's magic, his leadership," said Bunnell, "is his vision combined with his ability to demystify things and explain them in common language." Leadership is communication. In today's managerial world, leaders must persuade professionals to commit to an organizational vision. Strategy and execution align through inspiring rhetoric and purpose-driven leadership.

For Banner to become a great company, Fine believed employees at all levels needed a roadmap to understand and appreciate the company's strategic vision. Within Fine's first year, the leadership team created a five-stage vision to make Banner an industry leader by 2020. Their vision, detailed below, has stood the test of time.

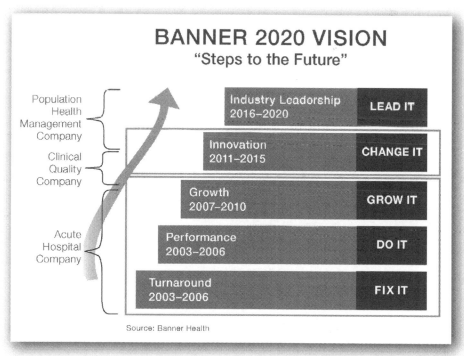

Having articulated this strategy, Fine started listening. "There was a lot of noise," he observed. "You have to pay attention to the noise that matters the most. In our case, we had to get the hog out of the ditch."

FIX IT (2000–2002)

Banner moved rapidly toward becoming an operating company and standardizing the company's business practices systemwide. Fine empowered decision-makers and reduced costs. He attacked operational performance, selling off rural assets and reinvesting in core markets. He closed the Fargo, ND, headquarters. Banner's operational performance improved as its balance sheet strengthened. Fine implemented a new organizational structure, switching key roles in the process. For example, Dr. John Hensing's responsibilities shifted from insurance contracting to integrating Banner's clinical and administrative functions systemwide.

In making that decision, Fine talked with Hensing. "I asked John what he had been doing. John explained to me how he managed insurance contracting. I told him we need to change his role!" Fine wanted Hensing to lead Banner's clinical transformation efforts. Fine observed, "It has taken more than a decade of work, but John has built high-quality clinical protocols through clinical consensus groups. He started that first day, had a free hand, my support and won people over. He positioned like-minded medical leaders in all facilities. Their sole focus is clinical quality."

Fine continued disrupting the status quo. Steve Orr had envisioned Banner's national company headquarters in Denver, CO. The plan was to build new corporate offices near Denver International Airport and close the Phoenix headquarters. Within three weeks of starting, Fine vetoed the move. He had specific concerns about the projected $6 million overhead cost and questioned the wisdom of moving corporate staff away from the company's primary market.

Sensing managerial role confusion and overlapping responsibilities, Fine also revamped Banner's leadership team. During his first six weeks, he met with the company's top 24 leaders. Fine clarified roles and reduced the senior team to 10 people. Some individuals assumed new roles within Banner and others left the company. Fine centralized decision-making and emphasized clinical quality and outcomes. Banner's Fix It triage ran two years. It streamlined operations, improved efficiency and generated sufficient cash flow to fund strategic growth. This included a thorough review of existing assets and tough decisions regarding which to keep and which to divest.

"We did a system-wide asset analysis in 2001," Fine says. "We arranged our products in a grid to evaluate performance. We identified our very important assets, and realized we needed to let go of some assets and businesses. We started by reducing our rural facility footprint. In each of our rural markets, we decided if it was better for that community if we continued running the local facility or sold it to a rural provider."

In 2001, Banner sold facilities and terminated leases in Iowa, Kansas, Minnesota, New Mexico, North Dakota and South Dakota. In communities where Banner divested, management took great care to leave the facilities with organizations that would do a quality job for the community. Banner also exited most of its long-term care entities, another business line that management ranked as nonessential.

Fine and the senior team streamlined Banner's profile to create clearer lines of responsibility with fewer direct reports. They focused on building fewer, larger regional markets. Accordingly, Banner invested heavily in northern Colorado, its second largest market. The organization also made investments throughout Arizona, in Fairbanks, Alaska and Nevada. By 2003, Banner had a cohesive leadership team, a rational facility mix and stable operations in high-potential markets. It was time for Banner to perform.

DO IT (2003–2006)

Between 2003–2006, Banner put more gas into its tank and revved its engine. Leadership upgraded the company's operating model by standardizing performance metrics and building balance-sheet strength. Leadership focused on process improvement that led to better clinical, operational and financial outcomes. Banner embraced its "inner-Deming" by continually reducing performance variance. Instead of running 20 GI labs 20 different ways, Banner established uniform protocols for running all of its GI labs.

During this period, performance and outcomes took precedent. Financial outcomes, medical outcomes, customer service outcomes and employee satisfaction and engagement outcomes continuously improved. Leadership's operating approach was hands-on and metrics-driven. Local markets retained their unique personalities while achieving process standardization, variance reduction and performance improvement. Discipline, transparency and accountability infused Banner's operating culture.

Banner renegotiated its partnership models in Greeley and in Fairbanks. Local authorities owned the facilities and contracted with Banner to operate them. Banner wanted tighter operational and strategic alignment, so that these facilities would integrate seamlessly into Banner's national care network. The new operating agreements were longer-term and blended operational performance with capital investment to achieve targeted performance objectives. This resulted in a classic win-win for the local owners and Banner. It also demonstrated Banner's ability to work effectively in partnership arrangements.

In 2001, Banner bought out physician investors in an underperforming cardiac hospital in Mesa. The group had balked at adopting Banner's cardiac treatment protocols and reigning in its over-utilizing members. They wanted out of the investment. Banner agreed even though Fine told the physicians they were making a mistake. Once Banner assumed operating control, patient volumes increased, outcomes improved, innovation continued and profits soared. In 2004, Baywood Heart Hospital almost doubled in size and became one of the nation's largest free-standing cardiac hospitals. Today, that center operates as Banner Heart Hospital.

With its operations running smoothly, it was time for Banner to grow through internal investment and external acquisition.

GROW IT (2007–2010)

By 2007, Banner was an effective operating company with a strong brand and cohesive culture. This translated into strong profitability and organizational cash flow. Leadership invested in strategic growth. "We were able to enter the multi-billion-dollar growth stage," recalled Fine. "Between 2007–2010, we built new campuses and closed a series of acquisitions, including purchasing Sun City Hospitals."

Banner facilities have a clean, distinctive look and feel. For many years, only the headquarters displayed the company name and logo. Local facilities maintained local branding. With flourish, Banner took its name systemwide. All facility names now begin with Banner and fly the Banner flag. Unifying Banner's facilities reinforced the organization-wide commitment to efficiency and quality: one standard of care at all Banner facilities.

Banner did not expand just to become bigger. Leadership believes strategic growth makes Banner better and stronger. Fine observed, "We set about getting bigger, not only to improve top line revenue at each facility but to expand the company's footprint. The greater the operating base, the more surface area there is over which to spread overhead expenditures and drive per-unit costs lower." Done right, bigger generates better outcomes, improves efficiency and saves money.

Banner's leaders took to the task of expanding the company through internal growth and acquisition while continuing their push to achieve consistently better clinical outcomes. In rapid succession, Banner built four new hospitals in metropolitan Phoenix. The first was 293-bed Banner Estrella Medical Center (Banner Estrella) in western Phoenix. BEMC incorporated state-of-the-art technology in an EMR system, including computerized physician order entry (CPOE). This technology helped improve clinical outcomes and reduce medical errors. Banner Estrella became Banner's franchise model for new hospitals with paper-light operations. The fourth new hospital, 53-bed Banner Ironwood Medical Center in Queen Creek, became the franchise model for smaller, community-centric facilities. In between were 177-bed Banner Gateway Medical Center in fast-growing Gilbert and 206-bed Cardon Children's Medical Center in Mesa.

In September 2008, Banner completed its $316 million purchase of Sun Health, a two-hospital system located amid the Del Webb retirement communities in Sun City. Banner immediately renamed the facilities, upgraded their technology platforms and eliminated 40 duplicative executive and administrative positions. Integrating the Sun Health facilities into Banner's network proceeded smoothly until a large cardiology group declared it would not follow Banner's cardiology protocols. The doctors believed their protocols were more appropriate for their patient population. They reversed position when asked if they were willing to accept the consequences (clinical, financial, reputational) if their outcomes were inferior to those generated with Banner's cardiology protocols. Discipline, transparency and accountability are powerful managerial tools.

The Sun Health acquisition included the nationally recognized Sun Health Research Institute (SHRI). Banner incorporated its own research activities under an expanded Institute with the Sun Health name. The Institute conducts path-breaking research in age-related diseases, particularly Alzheimer's and Parkinson's diseases.

By 2009, Banner Mesa (the hospital that originally brought LHS and Samaritan together) had reached the end of its useful life. Rather than demolish the building, Banner transformed Mesa into a simulation and training center. It was a bold strategic move within an industry that had yet to embrace simulation training.

Around that same time, I attended a black-tie gala dinner in Seattle benefiting Swedish Medical Center. Hospital galas follow a pattern. Midway through the festivities, there's a special donation request. This night, Swedish was raising money for a pediatric robot. The master of ceremonies highlighted how experienced care providers who *have not* worked together make more mistakes than less-experienced care providers who *have* worked together. No surprise there. Coordinated teams always are more effective than independent practitioners thrown together. The MC then sang the praises of team-based training. As with flight crews, medical simulation training for care teams reduces errors and improves outcomes. No surprise there either.

I was underwhelmed. I asked Deb Oyer, my Seattle physician friend, why robotic simulation was such a big deal. She outlined healthcare's standard training methodology: "See one. Do one. Teach one." Incredible. Medicine was only beginning to discover the benefits of coordinated simulation training. Other industries have used simulation training for decades. As a result of healthcare's antiquated training methods, people suffer. A senior physician once told me that new doctors operate on indigent patients and veterans because few complained when medical errors compromised their care. Banner clearly had a different vision.

Creating the Banner Simulation Education Center confirmed leadership's singular commitment to quality outcomes. Covering 55,000 square feet, the 55-bed virtual hospital is among the largest in the nation.[276] The center includes 55 computerized mannequins as patients, an ER, ICU units, neonatal ICU, pediatric ICU, a general pediatrics area, a medical-surgical floor, a labor and delivery suite and an OR.[277] Beyond upgrading care provider skills, simulation training saves millions each year by reducing nurse-training time. New nurses get to the bedside faster with proven experience and greater confidence.

Banner also has embraced telemedicine. It was among the first health systems to centralize ICU operations. Working with Philips, Banner established tele-ICU remote monitoring centers in Mesa, Arizona; Denver, Colorado; Santa Monica, California; and Tel Aviv, Israel. Centralized ICU monitoring enables skilled clinicians to monitor patients at multiple locations and respond immediately to patient emergencies. Banner's mortality rates dropped significantly and remain impressively low. Banner's success in tele-ICU established a foundation for a broader movement into telemedicine, which Banner employs to standardize care delivery throughout its massive seven-state (including Alaska) geographic footprint.

Facilities and programs are only as strong as the professionals that manage them. Recognizing this universal truth, Banner has invested heavily in leadership training. Most healthcare systems employ staffing rather than talent-driven hiring and professional development. In 2007, Banner hired Ed Oxford, former head of Motorola University, to advance the company's leadership training and talent-development programs. Today, hundreds of employees, including physicians, have completed extensive experiential-based leadership training. Program graduates are the vanguard of Banner's efforts to institutionalize performance improvement.

"Leadership training and leader placement are how we spread the culture of constant process improvement. Letting people know they aren't alone if they're really trying to do the right thing," observes

---

276 2009 Care Management Annual Report, Banner Health
277 *Ibid.*

Hensing, Banner's chief medical officer "Our system has a very progressive approach to talent development. This is the reason Banner can institute changes systemwide so effectively. We have buy-in from a whole stream of up-and-coming leaders who understand that being part of a system means applying best practices wherever they find them and wherever they're needed."

This kind of buy-in infuses a corporate culture that understands healthcare delivery has to improve and become more cost-effective. "Classroom training is only 10 percent of development. Coaching and experiential training are the other 90 percent," observes Bunnell. "Participants learn how to execute leadership roles within an environment that offers coaching and support." As Banner's developing leaders spread throughout the system, they become an effective guiding coalition for instituting organizational change. Bunnell cannot imagine Banner achieving its lofty performance goals without the active engagement and support of the company's emerging leaders, "They're the fuel that drives Banner's engines."

This growth and success occurred as Banner committed to becoming a clinical outcomes company. Fine summarizes this period as follows: "We grew, we advanced … That pushed us into the innovation stage."

Change It (2011–2015)
Having established systemwide clinical infrastructure, Fine took the bold step in March 2009 of publicly declaring that Banner would operate going forward as a clinical outcomes company. In Fine's words, Banner would "focus on reducing care variability and increasing care reliability to deliver consistently superior outcomes." To achieve this vision, Banner leadership restructured the organization to place care quality and management at the center of Banner's operating culture.

A strong, well-executed organizing principle galvanizes corporate cultures and differentiates successful companies. For example, Amazon's Bezos is legendary for his relentless focus on delivering value to customers. This principle drives Amazon's strategy. Amazon allows approved vendors to undercut its prices on its own website. Why?

It generates better value for customers. Amazon will undercut these partner vendors if their profit margins become too high. Why? It generates better value for customers.

Becoming a clinical outcomes company crystalized and reinforced Banner's strategy. Initiatives that improve clinical outcomes move forward irrespective of cost. It's remarkable what organizations can accomplish when metrics and mission align. Banner began measuring lives saved in its ICUs relative to APACHE (Acute Physiology and Chronic Health Evaluation) predictive algorithms in 2007. That year Banner saved 224 lives. When Banner declared itself a clinical quality company in 2009, the number had increased to 527. The big leap occurred in 2011 when the number of lives saved skyrocketed to 1,590. Today, Banner's annual number of lives saved exceed 2,000. Relative to APACHE's predictive algorithms, Banner's tele-ICU in 2013 yielded 33,000 fewer ICU days, 47,000 fewer hospital days and $89 million in cost avoidance.[278]

Banner achieves these remarkable ICU outcomes while having one of the nation's lowest ICU lengths of stay. Banner ICU patients survive more frequently, leave ICUs more quickly and cost less to treat: Win. Win. Win. Performance improvement is rarely linear. Organizational learning takes time and commitment. Banner's 2011 breakout performance was years in the making. There is no wiggle room when pursuing quality outcomes.

During the latter part of 2008, Fine underwent radiation and chemotherapy treatments for cancer diagnosed that July. It was during this time he realized that providing exceptional clinical care differentiates great healthcare companies. This set the stage for the March 2009 company announcement about clinical outcomes and the organizational restructuring. Fine explains, "Actions speak louder than words. Changing the focus has people thinking about the end game of excellent patient care. This was the lesson for me. It became clear to me that we needed to bring these words to life."[279]

---

278 HealthLeaders, *Telemedicine: Advancing from Pilot to Practice*, 2014
279 Banner Health, *Stretching Health*, 2009 Care Management Annual Report

These 2009 events hinted that Banner was moving toward the 2020 Vision's next evolutionary phase, "Change It." "Our product should be better than our competitors," Fine declared. Quality is Job 1. Outcomes matter. Patients count. Everything else is secondary. "It's easy enough to *say* quality should be Job 1, but physicians don't always go along with the program; there can be resistance," Fine noted. "You have to be willing to take on physicians' *captain-of-the-ship* mentality. Implementing one EMR platform systemwide became Banner's next big challenge.

Banner has worked continuously with Cerner to develop its EMR. The companies made a 10-year shared commitment in April 2015 to achieve full interoperability. "At Banner, we're convinced that the transformation of health care, better clinical outcomes for less cost, will largely occur through population health management plans that improve usage and services management in hospitals and clinics," said Fine in the press release announcing the Cerner agreement. "Effective and innovative electronic solutions will be at the heart of this transformation, and Cerner is an ideal partner and national leader in these efforts."[280]

Under Hensing, Banner has developed over 20 clinical consensus groups in specific disease cohorts. Each group develops and assesses outcomes-based treatment protocols for their clinical specialties. These protocols become part of Banner's systemwide EMR and standardize care delivery throughout the system.

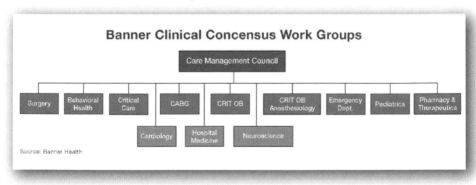

Commitment to quality outcomes led to rigorous benchmarking. Measurement improves performance. Banner measures quality,

---

280 https://www.bannerhealth.com/About+Us/News+Center/Press+Releases/
Press+Archive/2015/Banner+Health+Cerner+form+multi+year+strategic+partnership.htm

patient safety, mortality and patient satisfaction metrics with all practitioners at all facilities. The clinical consensus group protocols weren't universally accepted by all Banner physicians. Banner allowed dissenting clinicians to practice according to their own protocols provided they produced equivalent, reliable outcomes. Some did; most didn't. "It was a rude awakening," Fine admitted. "Everyone wasn't good." Employing evidenced-based protocols enables Banner to elevate B-level physicians into the A category. Discipline, transparency and accountability drive the process. Banner's culture doesn't tolerate medical prima donnas or sacred cows. Evidence drives decision-making.

Banner's singular focus on clinical excellence led to its path-breaking partnership with MD Anderson in 2011. An honest internal assessment concluded Banner's oncology services were not distinctive. Rather than rebuild this product line, the leadership team recognized the competitive advantage of aligning with a world-class oncology partner. "Our clear mission statement, 'We exist to make a difference in people's lives through excellent patient care,' led us to this decision," said Fine.

Banner is the only partnership where MD Anderson has agreed to shared naming rights. The partnership employs MD Anderson physicians, treatment protocols and support systems, including second opinions for complex cases. Although the MD Anderson partnership alienated some local oncologists, Banner's leadership believes that better treatment outcomes and customer experience will drive the venture's long-term success.

Achieving the best clinical outcomes is half of the value equation. The other half requires those outcomes to come at lowest cost. Banner is developing the care management capabilities necessary to manage population health risk. Banner was an inaugural member of the Pioneer Accountable Care Organization (ACO) program. The Centers for Medicare and Medicaid Services (CMS) program launched with much fanfare in December 2011. CMS expects Medicare beneficiaries enrolled in the program to receive higher-quality care at lower costs through enhanced care coordination.

While the Medicare Pioneer program has presented challenges for many participants (only 19 of the original 32 members remain in the program as of early 2016), Banner has prospered. It has achieved the highest cumulative shared-savings payments ($41 million) in the program's first three years. In a November 2013 interview with *Modern Healthcare*, Fine attributed Banner's Pioneer ACO success to its ability to manage the care costs of the highest users of healthcare services. Better care coordination improves quality outcomes at lower costs.

In addition to its Pioneer ACO, Banner has a small Medicaid insurance company and a Medicare Advantage plan. The organization also is preparing for bundled payments in orthopedics and cardiology by standardizing procedure delivery and enhancing care transitions. "The basic program needs to be changed so that providers like us are rewarded for reducing utilization," notes Bunnell. "When you look at things with a long-term view, you can take the position that you have to reduce costs in this country and you logically end up on the path we are following."

More broadly, Banner Health Network ("BHN") focuses on population health from a primary care perspective. The network has the following components: "3,000 Banner Health-affiliated physicians and advanced-practice providers; 15 Phoenix-area Banner Health hospitals; and numerous other medical facilities."[281] Primary care physicians coordinate and manage each member's care. Care teams also include pharmacists, nurse practitioners, nurse case managers and other health professionals collaborating to deliver the right care at the right time and place. BHN is at the center of Banner's efforts to transition to a population health management company, the final stage of the company's 2020 Vision.

Lead It! (2016–2020)

In February 2015, Banner made a big commitment to academic medicine when it acquired the University of Arizona Health Network ("UAHN") headquartered in Tucson. The deal included the University of Arizona Medical Center's two campuses; UAHN's faculty practice, University Physicians Healthcare; and UAHN's three health plans.[282] The University of Arizona and its medical school became Banner's exclusive academic partner through a remarkable 30-year affiliation agreement.[283]

---

281 https://www.bannerhealthnetwork.com
282 http://www.modernhealthcare.com/article/20141119/NEWS/311199966
283 *Ibid.*

UAHN had not been profitable in the years before the merger. Losses in its acute care and health insurance businesses overwhelmed revenue gains.[284] Per their agreement, Banner has pledged $500 million for UAHN's capital projects through 2020. It also has pledged $300 million for clinical research and agreed to pay off $146 million in UAHN debt.[285]

Fine delivered "tough love" to UAHN's academic physicians, "For you to succeed, we have to succeed." Banner must have a sustainable economic model to support UAHN's academic mission. Entrenched, unproductive business practices must disappear. No sacred cows. No prima donnas. Fine reiterated that Banner runs on three words, "Accountability, Discipline and Transparency"— words that hadn't existed in UAHN's lexicon. Banner plans to integrate UAHN physicians into Banner's care network, encourage their participation in Banner's clinical consensus work groups and hold them accountable for their performance. The acquisition gives Banner a major market presence in Tucson, but it comes with significant integration challenges as Banner simultaneously pushes to become a population-health management company.

Big challenges. Big opportunities. Time to think differently. As in 2001 and 2009, Fine and Banner's leadership team decided to reinvent the company. Going forward, Banner will strive to become a "Trusted Advisor and Health Steward" to its customers in healthcare's increasingly consumer-oriented marketplace. The leadership team envisions that Banner will operate "clinically integrated networks caring for whole communities that thrive under capitated payment models." To achieve this vision, Banner's leadership team developed the following six interrelated themes with strategies designed to "Enable (2015–2017), Scale (2016–2020) and Lead (2020+):

1. **Perfect the Consumer Experience:** Grow top-line revenues and engage customers/patients;

---

284 http://www.modernhealthcare.com/article/20150226/NEWS/150229916
285 *Ibid.*

2. **Deliver Seamless Access to Coordinated Care:** Create customer loyalty by providing care services when and where customers need and want them;

3. **Enable an Efficient Operating Unit:** Reduce per-unit costs while improving quality outcomes;

4. **Improve Care and Health:** Deliver better care outcomes through appropriate utilization, preventive care and health promotion;

5. **Acquire Members:** Increase market share by attracting members to the Banner Health Network without sacrificing financial sustainability; and

6. **Achieve Employee and Organizational Agility:** Develop and apply talent to optimize performance within nimble, accountable organizational structures.

To operationalize the new strategic vision and its integrated themes, the leadership team organized Banner into three divisions that mirror functions found in large manufacturers: Growth; Design; and Delivery. Corporate support functions reinforce and enhance each division's performance.

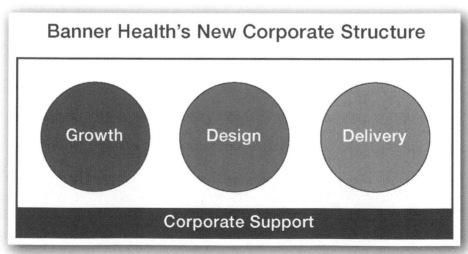

Growth encompasses all activities related to increasing revenues, including marketing, insurance products, increasing covered lives, partnerships and new ventures. The Design Division will develop Banner's health products and services, so the company has the resources and capabilities to deliver the right care, in the right place, at the right time and right price. Their activities encompass care protocols, patient engagement, telemedicine, virtual care and care transitions. Delivery executes. It provides efficient integrated care tailored to Banner's academic and community enterprises. Corporate support leads organizational strategy, executes mergers and acquisitions and delivers all support services as needed to each division.

Borrowing terminology from manufacturing enables Banner to break free from healthcare's current transaction-based paradigm. The leadership team believes Banner's future requires the company to embrace consumerism, deliver value and engineer continuous performance improvement. Like a phoenix rising from the ashes, Banner rises from the desert and across the West with value-driven services that deliver better, more convenient and affordable healthcare.

Banner's "Fine"est Hour

Banner is still a teenager. It has grown to become a prominent and highly respected health system. Banner's story of performance, growth and innovation roots itself in great governance and leadership. Superior execution occurs as a by-product of a high-functioning board-management relationship that creates the dynamic tension necessary to drive the company forward.

Banner's story also demonstrates the power of bottom-up, market-focused evolutionary growth. The desire to play offense and seize opportunities underlies the restlessness Banner exudes as its footprint, capabilities and ambitions expand. In this sense, Banner reflects the personality and proclivities of its long-time CEO Peter Fine. Misery is optional. Banner chooses optimism infused with discipline, transparency and accountability. Banner plans the work and works the plan with enthusiasm, energy and excitement. The healthcare marketplace has come Banner's way. This is its time.

SECTION IV: Advance

OUR GREATEST CHALLENGE

If you want to do something new, stop doing something old.
PETER DRUCKER

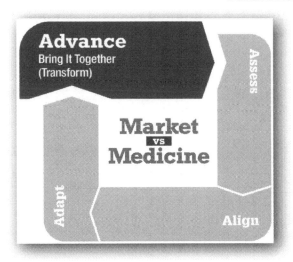

- Chapter 12: Nature's Cruel Trick

- Chapter 13: Embracing Pluralistic Healing

- Chapter 14: Nudging Toward Wellness

E very other February, Intermountain Healthcare sponsors its Mind Share conference in Park City, Utah. Healthcare leaders assemble to compare notes on industry transformation. Some also ski. At the 2014 Mind Share, Intermountain CEO Charles Sorenson told the story of an obese Intermountain patient who complained about problems with his medications. The patient wrote his nine medications on the back of a Burger King receipt to make sure he got them right. Charles projected the receipt on to a large presentation screen and observed, "The patient's problem wasn't the medications on the back of the receipt, it was the food on the front of the receipt: five Whoppers; three large french fries and a large Mountain Dew." The patient's medications treated the symptoms, not the root causes, of his chronic disease.

I left for the Salt Lake City Airport with Sorenson's story still fresh in my mind. Going through airport security, I watched the young woman in front of me clear the screening process. Not even 30 years old, she weighed at least 300 hundred pounds and wheeled an oxygen canister to assist her breathing. It took awhile for her to unhook the canister and maneuver through the metal detector. Two thoughts entered my mind. The first was empathy. I imagined how compromised her life must be by her medical condition. The second thought was more global. This type of person didn't really exist in America 30 years ago. I wondered what had happened in history, economics and culture to cultivate America's obesity epidemic and the massive chronic disease it triggers. That question became the impetus for this book's fourth and final section, *Advance*.

The first three sections of *Market vs. Medicine* identify structural flaws in American healthcare and predict how sustained and disruptive innovation will transform healthcare payment and delivery. Yet, healthcare delivery accounts for only about 10 percent of health status. Lifestyle choices, genetics, social determinants of health and environmental triggers account for the other 90 percent. Fixing healthcare delivery alone will not reverse the chronic disease epidemic that is crippling the country. America must reverse the root causes of chronic diseases to prosper as a nation and a people.

Advance tackles this larger challenge of improving societal health and wellness by enabling individuals to make better, more consistent lifestyle choices while living within healthier communities.

- Chapter 12, *Nature's Cruel Trick,* explores why the human body and brain are ill-suited for modern living. It considers how poor social and economic circumstances (poverty, loneliness, limited autonomy, abusive relationships, isolation) combined with massive consumption of processed foods trigger stress-related illnesses, particularly chronic diseases.

- Chapter 13, *Embracing Pluralistic Medicine,* postulates that more holistic integration of Eastern and Western medicines could improve health outcomes. The discussion expands beyond the Newtonian view of the body as a machine by considering how the application of quantum mechanics within biological science could advance medical understanding, diagnosis and treatment.

- Chapter 14, *Nudging Toward Wellness,* examines how increasing public awareness of health, wellness and lifestyle issues is changing consumption patterns in positive ways. It considers how the application of behavioral psychology can improve lifestyle decision-making and individual wellness and evaluates how understanding the body's relaxation mechanisms can reduce stress, trigger self-repair and promote disease prevention.

Throughout, *Advance* examines the potential for improving societal health and wellness by doing the following:

- Identifying the broad evolutionary and industrial forces driving negative wellness trends;

- Exploring the brain's capabilities, limitations and biases to adapt heathier behaviors within the construct of modern life;

- Considering how more expansive, pluralistic approaches to medical treatment could contribute to both improved individual healing and better societal health;

- Examining how social and economic conditions can influence health status in positive and negative ways;

- Evaluating the potential for genetic and epigenetic interventions to cure chronic disease; and

- Detailing how behavioral economics can play a constructive role in nudging individuals toward healthier choices.

America must both transform its healthcare system and develop a transformative culture of health and wellness to counter modern life's negative influences. It's this generation's greatest challenge. As Cleveland Clinic CEO Toby Cosgrove observes, "The state of our nation depends on the state of our health."[286]

---

286 http://health.clevelandclinic.org/2013/04/how-a-healthier-lifestyle-will-reduce-the-deficit/

CHAPTER 12

NATURE'S CRUEL TRICK

*Perhaps our greatest distinction as a species
is our capacity, unique among animals, to
make counter-evolutionary choices.*
JARED DIAMOND

*We are living in a world today where lemonade
is made from artificial flavors and furniture
polish is made from real lemons.*
ALFRED E. NEUMAN

*When you go to the grocery store, you find that the cheapest
calories are the ones that are going to make you the
fattest—the added sugars and fats in processed foods.*
MICHAEL POLLAN

D uring the financial crisis, I took some kids to see *WALL-E*, an animated Disney film. Set 700 years in the future, the movie chronicles a love story between two robots. WALL-E is the last robot left cleaning a despoiled and abandoned Earth. WALL-E's name is short for "Waste Allocation Load Lifter—Earth class." One day, WALL-E spies an Earth probe named Eve, becomes smitten and follows her back to a massive spaceship housing what's left of the human race.

In the movie, our future selves spend their days plugged into entertainment systems travelling through expansive shopping malls on automated scooters. These humans are overfed, self-absorbed, immobile and consumed by trivial concerns. They cannot walk under their own power and rely on machines to provide material comfort and support.

Inside the sold-out movie theater, the irony was inescapable. The audience sat in oversized seats with large cup holders absorbed in a digital world while gulping sodas and gorging on giant buckets of popcorn. I couldn't believe this was a children's movie! Disney's dystopian vision for our collective future was disconcerting, directionally correct and apocalyptic.

Nature's Cruel Trick

The American lifestyle causes unprecedented and increasing levels of disease, disability and medical expenditures. Significant biological, and environmental factors contribute, fostering deeply-engrained and unhealthy behaviors that are difficult to reverse. To survive in the Serengeti, humans learned to walk long distances, think on our feet, live in cooperative communities, respond quickly to threats and eat mostly plants. Evolution enabled humans to live off the land and avoid saber-toothed tigers, but it did not equip us for office work, abundant food and prolonged stress. Our modern lifestyle causes heart disease, cancer, osteoporosis, depression and dementia. It contains too much of the following disease-causing factors:

- **Inactivity:** too much sedentary work and entertainment;

- **Chronic Stress:** Fight-or-flight mechanisms trigger prolonged adrenalin and cortisol release that damage the immune system;

- **Overeating:** More people die from eating too much food than too little;

- **Bad Food:** Unhealthy processed foods short-circuit the body's systems for regulating nutrient consumption and overload the body with excess sugar, fat and salt triggering chronic disease; and

- **Sleep Deprivation:** Too little sleep impairs decision-making and weakens the immune system.

Lifestyle and environment weave together and influence human behavior. Throughout daily living, the mind receives environmental signals and prepares the body for action. The mind does this through targeted release of biochemical hormones. Unfortunately, modern life often overwhelms the natural defenses our body employs to navigate a dangerous world. The following environmental factors stimulate the unhealthy behaviors listed above:

- **Stimulus Overload:** People are constantly bombarded with sophisticated emotional messaging;

- **Isolation:** Wired to live in close-knit, social communities, isolated individuals experience more depression and disease;

- **Inequality:** Low-income individuals are disproportionately obese and suffer from chronic disease, stress-related illness and depression. Complex environmental factors relating to food access, economic insecurity and dysfunctional communities drive this pathology; and

- **Expectations:** People believe that pharmacological and medical breakthroughs will compensate for unhealthy lifestyle choices.

According to molecular biologist Dr. John Medina in *Brain Rules: 12 Principles for Surviving and Thriving at Work, Home, and School,* modern life inhibits our natural abilities. We live in high-stress environments even though stressed brains are less effective.[287] We live sedentary life-styles even though exercise improves cognition. We multi-task even though our brains do not have sufficient bandwidth to focus on multiple tasks simultaneously.[288]

The conclusion is inescapable: Human beings are not built for modern society. Nature has played a cruel trick on us. The defense systems that the body has evolved to survive in nature are counterproductive in modern living and working environments. Instincts make it harder, not easier, for people to make healthy choices. To appreciate why, it is essential to understand how the human brain has evolved.

Three Brains in One

The human brain is large, takes years to develop and consumes 20 percent of the body's energy. It manages human relationships, facilitates collaboration and understands others' perspectives. Dr. Paul MacLean, the influential Yale neuroscientist, theorized that the human brain evolved in stages as three separate brains to solve problems in outdoor environments. He named this the "triune" brain, literally three brains in one.

The brain stem, or reptilian brain, controls vital functions, such as breathing. The paleo-mammalian brain, or limbic system, creates emotions, fears and pleasures as it interprets sensory information. The neocortex, or human brain, controls speech, vision and memory as well as uniquely human cognitive functions, including problem-solving, emotional control and intellectual focus.

The brain's architecture has evolved over millennia and contains multiple shortcuts and inbred bias. These memory and bias quirks influence decision-making. People believe they act rationally; however, the vast majority of human behavior is instinctive and habitual. Malcolm Gladwell, best-selling author of *The Tipping Point*, equates the brain's rational and instinctive influences on behavior to a boy riding

---

287 http://www.brainrules.net/about-brain-rules
288 *Ibid.*

an elephant. The boy thinks he's in control, but it's the elephant setting the course. Unfortunately, that instinctive elephant is ill-equipped to manage the stresses of modern living. Expansive chronic disease is the consequence.

Stress, Relaxation and Disease

Mind-body interactions influence individual susceptibility and responsiveness to disease. The body's limbic system monitors sensory information and triggers chemical responses to external stimuli. When sensing stress, the limbic system triggers fight-or-flight mechanisms that prepare the body for immediate physical action. Blood flows from the brain to our muscles. Glands flood our system with stress hormones, most notably adrenaline and cortisol. When relaxed, the limbic system floods our bodies with natural endorphins, dopamine, serotonin and oxytocin (EDSO) that lower stress, reduce pain and promote healing. Restful sleep, meditation, deep breathing, a nurturing environment and exercise can trigger release of healing hormones.

The limbic system's sensors are crude. They respond to stress but cannot evaluate its sources. A sabre-tooth tiger, financial worry or a tyrannical boss all trigger the same chemical release. Modern life creates prolonged stresses that flood the body with excessive stress hormones and damage immune systems. Prolonged stress also stifles the release of relaxation hormones. Afraid, angry and depressed people get sick more often and die younger.

It starts in childhood, as Ashley Winning from the Harvard T.H. Chan School of Public Health discovered when researching connections between childhood stress and disease.[289] Winning examined data from the 1958 British Birth Cohort Study that followed the diet, habits and emotional health of 6,714 children born the same week in 1958.[290] She found that "even the adults who had lower distress levels were at

---

289 http://www.npr.org/sections/health-shots/2015/09/29/444451363/childhood-stress-may-prime-pump-for-chronic-disease-later
290 *Ibid.*

higher risk of chronic illness if they had experienced higher levels of distress during childhood."[291]

Stress contributes to heart disease, asthma, obesity, diabetes, head-aches, gastrointestinal issues, depression and anxiety, Alzheimer's, accelerated aging and even premature death.[292] Prolonged stress (such as that caused by loneliness) is particularly damaging. "Loneliness and social isolation are as much a threat to our health as obesity."[293] The impact of loneliness on hormone levels, impulsive behavior and sleep, for example, can impair cognitive function, compromise the immune system and lead to chronic disease.[294]/[295]

Dr. Herbert Benson's research, by contrast, suggests a relaxed brain enables the body to heal itself.[296] Benson is the director emeritus of the Benson-Henry Institute (BHI), and mind-body medicine professor of medicine at Harvard Medical School. He's a pioneer in mind-body medicine and how the body's mechanisms counter-act the harmful effects of stress.[297] In researching religious and secular literature, Benson discovered multi-cultural strategies for calming the mind. Benson then designed clinical studies to validate his theory that almost every culture developed techniques for "breaking the train of everyday thinking."[298] He named this mind-body effect the "relaxation response." His studies have demonstrated that the relaxation response is an "effective therapy for stress-related disorders: anxiety, mild and moderate depression, undue anger and hostility, insomnia, high blood pressure, premenstrual tension, menstrual cramps, rheumatoid arthritis and IBS."[299]/[300]

---

291 Ibid.
292 http://www.webmd.com/balance/stress-management/features/10-fixable-stress-related-health-problems
293 http://www.everydayhealth.com/news/loneliness-can-really-hurt-you/
294 Ibid.
295 https://www.psychologytoday.com/articles/200308/the-dangers-loneliness
296 https://www.bensonhenryinstitute.org/about/dr-herbert-benson
297 Ibid.
298 http://brainworldmagazine.com/dr-herbert-benson-on-the-mindbody-connection/
299 Ibid.
300 http://brainworldmagazine.com/dr-herbert-benson-on-the-mindbody-connection/#sthash.yTu84nrG.dpuf

Most human behavior is habitual. We respond without thinking to environmental cues carved into our neural circuitry. This works well except when our habits (e.g. afternoon cookies) reinforce unhealthy behaviors. Overcoming bad habits requires developing new neural pathways that ignore salient environmental cues and redirect behavior. This is difficult because the old neural pathways don't disappear. Ask anyone who has tried to quit smoking. It requires willpower to follow desired behaviors long enough (at least six weeks) to build neural circuity strong enough to overpower existing pathways.

Not surprisingly, it's easier to develop new habits when relaxed than stressed. Stress zaps willpower and reduces people's ability to break bad habits and adhere to new positive behaviors. In their 2011 book, *Willpower: Rediscovering the Greatest Human Strength,* social psychologist Roy F. Baumeister and *New York Times* science writer John Tierney conclude that willpower is a limited resource, and its effectiveness fluctuates with sugar glucose levels.[301] When glucose levels are low, human behavior is more impulsive. This is why people often crave sweet, salty and fat-laden foods when stressed.

Sendhil Mullainathan, a behavioral economist at Harvard, and Eldar Shafir, a psychologist at Princeton, go even further.[302] Their research shows that stressed individuals have limited bandwidth and engage in tunnel thinking.[303] Individuals with bandwidth scarcity cannot see the bigger picture or engage in longer-term planning. Available energy focuses on solving an immediate crisis, such as meeting a deadline or making a rent payment. Under stress, IQ declines and bad decision-making ensues. This explains why low-income people suffer disproportionate stress levels and experience disproportionate levels of chronic disease.[304]

The health consequences of these insights into human behavior and mind-body connectivity are profound. The stresses of modern life compromise the body's ability to relax and promote self-healing.

---

301 http://www.nytimes.com/2011/11/27/opinion/sunday/willpower-its-in-your-head.html?_r=0

302 http://opinionator.blogs.nytimes.com/2013/09/25/escaping-the-cycle-of-scarcity/

303 *Ibid.*

304 http://harvardmagazine.com/2015/05/the-science-of-scarcity

Instead, prolonged stress diminishes people's capacities to develop healthier habits by depleting willpower, stimulating tunnel thinking and triggering impulsive behaviors. Modern life itself has become a breeding ground for chronic disease. Quirky brain function and mind-body mechanisms designed for wilderness survival capitulate before prolonged stresses (e.g. loneliness) and counter-productive environmental stimuli (e.g. mass marketing of fast foods). The pace of negative lifestyle change is accelerating and spreading worldwide. Reversing these negative lifestyle trends is this generation's greatest challenge.

How Bad is It?

Eighty-six percent of U.S. healthcare spending gets directed toward treatment for chronic disease such as diabetes, heart disease, chronic obstructive pulmonary disease (COPD), high blood pressure (hypertension), cancer, acid reflux and asthma.[305] At least half of America's 117 million adults have one chronic disease; one in four adults have at least two chronic diseases. Cancer and heart disease account for 48 percent of all deaths.

Chronic diseases account for seven of the top ten causes of death. Much chronic disease is caused by high-risk behaviors (poor nutrition, tobacco use, lack of exercise and excessive alcohol consumption). It's preventable and treatable. Diabetes statistics alone are staggering. Almost 30 million Americans (one of every eleven people) have diabetes; however, one out of four of them don't know they have the disease. 86 million adults (one in three) are pre-diabetic; 90 percent are unaware they're pre-diabetic and up to 30 percent of them will develop diabetes within five years.

Type 2 Diabetes used to be called adult-onset diabetes. There was no Type 2 diabetes in children in 1980. Today, more than 5,000 children are diagnosed each year with this disease. Many thin people are at risk for diabetes without knowing it. This condition is known as TOFI or "thin on the outside, fat on the inside."

305　CDC Factsheet

The cost to society from diabetes is astronomical and growing: around $245 billion in annual medical costs and lost work wages. Average medical costs are twice as high for diabetics than for non-diabetics.

What Went Wrong?

Consumption of processed and fast foods increased dramatically beginning in the 1980s. Ironically, this shift coincided with the beginnings of the low-fat movement. Portion sizes ballooned. Activity levels plummeted. The American waistline expanded. In 1990, no state had more than 15 percent of its adult population categorized as obese. Today, no state has less than 20 percent of its adult population categorized as obese, and the national average is approaching 35 percent.[306] As food-consumption patterns shifted, industrialized agriculture emerged to meet market demands for tasty processed food at very low prices. This one-two punch introduced unhealthy amounts of sugar, fat, salt, antibiotics and pesticides into the American diet and spawned epidemic levels of chronic disease.

During the 1990s, scientists at major food companies became concerned about the link between increased processed-food consumption and higher obesity levels. The food industry attempted and failed to self regulate. Michael Moss, a Pulitzer-prize winning investigative reporter, chronicled the infamous effort in his 2013 book *Salt Sugar Fat: How the Food Giants*

Hooked on Processed Foods

Early in April 1999, the presidents and CEOs of the nation's leading food companies met at Pillsbury's Minneapolis headquarters to discuss America's growing obesity epidemic.[307] Top executives from Nestlé, Kraft, Nabisco, General Mills, Procter & Gamble, Coca-Cola and Mars attended, reviewed the evidence and heard the scientists' plea for self-

---

306 http://stateofobesity.org/adult-obesity/

307 http://www.nytimes.com/2013/02/24/magazine/the-extraordinary-science-of-junk-food.html

regulation. General Mills refused to play ball. CEO Stephen Sanger reportedly dismissed all health concerns by saying, "Don't talk to me about nutrition. Talk to me about taste..."[308] His stance ultimately torpedoed industry attempts to reign in its unhealthy production practices. This behavior mirrors that of 1960s-era tobacco company executives: They ignored health concerns, fought regulation and vigorously peddled cancer sticks to an unsuspecting public. A decade later, General Mills, together with Disney, Nestle, and Kellogg, killed federal efforts to draft voluntary nutrition guidelines.[309]

Processed foods taste like cardboard. Moss details how scientists isolate each processed food's "bliss point"— the right mix of sugar, fat and salt that optimizes palatability. Given their limited availability in nature, the body craves sugar, fat and salt. The brain rewards their consumption by releasing neurotransmitting chemicals like dopamine. A dopamine buzz makes us want more and overcomes the body's defenses against overeating. When commercials for Lay's Potato Chips say, "You can't eat just one," they are literally telling the truth. Sophisticated laboratories engineer the synergistic combinations of sugar, fat and salt required to achieve each processed food's bliss point. Doritos, for example, relies on a complicated balance of flavors that trigger us to keep eating but lacks any one overriding flavor that would signal the brain to stop. This contradiction is known as sensory-specific satiety.[310]

Industrialization of the food supply supported the massive consumption of fast and processed foods. Factory farms replaced small- and medium-sized animal farms as principal suppliers for the food industry. Agribusiness has exercised growing influence over what we eat and how much we pay for it.[311] The advocacy group, Food & Water Watch, attributes the proliferation of factory farms to several factors: unchecked food-company mergers, corporate acquisitions, and lax environmental rules and enforcement.[312] The waste generated by fac-

308 *Ibid.*
309 http://thinkprogress.org/health/2013/02/28/1642911/big-food-lets-move/
310 *Ibid.*
311 http://www.factoryfarmmap.org/wp-content/uploads/2010/11/FactoryFarmNation-web.pdf
312 https://www.foodandwaterwatch.org/news/factory-farms-continue-dominate-us-

tory farming introduces a nasty brew of environmental and health problems.[313] In an interview discussing his book *Pig Tales*, author Barry Eatabrook describes how waste runoff from pig farms endangers safe drinking water in Des Moines, IA.[314] Centralized food production endangers both our health and our environment.

Factory farms instituted corn feeding to make animals grow faster, larger and more uniform before slaughter. In closely controlled living conditions, disease and bacteria spread among animals in viral fashion.[315] Industrialization also increases the risk for foodborne bacteria, such as e coli and salmonella. As a consequence, factory farms use high levels of antibiotics to control disease. In the United States, more than 70 percent of all antibiotics go to animals.[316] The FDA has approved 685 different drugs for use in animal feed.[317] Agribusiness mixes the drugs into feed and water to prevent illness and promote growth. Antibiotic-fed animals need to eat less feed to reach a given weight.[318] While beneficial to animal production, widespread antibiotic use in animals has spurred the rise of drug-resistant bacteria that promote disease. As early as 1977, the FDA warned about the nontherapeutic use of antibiotics in animals leading to drug-resistant superbugs in livestock and humans.[319] The CDC reports that over 2 million Americans each year become infected with drug-resistant bacteria and at least 23,000 die from these infections.[320] This is a major public health concern.

---

livestock-industry

313 http://www.factoryfarmmap.org/wp-content/uploads/2010/11/FactoryFarmNation-web.pdf

314 http://www.npr.org/books/titles/403318353/pig-tales-an-omnivores-quest-for-sustainable-meat

315 http://www.pbs.org/wgbh/pages/frontline/shows/meat/industrial/consolidation.html

316 http://www.nytimes.com/2015/10/20/business/energy-environment/taking-on-the-superbugs-antibiotics.html

317 http://www.washingtonpost.com/news/wonkblog/wp/2013/12/14/the-fda-is-cracking-down-on-antibiotics-at-farms-heres-what-you-should-know/

318 *Ibid.*

319 *Ibid.*

320 http://www.cdc.gov/drugresistance/

The Mass-Produced American Diet

Mass-produced food enables McDonald's to charge low prices for burgers, fries and other gourmet fare. McDonald's latest marketing campaign is "The McPick 2 Menu." It welcomes customers "to a mouth-watering mix-and-match menu" that lets them pick two of the following items for $2: a McDouble cheeseburger; a McChicken sandwich; world-famous fries and mozzarella sticks. At least the chicken sandwich has some lettuce. Dine-in establishments are equally adept at getting us to eat and spend more. Like their fast food cousins, sit-down retailers have the highest margin in the least-healthy foods and drinks. Americans eat ever-unhealthier foods while spending less money.

Menus often show small, medium and large portions at different price points. Customers perceive a deal if they order the cheapest portion. In reality, that's where the restaurant maximizes its profit. The strategy is called bracketing. Customers don't realize the restaurant always intended to sell the smaller portion at the advertised price; they just used the larger, higher-priced portion as a decoy.[321]

As schools stopped preparing meals to cut costs, fast food companies moved into this booming market. In 2011, school food service was a $9.5 billion industry. To further augment revenues, schools sell pouring rights to big beverage companies. In 2005, nearly half of all public elementary schools and approximately 80 percent of public high schools had a direct, exclusive-rights contracts with either Coke or Pepsi.[322] That number dropped between 2007 and 2012 but remains above 70 percent.[323]

The Healthy, Hunger-Free Kids Act of 2012 established new nutrition guidelines for the National School Lunch Program. Choices must now be low-fat, low-sodium and low-calorie. Schools have to serve lean proteins, fruits and vegetables and whole grains instead of french fries, PB&J and all the greasy, fried lunchtime favorites. Unfortunately, school nutrition directors report more tossed-out food than ever

---

321 http://www.businessinsider.com/restaurant-menus-spend-more-money-2014-7

322 www.motherjones.com/tom-philpott/2012/08/schools-limit-campus-junk-food-have-lower-obesity-rates

323 http://www.medicalnewstoday.com/articles/271150.php

before.[324] A 2014 report announced that 1 million kids had stopped buying school lunches after the new guidelines took effect.[325]

Notorious King Sugar

Sugar is in 80 percent of the food we eat. The average American consumes 40 teaspoons per day, which is four to six times recommended levels. The American Heart Association recommends women limit their added sugar to approximately 6 teaspoons per day. They suggest men consume no more than 9 teaspoons per day of added sugar.[326] Increased sugar consumption is the single-biggest factor driving skyrocketing obesity levels and the related explosion in chronic disease.

Over the past 30 years, per capita American sugar consumption has increased dramatically.[327] The uptake corresponds with the rise of high fructose corn syrup (HFCS). Food scientists created HFCS in 1957 by using enzymes to convert glucose in corn syrup to fructose. HFCS is as sweet as table sugar (sucrose) but costs less, aided by large government subsidies for corn production. Use of HFCS accelerated after the FDA found the artificial sweetener "generally recognized as safe" in 1976.[328] Coke began using HFCS to sweeten its soft drinks in 1980 and most beverage manufacturers followed suit quickly thereafter.[329] Digestively, HFCS behaves like any other sugar: It turns into fat as it moves from the liver to the pancreas. Like all sugars, HFCS lights up the same part of the brain as cocaine.[330]

---

324 http://www.nytimes.com/2015/09/27/sunday-review/why-students-hate-school-lunches.html?action=click&contentCollection=N.Y.%20%2F%20Region&module=MostPopularFB&version=Full&region=Marginalia&src=me&pgtype=article&_r=0

325 http://www.washingtontimes.com/news/2014/mar/6/1m-kids-stop-school-lunch-due-michelle-obamas-stan/?page=all

326 http://www.heart.org/HEARTORG/GettingHealthy/NutritionCenter/HealthyDiet-Goals/Sugar-101_UCM_306024_Article.jsp#.VkkUjsomqmA

327 Ibid.

328 https://en.wikipedia.org/wiki/High_fructose_corn_syrup

329 http://earthsky.org/human-world/a-brief-history-of-high-fructose-corn-syrup

330 http://www.forbes.com/sites/jacobsullum/2013/10/16/research-shows-cocaine-and-heroin-are-less-addictive-than-oreos/

Although HFCS has become notorious in many policy circles (Mayor Bloomberg's 2012 attempt to limit soda consumption in New York City targeted HCFS[331]), it is no more or less dangerous than other forms of sugar. Sugar itself is the villain. All sugars (refined, brown, fruit concentrate and HFCS) contribute to sugar over-consumption and its negative health effects. Neuroscientist Joseph Schroeder demonstrated that high-fat and high-sugar foods stimulate the brain in the same way that drugs do.[332] Sugar affects behavior, including impulse control and energy levels.

High-sugar foods are addictive. The more we eat, the more we want. The feedback loop is vicious. In the 2015 documentary *That Sugar Film*, Australian actor Damon Gameau consumed 40 teaspoons of sugar per day (the average Australian consumption level) from so-called healthy processed foods (yogurt, fruit drinks, granola bars—no ice cream) for 60 days. Gameau kept his calorie intake and exercise regimen constant. The result? He gained 15 pounds, added four inches to his waist, became moody, felt rotten, lost his ability to concentrate and developed signs of pre-diabetes, heart problems and non-alcoholic fatty liver disease. Once Gameau stopped the experiment, it took 60 days of eating whole foods and drinking water to reverse the damage.[333]

Rugged Americans?

The average American is inactive more than eight waking hours per day. No age group older than 30, on average, undertakes more than 30 minutes of moderate or vigorous activity per day."[334] According to a 2012 circular from the American Heart Association, 65 percent of American adults routinely "sit instead of stand, drive instead of walk, and ride the elevator instead of walking up stairs."[335]

---

331 http://earthsky.org/human-world/a-brief-history-of-high-fructose-corn-syrup
332 *Ibid.*
333 http://www.ctvnews.ca/health/the-drastic-results-of-eating-healthy-foods-with-added-sugar-1.2457334
334 http://www.theverge.com/2015/1/22/7870707/bmj-sedentary-job-health-riskst
335 http://circ.ahajournals.org/content/126/1/e3.full

The rate of heart attacks and atherosclerosis is increasing in adults as young as 35 to 45 years of age.[336] Why? Born in the 1970s and 80s, this generation grew up on processed food, video games and the Internet. Stresses of daily living contribute to sleep deprivation, slowing metabolisms and weight gain. Welcome to WALL-E world.

In 2011, Canadian physician Kevin Patterson served at the Canadian Combat Surgical Hospital in Kandahar, Afghanistan. He noticed a radical difference between Western and non-Western body types. Western soldiers had organs wrapped in fat. "Typical Afghan civilians and soldiers were 140 pounds or so as adults. When we operated on them, what we were aware of was the absence of any fat or any adipose tissue underneath the skin," Patterson recorded. "Of course, when we operated on Canadians or Americans or Europeans, what was normal was to have most of the organs encased in fat. It had a visceral potency to it when you could see it directly there."[337]

Patterson cites the rise in obesity as a trigger. "Type 2 diabetes historically didn't exist, only 70 or 80 years ago," says Patterson. "And what's driven it, of course, is this rise in obesity, especially the accumulation of abdominal fat. That fat induces changes in our receptors that cells have for insulin. Basically, it makes them numb to the effect of insulin."[338]

The American Heart Association sums up the threat: "We can now conclude that today our toxic lifestyle is trumping our advances in medical science. That is why, in this era of debates over optimal systems for delivering health care, if we do not develop effective strategies that promote healthy lifestyles, then whatever health care system we do adopt will be overwhelmed by chronic disease and will ultimately fail. It will also contribute to bankrupting our country because of the excessive cost in trying to treat diseases too late in their natural histories."[339]

Socio-economic realities foster unhealthy lifestyles and rising obesity. Lower income neighborhoods traditionally offer fewer healthy

336 Ibid.
337 http://www.npr.org/2011/03/24/132745785/how-western-diets-are-making-the-world-sick
338 *Ibid.*
339 http://circ.ahajournals.org/content/126/1/e3.full

food choices. Financial circumstances often limit nutritional choices. These factors have lasting dietary impacts. Research indicates that the earlier children are exposed to junk food, the more likely they are to suffer dangerous, life-long health problems.[340] The "bowling-alone" phenomenon exacerbates these trends. Societal disconnection incubates disease. Socially isolated individuals are prone to depression and less likely to exercise and eat well.

The Calories-In, Calories-Out Myth

There's a myth that all calories are created equal. "Calories in are not the same as calories out," according to Dr. David Ludwig, director of the obesity program at Boston Children's Hospital. Sugar calories are less filling and disproportionately cause weight gain and increase body fat. Notes Ludwig, "Highly processed foods undermine our metabolism and overwhelm our behavior."[341] Dr. Dariush Mozaffarian of Harvard Medical School studies how different foods affect weight gain. Echoing Ludwig, Mozaffarian notes, "Fat, protein and carbohydrates influence satiety, metabolic rate, brain activity, blood sugar and the hormones that store fat in very different ways."[342]

Drs. Ludwig and Mozaffarian are among several obesity experts and nutrition scientists featured or quoted in "Fed Up," the controversial 2014 documentary produced by Katie Couric and Laurie David, producer of "An Inconvenient Truth." The film explores why childhood obesity is so prevalent, despite watchful attempts to curb calories and exercise more. It concludes that calories are not equal and exercise alone is not sufficient to overcome the effects of unhealthy eating.

First Lady Michelle Obama's "Let's Move!" campaign emphasizes exercise in its effort to reduce childhood obesity. Interestingly, when the program kicked off in 2010, it advocated healthier foods, better food labeling and more exercise to improve childhood well-being.[343]

---

340 http://www.medicaldaily.com/unhealthy-eating-habits-begin-early-infancy-formula-feeding-junk-food-should-be-avoided-308916

341 http://well.blogs.nytimes.com/2014/05/09/fed-up-asks-are-all-calories-equal/

342 Ibid.

343 http://www.politico.com/story/2013/10/michelle-obama-policy-initiatives-big-busi-

Supporters hoped the campaign would stare down Big Food[344] and clarify the health risks associated with processed foods, sweeteners and fats. During its first year, Let's Move! preached a tougher healthy-food message. Then it shifted emphasis to favor exercise and personal fitness, side stepping Big Food's role in childhood obesity.[345]

The revamped Let's Move! campaign found more corporate support. Coke, Pepsi, Nestle, Kellogg, General Mills, Nike, Reebok, Disney and Nickelodeon are among the corporations sponsoring the Partnership for a Healthier America, the nonprofit supporting Let's Move! To its credit, Walmart pledged to open stores in urban food deserts devoid of healthy grocery options and "to reduce salt, sugar and fat content in their products over five years."[346] The food industry felt the implicit challenge raised by Let's Move! and increased their lobbying activities. A 2012 Reuters special report tabulated that 50 food and beverage groups had devoted more than $175 million toward lobbying since President Obama took office, doubling the $83 million spent during the last three years of the George W. Bush Administration. Disney, Nestle, Kellogg and General Mills scuttled an initiative, favored by Mrs. Obama, to promote healthier food marketing to children.[347]

In a nuanced public relations move, Coca-Cola donated $1.5 million in 2014 to found the nonprofit Global Energy Balance Network (www.gebn.org). GEBN highlighted the need for energy balance, offsetting caloric intake with enough physical activity to burn those calories. The group's stated mission is: "To connect and engage multi-disciplinary scientists and other experts around the globe dedicated to applying and advancing the science of energy balance to achieve healthier living."[348] It funded major research projects at the University of Colorado School of Medicine and the University of South Carolina.

ness-99069_Page2.html

344 http://thinkprogress.org/health/2013/02/28/1642911/big-food-lets-move/
345 *Ibid.*
346 http://thinkprogress.org/health/2013/02/28/1642911/big-food-lets-move/
347 http://www.reuters.com/article/2012/04/27/us-usa-foodlobby-idUS-BRE83Q0ED20120427
348 https://gebn.org/about

In a 2014 editorial, GEBN members argued that increasing physical activity for weight loss was more achievable than reducing calories.[349] The Mayo Clinic supports the counter view that diet trumps exercise with respect to weight loss. "For most people, it's possible to lower their calorie intake to a greater degree than it is to burn more calories through increased exercise," wrote Dr. Donald Hensrud.[350]

On November 9, 2015, the University of Colorado School of Medicine announced it would return the $1 million Coca-Cola donated to fund the GEBN.[351] GEBN disbanded in December, 2015, after revelations by *The Associated Press* of Coke's role in managing the organization. In a concurrent announcement, Coke CEO Muhtar Kent announced that he had accepted the retirement of Coke's Chief Science and Health Officer Rhona Applebaum. Applebaum had managed Coke's relationship with GEBN.[352]

Say Cheese!

The United States Department of Agriculture (USDA) promotes American agricultural produce and generates national nutritional standards. Conflicts abound. It is impossible for one organization to promote healthy eating while promoting and subsidizing corn, sugar, wheat and dairy products. Simultaneously policing nutrition and hawking cheese invite psychotherapy.

In 1976, Senator George McGovern investigated links between diet and coronary disease. Expert testimony identified dietary fat as the principal culprit and pushed Congress to recommend healthy carbs over fatty foods. So began America's embrace of low-fat diets.[353] As

349 http://www.touchendocrinology.com/articles/what-causing-worldwide-rise-body-weight

350 http://www.mayoclinic.org/healthy-lifestyle/weight-loss/expert-answers/weight-loss/faq-20058292

351 http://www.foodpolitics.com/2015/11/university-of-colorado-returns-coca-cola-funding-for-global-energy-balance-network/

352 http://www.cbsnews.com/news/anti-obesity-group-funded-by-coke-global-energy-balance-network-disbanding/

353 http://www.npr.org/sections/thesalt/2014/03/28/295332576/why-we-got-fatter-during-the-fat-free-food-boom

dairy producers removed fat from milk, they accumulated enormous quantities of milk fat and sought alternative uses. "Cheese, Glorious Cheese" came to the rescue.

In 1983, Congress established the National Dairy Promotion and Research Board within the Department of Agriculture to create demand-building products for the dairy industry. In 1995, the National Dairy Promotion and Research Board and the United Dairy Industry Association created Dairy Management Inc. (DMI) to "coordinate national and local dairy promotion programs."[354] DMI receives most its funding from government-mandated taxes and government subsidies.[355] With continuous support from the Department of Agriculture, DMI works with industry to create and market new products in both the U.S. and overseas. With sales slumping in 2009, DMI helped Domino's create new pizzas with 40 percent more cheese and paid $12 million to market them. Domino's sales soared by double-digits as consumers devoured its cheesier pizzas. Each slice contained two-thirds of the Department of Agriculture's own recommended daily level of saturated fat.[356]

Marketing works. Egged on by government-funded advertising, tantalizing (and fat-laden) products, high-minded nutrition claims and clever slogans, Americans now consume record levels of cheese. In 2010, Americans gobbled up 23 pounds of cheese annually vs. just 8 pounds in 1970.[357] Cheese has become our largest source of saturated fat. An ounce of cheese contains as much saturated fat as a glass of whole milk.

Food companies influence the USDA's policy positions on nutritional standards. Schwan Food Company of Marshall, Minnesota, is a privately held company with a lot of dough invested in frozen pizzas. With $3 billion in annual sales, Schwan supplies 70 percent of the pizza served in schools.[358] Confronting proposed USDA guidelines in 2011

354 www.dairy.org/about-dmi/history

355 http://www.nytimes.com/2010/11/07/us/07fat.html

356 *Ibid*

357 http://cspinet.org/new/pdf/changing_american_diet_13.pdf

358 http://www.mprnews.org/story/2011/11/18/schwan-foods-pizza-as-vegetable-minnesota-delegation

that would eliminate frozen pizza from federally subsidized school-lunch programs, Schwan went to work. Together with the American Frozen Food Institute, Schwan spent $450,000 on lobbying to eliminate the proposed language governing pizza ingredients.[359]

Senator Amy Klobuchar of Minnesota is among the Senate's more liberal members and an ardent advocate for improved children's nutrition. She was an original sponsor of 2010 legislation that empowered the USDA to tighten the nutritional rules for school lunches. At the critical moment, Senator Klobuchar authored a letter to Secretary of Agriculture Tom Vilsack endorsing Schwan's position. Her letter contained language identical to that found in the Senate testimony of a Schwan executive two months earlier. In the end, the new guidelines recognize tomato sauce as a vegetable and millions of kids eat Schwan frozen pizza in subsidized school lunch programs every day. For her part, Senator Klobuchar said she supported the legislation "because she believes children should be served healthy foods."[360]

Sugar's Daddy

In 2003, HHS Secretary Tommy Thompson killed attempts by the World Health Organization (WHO) to limit recommended sugar consumption. Concerned about rising obesity and related chronic disease throughout the world, WHO sought to limit sugar intake to 10 percent of total daily caloric consumption. Thompson threatened to cut the United States' $406 million in WHO funding if it implemented this guideline.[361] The threat succeeded. A year later when the WHO released its global health strategy on diet and health, it excluded the 10 percent sugar-consumption guideline.[362] It took until 2015 for WHO to issue that guidance.

---

359 *Ibid.*

360 http://www.mprnews.org/story/2011/11/18/schwan-foods-pizza-as-vegetable-min-nesota-delegation

361 http://www.theguardian.com/society/2003/apr/21/usnews.food

362 http://www.newsweek.com/report-sugar-lobby-threatens-organizations-buries-sci-ence-health-effects-256529

Congress passed mandatory food labeling guidelines in 1990. Food labels contain the amounts of fat, cholesterol, sodium, carbohydrates, sugars and protein included in each serving. These labels also identify the product's percentages of recommended daily consumption targets. Sugar is the only ingredient exempt from this requirement.[363] This is about to change. In January 2016, HHS and USDA announced new dietary guidelines that included a suggested a 10 percent limit on the percentage of calories that come from added sugars.[364] The Sugar Association released a hard-hitting statement questioning the scientific basis for the guidance and predicting its reversal.[365]

The sugar lobby is powerful. The *Wall Street Journal* suggests the sugar subsidy may be the worst of America's farm subsidies. That's saying something. The American government grants non-recourse loans annually to sugar farmers at a guaranteed price-per-pound that is roughly twice the global market price. The government sustains this high price for U.S. consumers by imposing tariffs on foreign sugar imports.[366] The net result is that Americans not only consume way too much sugar, we pay twice as much as we should for it. Gluttony and greed align.

The New Yorker reports, "at least half our calories come from food that is subsidized by the government."[367] By comparison, very few federal subsidies exist to incentivize farmers to grow a greater selection of vegetables.[368] Federal policies help keep prices low for corn and the sugar-based products that make Americans sick.

Implications

The American lifestyle poses great risk to our national quality of life, standard of living and productivity. Ancillary costs (human,

---

363 http://www.accessdata.fda.gov/scripts/cdrh/cfdocs/cfcfr/CFRSearch.cfm?fr=101.9

364 http://www.hhs.gov/about/news/2016/01/07/hhs-and-usda-release-new-dietary-guidelines-encourage-healthy-eating-patterns-prevent-chronic.html

365 http://www.sugar.org/2015-dietary-guidelines-for-americans-recommendation-for-added-sugars-intake-agenda-based-not-science-based/

366 http://www.wsj.com/articles/rubio-and-big-sugar-1446769246

367 http://www.newyorker.com/magazine/2015/11/02/freedom-from-fries

368 *Ibid.*

environmental, social, economic) are enormous. Current trends are not sustainable. The increasing cost of treating chronic disease drains resources from other more productive areas of the economy.

Human decision-making has inherent biases and limitations that contribute to increasing obesity levels and chronic disease. The pressures of modern living, particularly its prolonged stresses, compromise Americans' ability to make healthy lifestyle choices. Sophisticated product design and marketing short-circuit the body's natural defenses. The result is fatter, sicker people with ever-higher levels of chronic disease and limited resources for combatting the sources of their chronic disease.

The American government appears hopelessly captured by special interests that influence public expenditures and regulations to benefit corporate interests. It's not a coincidence that six of the 10 wealthiest U.S. counties are in the Washington, D.C. metro area.[369] Highly paid professionals wage war each day to nudge government activity in ways that favor their clients. As with medical care, societal demands for better, safer, healthier food conflict with powerful entrenched interests. The overall health of the American people suffers as a consequence.

America's rugged individualism and its obesity go together like love and marriage. America society blames obese individuals for their inability to control their weight. In turn, these individuals often blame themselves when they fail to lose weight, as they almost always do. While individual lifestyle choices contribute to the nation's obesity crisis, American culture also shoulders significant responsibility. Assigning individual blame shifts responsibility away from counterproductive corporate and governmental actions. Unfortunately, entrenched interests don't relinquish their privileges without a fight. America and Americans win when the playing field tilts toward value and away from influence.

A core premise of *Market vs. Medicine* is that bottom-up, market-driven change is the most effective way to improve the nation's health and well-being. Consumer purchasing decisions move markets. Walmart's commitment to sell organic food and stop carrying milk with hormones illustrates

---

369 http://www.valuewalk.com/2015/03/the-ten-richest-counties-in-america-will-surprise-you-infographic/

how consumer preferences can drive positive societal change. Walmart's research revealed that 91 percent of their customers "would consider buying organic if it were affordable." In April 2014, Walmart announced it would sell its *Wild Oats* organic products at prices 25 percent lower than brand-name competitors.[370]/[371] Making organic foods more accessible and affordable will increase consumer demand for the organic products. Other retailers (think Amazon) will capitalize on changing consumer preferences. Individual purchasing decisions move markets.

Shifting demand curves is essential to transforming American healthcare. Making smart medical and lifestyle decisions easier and more cost-effective is the key to success. To advance, American healthcare must expand its understanding of diagnosis and treatment while using disruption, innovation and behavioral science to empower individuals to take control of their health and wellness. It's the American way.

370 http://www.nytimes.com/2014/04/10/business/walmart-to-offer-organic-line-of-food-at-cut-rate-prices.html?_r=0

371 http://www.bloomberg.com/bw/articles/2014-11-06/wal-mart-promises-organic-food-for-everyone

CHAPTER 13

Embracing Pluralistic Healing

It's supposed to be a professional secret, but I'll tell you anyway. We doctors do nothing. We only help and encourage the doctor within.
ALBERT SCHWEITZER, M.D.

The art of medicine consists in amusing the patient while nature cures the disease.
VOLTAIRE

During World War II, Stamatis Maraitis migrated to the U.S. from Greece seeking treatment for a hand mangled in a munitions accident. He became a painter, married a Greek-American woman (Elpiniki) 13 years his junior, moved to Florida and bought a three-bedroom house where they raised three children. Stamatis was a hard worker, dedicated family man a three-pack-a-day smoker. By the mid-1970s, Stamatis was in his early 60s and suffering shortness of breath. Multiple doctors diagnosed with him terminal lung cancer. He had between six and nine months to live. Stamatis and Elpiniki returned to his ancestral home on the Greek island of Ikaria. Stamatis wanted to spare his wife the high cost of a U.S. funeral and be buried with his ancestors. He was very sick.

Within months, his health improved dramatically. His cancer went into remission and he remained healthy and alive for 36 additional years, surviving Elpiniki (who died at 85) *and* the doctors who had diagnosed his cancer.

Author Dan Buettner documents Stamatis' remarkable story in a 2012 *New York Times* article, "The Island Where People Forget to Die."[372] At first, Stamatis was bed-ridden. Elpiniki and his elderly mother cared for him. They ate traditional, plant-based whole foods grown in the garden. Stamatis attended the island's Greek Orthodox chapel where he reconnected with childhood friends. They'd stop by his house every afternoon for lively conversation lubricated with locally produced wine. "At least I'll die happy," he thought. Instead, his strength increased and he began taking daily walks in the hilly terrain. Stamatis planted a garden and worked in the vineyards. He often frequented a local tavern where he socialized and played dominoes late into the night. When asked decades later how he overcame his lung cancer, Stamatis replied, "It just went away."

Like Stamatis, most of Ikaria's residents live long, productive lives. Many centenarians inhabit Ikaria, living simply as they have for generations. Buettner studies longevity in cultures where people live the

372 http://www.nytimes.com/2012/10/28/magazine/the-island-where-people-forget-to-die.html?_r=0

longest. He terms these regions "Blue Zones"[373] and has written a book describing them with that title. After visiting Ikaria, Buettner realized that multiple factors contribute to long-living communities. "For people to adopt a healthful lifestyle," he wrote, "they need to live in an ecosystem, so to speak, that makes it possible. As soon as you take culture, belonging, purpose or religion out of the picture, the foundation for long healthy lives collapses. The power of such an environment lies in the mutually reinforcing relationships among lots of small nudges and default choices."[374]

Buettner has learned a great deal about Blue Zones. He discovered that Blue Zone residents, like Stamatis, consume plant-rich diets free of fatty, greasy foods and low in sugar. They engage in daily physical activity and enjoy socializing regularly with friends and neighbors. They take time to relax, are spiritual and committed to their families.[375]

The qualities of Blue Zone living can overcome the pressures of modern living. As Stamatis discovered, the body can heal chronic disease. More expansive application of treatment approaches and philosophies generates better outcomes. In pluralism there is medicinal power. Enhanced health and wellness follow.

Mind and Medicine

During his 2015 State of the Union address, President Obama articulated a medical future where genetic discovery shapes tailored therapies that eradicate disease. Notice the President's language:

> *Doctors have always recognized that every patient is unique...and tried to tailor their treatments...to individuals. You can match a blood transfusion to a blood type...What if matching a cancer cure to our*

---

373 The five Blue Zones are: Ikaria, Greece; Okinawa, Japan; Ogliastra Region, Sardinia; Loma Linda, Calif.; and Nicoya Peninsula, Costa Rica.

374 *Ibid*

375 http://www.npr.org/sections/thesalt/2015/04/11/398325030/eating-to-break-100-longevity-diet-tips-from-the-blue-zones

genetic code was just as easy, just as standard? What if figuring out the right dose of medicine was as simple as taking our temperature?[376]

President Obama's statement and his Precision Medicine Initiative trumpet the virtues of pure biomedical research. Its proponents adhere to a Newtonian view of the body as machine. With enough genetic knowledge, they believe physicians can manipulate individual genomes to engineer cures. In this worldview, unlocking complex cause-and-effect relationships solves medical mysteries.

Medical science will discover many more breakthrough treatments through proven research methodologies (e.g. randomized controlled trials); however, the genome-specific focus is too narrow. There is little recognition in Western medicine that other factors also influence physical health.[377] Medical science cannot explain spontaneous remissions (remember Stamatis), the placebo effect or correlations between loneliness and high disease levels.

Emotions, relationships, mindsets, lifestyle and beliefs influence how well or poorly individuals heal. Factors influencing individual response to disease are interrelated and irreducibly complex. Western medicine needs a wider lens to understand them and a greater tolerance for observational studies to determine what works. A more pluralistic understanding of healing dynamics leads to better treatments and better health outcomes. American medicine has much it can learn from the rest of the world.

East Meets West and Vice Versa

I met world-renowned surgeon Dr. Naresh Trehan on my first trip to India in 2004. His Escorts Heart Institute and Research Center in Delhi had procured Asia's first Da Vinci surgical system.[378] Trehan invited me to tour the facility and watch him perform robotic cardiac bypass surgery. Within minutes of arriving, hospital staff put me in scrubs and ushered me into an operating room. Other surgeons

376 President Obama, January 30, 2015, State-of-the-Union Address
377 https://umm.edu/health/medical/altmed/treatment/mindbody-medicine
378 http://archivehealthcare.financialexpress.com/201202/market03.shtml

prepared patients for Trehan's magic while he shuttled between operating rooms. At the critical moment, he redirected arterial blood flow through a newly attached healthy vein. Nobody ties surgical knots like Trehan. It helps that he's ambidextrous. Using this efficient system, Trehan performs up to 20 surgeries in a day.

After the surgeries, Trehan and I retreated to his office where we became fast friends. He shared his plans for building a super-specialty medical enterprise on 43 acres near the Delhi Airport in Gurgaon, called Medanta MediCity. As luck would have it, Trehan's daughter, Shyel, and future son-in-law, Pankaj, were moving to Chicago, so Pankaj could attend Northwestern University's Kellogg School of Business. During the next few years, we met several times in Chicago and Delhi to discuss plans for Medicity. It's the only construction site I've visited where workers wore hardhats and flip flops. Donkeys carried materials between floors in what would become a world-class destination medical enterprise. In December 2009, Medanta Medicity opened its doors to patients and quickly filled to capacity. Medanta Medicity has 1,250 beds, 350 of which are designated critical care, and 45 operating rooms[379] as well as 32 institutions, departments and divisions supporting 20 specialties.

Trehan is among the world's most skilled cardiothoracic surgeons. Although U.S. trained, he incorporates India's Ayurvedic medicine, the world's oldest holistic healing system, into Medanta's treatment protocols. Trehan believes Western medicine is "outside in," or invasive and reductionist. Eastern medicine is "inside out," or holistic and integrative. Trehan believes the optimal delivery system should be pluralistic and apply evidenced-based therapies from both disciplines. Consequently, Medanta's Department of Integrative Medicine synthesizes modern technology with time-tested Ayurvedic practices. Medanta applies "the immense wealth of medical knowledge represented by the science of Ayurveda for patient care and health promotion."[380] Medanta specifically takes an integrative approach to managing cardiac insufficiency, pulmonary hypertension, rheumatism and diabetes among other diseases.

---

379 *Ibid.*
380 http://www.medanta.org/department_integrative_medicine_holistic_therapies.aspx

A Medanta patient experience illustrates the healing power of pluralistic approaches to health and wellness. Unable to walk with a condition that had confounded specialists all over the globe, an Arab sheik visited Medanta for a consultation. A neurological examination revealed improper signaling between the sheik's brain and his legs that prevented his walking. There was nothing Western medicine could do to improve the sheik's condition. Trehan asked the sheik if he would consider Ayurvedic therapies. He agreed. The massage and herbal treatments were so successful that the therapist accompanied the sheik back to Abu Dhabi, where treatments continued and the sheik made a full recovery. Pluralistic medicine succeeded where Western medicine alone had failed.

Despite clear evidence that Eastern medicine has therapeutic value, it takes a back seat to Western medicine. Western medicine's protocols are better documented, highly technological and research-driven. Through the generations, Ayurvedic practitioners (traditional healers in India) have passed their treatments to chosen successors through experiential learning. Consequently, Ayurvedic medicine suffers from uneven documentation, limited practitioner credentialing, outcomes variation and fraudulent practices. Ayurveda cannot achieve parity with Western medicine until it professionalizes training, research and protocol development.

While its acute interventions are oftern successful, Western medicine is losing the battle against chronic disease. Chronic disease has multiple, inter-related causal factors that defy reductionist cause-and-effect prevention and treatment solutions. Interventionist medicine can amputate a diseased limb but does not prevent the diabetes that necessitates the amputation. Engineered therapies underperform natural defenses—eating oranges provides more therapeutic benefit than vitamin C tablets. Properly applied, holistic therapies can diagnose chronic diseases earlier and treat them more effectively. Achieving lifestyle balance through diet, meditation and integrative treatments can offset the disease-promoting stresses of modern living.

Given its advanced knowledge of Western medicine, Ayurvedic expertise and diverse population, India has the ideal ecosystem to develop, test and advance pluralistic therapies for chronic disease.

Interventionist medicine has traveled east. It's time for integrative medicine to travel west.

The journalist T.R. Reid sought treatment for his "bum" shoulder all over the world. He chronicled his international medical journey in *The Healing of America: A Global Quest for Better, Cheaper, and Fairer Health Care.*[381] In his book, Reid contrasts healthcare delivery systems in, France, Britain, Germany, Switzerland, Taiwan and Japan in the following passage:

> *In America, they wanted to do the high-tech, most aggressive, most expensive thing. They wanted to cut out my shoulder and put in a piece of titanium. It was about a $50,000 operation. In France, Germany, and Japan, they would have done that, and it would have cost me $5,000 in France, but those doctors suggested other things: cortisone shots, physical therapy.*[382]

Reid reported that neither Western nor Eastern treatments completely cured his shoulder[383] but the most effective treatment came through Ayurvedic massage during a one-month stay at an Indian ashram. "It gave me more movement and much less pain."[384] This type of solution defies western cause-and-effect treatments. Eastern medicine sees and evaluates the whole person. It views the body as a coordinated energy system and seeks to restore balance and wholeness. Ayurveda relies on deep human connection between care provider and patient to promote healing. Disconnection and disease are one and inseparable. This is why integrative approaches offer promise in treating chronic disease.

Native Wisdom

In the 1980s, the University of Alberta funded a five-year grant to study how First Nations' healer Russell Willier treated psoriasis on the

381   T.R. Reid, "The Healing of America: A Global Quest for Better, Cheaper, and Fairer Health Care," Penguin Books, 2009, 2010

382   http://khn.org/trreid/

383   http://www.pbs.org/wgbh/pages/frontline/sickaroundtheworld/etc/notebook.html

384   *Ibid.*

Sucker Creek Reserve in northern Alberta, Canada.[385] The study analyzed Willier's treatment of 10 non-First Nations' psoriasis patients. Psoriasis is a chronic illness where pharmacological treatments have had limited efficacy and generate painful side effects. Stress and a genetic predisposition for psoriasis seem to trigger outbreaks. An interdisciplinary team observed Willier as he gathered plants, led healing sweat-lodge ceremonies and documented patients' clinical progress. The Willier study aroused negative attention from Canada's medical community. One Edmonton attorney wrote the university's dean demanding to know why the university was "funding research on witch doctors."[386]

No good deed goes unpunished. Willier's treatment significantly outperformed pharmacological treatments. Despite this, the Alberta government defunded the research project, revoked its commitment to fund a native medicine clinic and stymied expansion of Willier's practice. Today, widespread interest in alternative, complementary and integrative medicine creates a more conducive environment to research and document the effectiveness of non-Western medical therapies. Expanded clinical studies and documentation will help Western practitioners incorporate less-understood practices into the mainstream.

Dr. Andrew Weil is a leading authority on integrative medicine. He earned an A.B. degree in biology (botany) from Harvard in 1964 and an M.D. from Harvard Medical School in 1968.[387] He has traveled widely studying how different cultures use medicinal plants and alternative healing techniques to treat illness and injury. Weil has written countless books, articles and newsletters sharing his knowledge and philosophies about integrative medicine. He also has counseled countless patients, including Chicago's long-time first-lady Maggie Daley, in using alternative therapies to battle cancer and other chronic diseases. Weil's acclaimed book, *Healthy Aging: A Lifelong Guide to Your Physical*

385 https://books.google.com/books?id=QIaIBAAAQBAJ&pg=PT8&lpg=PT8&dq=dr+david+young+psoriasis+sweat+lodge&source=bl&ots=GL86MRtpfX&sig=GuJ-qxmxSQGf XfDkDeo-p46kB4&hl=en&sa=X&ved=0ahUKEwiahc6inqfJAhXFax4KHTWADwgQ6AEIOz AC#v=onepage&q=dr%20david%20young%20psoriasis%20sweat%20lodge&f=false
386 *Ibid.*
387 http://integrativemedicine.arizona.edu/about/directors/weil

and Spiritual Well-Being, lays out the holistic principles of integrative medicine:[388] [389]

- A partnership between patient and practitioner in the healing process

- Appropriate use of conventional and alternative methods to facilitate the body's innate healing response

- Consideration of all factors that influence health, wellness and disease, including mind, spirit and community as well as body

- A philosophy that neither rejects conventional medicine nor accepts alternative therapies uncritically

- Recognition that good medicine should be based in good science, be inquiry driven, and be open to new paradigms

- Use of natural, effective, less-invasive interventions whenever possible

- Use of the broader concepts of promotion of health and the prevention of illness as well as the treatment of disease

- Training of practitioners to be models of health and healing, committed to the process of self-exploration and self-development

Americans Flock to Alternative Medicine

The American people are voting for alternative medicine with their pocketbooks. The NIH reported that approximately one third of Americans use some form of non-conventional medicine for their

388 Andrew Weil, M.D., "Healthy Aging: A Lifelong Guide to Your Physical and Spiritual Well-Being," First Anchor Books, 2007

389 http://www.drweil.com/drw/u/ART02054/Andrew-Weil-Integrative-Medicine.html

healthcare.[390] The government surveyed 89,000 American adults in 2002, 2007 and 2012 to ascertain trends in the use of complementary health approaches.[391] The following chart details the most common complementary health approaches:

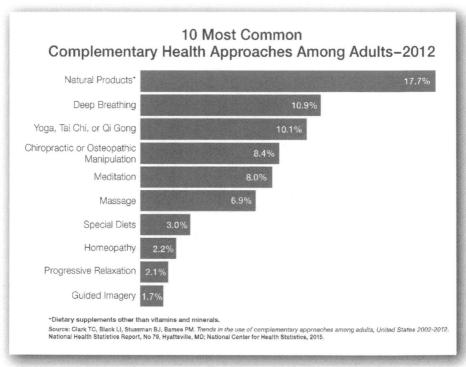

10 Most Common Complementary Health Approaches Among Adults–2012

Natural Products*	17.7%
Deep Breathing	10.9%
Yoga, Tai Chi, or Qi Gong	10.1%
Chiropractic or Osteopathic Manipulation	8.4%
Meditation	8.0%
Massage	6.9%
Special Diets	3.0%
Homeopathy	2.2%
Progressive Relaxation	2.1%
Guided Imagery	1.7%

*Dietary supplements other than vitamins and minerals.
Source: Clark TC, Black LI, Stussman BJ, Barnes PM. *Trends in the use of complementary approaches among adults, United States 2002-2012.* National Health Statistics Report, No 79, Hyattsville, MD; National Center for Health Statistics, 2015.

A 2013 *Chicago Magazine* article cited statistics from the CDC claiming "38 percent of adults turned to (complementary and alternative medicine) in 2007, spending nearly $34 billion."[392] The same article noted that "the percentage of U.S. hospitals offering such treatments has zoomed: from 14 percent in 2000 to 42 percent in 2010, according to the American Hospital Association." [393] This includes Cleveland Clinic, an institution traditionally associated with high-tech, complex care delivery.

---

390 http://www.cdc.gov/nchs/data/nhsr/nhsr079.pdf

391 *Ibid.*

392

393 http://www.chicagomag.com/Chicago-Magazine/August-2013/Integrative-Medicine/

In January 2014, Cleveland Clinic opened the Chinese Herbal Therapy Clinic within its Center for Integrative Medicine. The world-renowned health system was among the first in the U.S. to have a Chinese herbalist on staff.[394]/[395] The move came just two years after Ohio changed its laws to allow prescriptions of herbal blends within a clinical practice. The clinic's new service accommodates patients' preference for integrative approaches to managing and treating chronic disease. Physicians supervise application of herbal therapies to minimize risks of drug-herb interaction. The licensed herbalist prescribes proven herbal remedies to treat chronic diseases, pain, hormonal imbalances, digestive issues, sleep problems and even in-fertility.[396] The Cleveland Clinic promotes integrative medicine at all stages of care and operates the Center for Pediatric Integrative Medicine to offer alternative treatments such as hypnosis, guided imagery, Reiki, therapeutic touch, acupuncture and acupressure to its youngest patients.[397]

Other well-known U.S. hospitals offering integrative medicine include several grantees selected by the prominent Bernard Osher Foundation.[398] The Osher Centers for Integrative Medicine operate at Harvard Medical School and Brigham and Women's Hospital in Boston; Northwestern University in Chicago; University of California, San Francisco; and Vanderbilt University, Nashville, Tennessee. In Minnesota, the Penny George Institute for Health and Healing at Allina Health is the largest integrative medicine center embedded within a health system.[399]

---

394 https://my.clevelandclinic.org/about-cleveland-clinic/newsroom/releases-videos-newsletters/2014-3-5-cleveland-clinic-among-first-in-the-us-to-open-hospital-based-chinese-herbal-therapy-clinic

395 http://www.foxnews.com/health/2014/04/23/top-hospital-opens-up-to-chinese-herbs-as-medicines.html

396 *Ibid.*

397 https://my.clevelandclinic.org/childrens-hospital/specialties-services/departments-centers/integrative-medicine

398 http://www.osherfoundation.org/index.php?medicine

399 http://www.allinahealth.org/Penny-George-Institute-for-Health-and-Healing/

The Raby Institute for Integrative Medicine at Northwestern incorporates Dr. Theri Griego Raby's integrative medical model.[400] [401] The institute culminates Raby's career-long effort to bring integrative medicine to her patients. She began lobbying in 1996 for an integrative medicine center at Northwestern Memorial Hospital. Twelve years later, she founded the Raby Institute at Northwestern. The institute stresses constant, high-level communication between Northwestern's integrative practitioners and physicians. Treatments combine primary care services with alternative medical practices, including naturopathic medicine, traditional Chinese medicine, medical acupuncture, homeopathy, massage therapy and functional medicine (understanding the underlying causes of disease).

Holistic healing comes naturally to Raby. Born and raised in Albuquerque, New Mexico, she received her degree in allopathic medicine from the University of New Mexico. Her experiences with cross-cultural healing fueled her graduate and post-graduate work in holistic medicine. She sees herself as a healthcare "change agent."[402] Raby advocates tirelessly for integrative medicine, even supporting legislation to license naturopathic doctors in Illinois.[403] She cultivates patients' innate power to heal themselves and lead fully engaged, healthy lives.

Not surprisingly, Weil also is at the forefront of advancing integrative medicine. He founded the Arizona Center for Integrative Medicine at the University of Arizona College of Medicine in 1994. The center conducts education, clinical care and research in integrative medicine.[404] It operates "upon the premise that the best way to change a field is to educate the most gifted professionals and place them in settings where they can, in turn, teach others."[405] Today, the center leads international efforts to "develop a comprehensive curriculum in integrative medicine."[406]

400 http://www.rabyintegrativemedicine.com
401 http://www.rabyintegrativemedicine.com/pages/theri_griego_raby/34.php
402 http://www.rabyintegrativemedicine.com/pages/theri_griego_raby/34.php
403 Ibid.
404 http://integrativemedicine.arizona.edu
405 Ibid.
406 Ibid.

Integrative medicine's pioneers highlight the need, potential and demand for more holistic, patient-centric approaches to treating disease, particularly chronic diseases. While extremely promising, their efforts confront a medical mindset rooted in Newtonian physics and dedicated to reductionist research and therapies. No area of medicine illustrates this passion for precision engineering more than genetics.

Genetics, Epigenetics and Disease

Genetics-based therapies represent the pinnacle of medical science. Billions of dollars have poured into research to sequence genomes and develop tailored therapies. This is the basis for President Obama's Precision Medicine initiative and his "moonshot" program to cure cancer announced at his last State of the Union Address in January 2016. Other than some hereditary genetic markers for rare diseases and limited ability to assess individual responsiveness to some therapies, there is little to show for all the investment.

As the world crossed into the new millennium, President Clinton announced the completion of the first human genome map. Hope was in the air: new medicine for a new age. Clinton predicted that genetic discovery would "revolutionize the diagnosis, prevention and treatment of most, if not all, human diseases."[407] Accompanying the President, NIH genome director Francis Collins predicted that genetic diagnosis of diseases would occur within 10 years and genetic treatments would begin within 15 years. "Over the longer term, perhaps in another 15 or 20 years," Collins observed, "you will see a complete transformation in therapeutic medicine."[408]

Not so much. By 2010, the promise of more effective treatments remained largely unmet. The *New York Times* reported geneticists were "almost back to square one in knowing where to look for roots of common disease."[409] It appears now that a host of rare genetic variants combine to cause common diseases rather than a single, easily identifi-

407 http://www.nytimes.com/2010/06/13/health/research/13genome.html?pagewanted=all

408 *Ibid.*

409 *Ibid.*

able gene.[410] Six years later, science is still far away from personalized medicine and designer drugs. Genetic origins of disease may be irreducibly complex and may not be discoverable. When asked in 2010 whether medical science could understand the genetic origins of disease, Human Genome Project leader Eric Lander responded, "The only intellectually honest answer is that there's no way to know."

Core to genetic research is a reductionist belief in finding single causal elements: that flipping molecular switches off or on can prevent or cure disease. Drug side effects demonstrate the risks of manipulating human physiology. For example, the drugs physicians use to treat restless leg syndrome[411] often causes impulse control disorders, such as compulsive gambling and hyper-sexuality.[412] Side effects are still effects and they illustrate the fallibility of applying systematic solutions to treat specific illnesses. Different parts of the body can and do react differently to pharmacological intervention. Implicit in genetic research is the promise of overcoming side effects (no more compulsive gambling) through precise manipulation of targeted genes. That may be a chimera.

Despite the lack of breakthrough success, academic centers continue investing in expensive biomedical facilities and research. If anything, the pace has become more frenetic. An August 2015 *New York Times* editorial discussed "academic poaching" and how "states from coast to coast are using public funds to help their medical schools recruit scientific stars from other states or to prevent their own stars from being lured away by lucrative offers." Major universities are tripping over themselves to announce new or expanded centers of biomedical research. Over 150 American universities received over $1 million in NIH research grants in fiscal year 2016.[413] Given this enormous expenditure and the uncertainty of breakthrough outcomes, should there

---

410 *Ibid.*

411 Restless leg syndrome affects approximately ten percent of the population. Symptoms include prickling or tingling in the legs and an urge to move the legs. Symptoms are more noticeable at rest, such as during bedtime or a long car ride. Source: http://www.sciencedaily.com/releases/2010/12/101206135718.htm

412 http://www.dailymail.co.uk/health/article-2802936/drugs-parkinson-s-disease-turn-patients-gamblers-sex-addicts-compulsive-shoppers.html

413 https://report.nih.gov/award/index.cfm

be a Plan B? Turns out that manipulating external environmental factors can flip genetic switches and achieve remarkable improvement in health outcomes.

There are few purely genetic diseases. They include cystic fibrosis, hemophilia and certain childhood cancers. Almost all disease results from the interaction between genetic predisposition and external factors, such as diet, exercise, stress, smoking, environmental exposure and loneliness. These external factors are at the core of epigenetics. Epigenetics studies how genes express themselves in response to environmental influences. Epigenetics explains why three-pack-a-day smoker Stamatis contracted lung cancer. It also explains how his body cured the terminal cancer once he returned his Greek island home and resumed a traditional way of living.

Genetic medicine manipulates DNA to change the genotype. Epigenetics studies how to manipulate the environment to prevent harmful genetic triggers from turning on. In contrast to genetic-based treatments, epigenetic-based treatments have more more practical and immediate effect in treating disease, particularly chronic disease. That's why Popeye eats his spinach. Turns out it is easier to the manipulate the human environment than it is human DNA.

Epigenetics research reveals that multiple factors have a profound impact on each individual gene expression and human health. While biologists once believed that genes were static except for internal mutation, researchers now understand that environmental factors alter genes throughout life and even across generations. These factors include diet, stress, lifestyle choices and even ancestral behaviors.[414] [415]

In a landmark Duke University study, professor Randy Jirtle and post-doctoral student Robert Waterland demonstrated that environmental factors stimulate genetic change.[416] Their experiment employed agouti mice, so named because they carry the agouti gene that renders them yellow, obese and susceptible to chronic diseases. Jirtle and Waterland fed female mice a nutrient-rich diet before conception

---

414 http://discovermagazine.com/2013/may/13-grandmas-experiences-leave-epigenetic-mark-on-your-genes

415 http://www.radiolab.org/story/251885-you-are-what-your-grandpa-eats

416 http://discovermagazine.com/2006/nov/cover

and assessed that diet's impact on the mice's offspring. A November 2006 article titled *DNA is Not Destiny: The New Science of Epigenetics* from *Discover* magazine explains the experiment and its remarkable results:

> Typically, when agouti mice breed, most of the offspring are identical to the parents: just as yellow, fat as pincushions, and susceptible to life-shortening disease. The parent mice in Jirtle and Waterland's experiment, however, produced a majority of offspring that looked altogether different. These young mice were slender and mousy brown. Moreover, they did not display their parents' susceptibility to cancer and diabetes and lived to a spry old age. The effects of the agouti gene had been virtually erased.
>
> Remarkably, the researchers effected this transformation without altering a single letter of the mouse's DNA. Their approach instead was radically straightforward—they changed the moms' diet. Starting just before conception, Jirtle and Waterland fed a test group of mother mice a diet rich in methyl donors, small chemical clusters that can attach to a gene and turn it off. These molecules are common in the environment and are found in many foods, including onions, garlic, beets, and in the food supplements often given to pregnant women. After being consumed by the mothers, the methyl donors worked their way into the developing embryos' chromosomes and onto the critical agouti gene. The mothers passed along the agouti gene to their children intact, but thanks to their methyl-rich pregnancy diet, they had added to the gene a chemical switch that dimmed the gene's deleterious effects.[417]

A simple dietary change in one generation of mice dramatically reduced the next generation's risk for cancer and diabetes. Clinicians rarely consider the nuances of environmental factors in treating illnesses. They diagnose symptoms and prescribe therapies to alleviate

417 http://discovermagazine.com/2006/nov/cover

them. Payment mechanisms support this fragmented approach. As the agouti mice experiment proves, however, environmental stimuli can turn genetic switches on or off—activating or deactivating genetic proclivity for disease. The holistic science of epigenetics explains how positive lifestyle modification (e.g. eating a better diet) prevents and even reverses chronic disease.

Positive environmental stimuli can foster, prevent and reverse chronic disease. The opposite is also true. Since the late 1970s, negative epigenetic interactions have triggered explosive growth in obesity and chronic disease. Consuming processed food laden with sugar, fat and salt overwhelms the body's natural defenses against overeating. Epigenetics both causes and prevents chronic disease. As the agouti mice experiment demonstrates, environmental factors flip genetic switches that trigger chronic disease on or off.

Epigenetics and Bill Clinton

Chelsea Clinton's orders were clear. Her father had to lose weight if he wanted to walk her down the aisle for her upcoming wedding. Chelsea Clinton's admonition came after the former president underwent cardiac surgery in February 2012 to place two stents in clogged arteries. This surgery occurred six years after former President Bill Clinton's 2004 quadruple bypass surgery. Chelsea Clinton, a long-standing vegan, wanted her father to change his diet and exercise more. Bill Clinton decided to follow his daughter's example. He became a near-vegan, exercised, lost 35 pounds (back to his high school weight) and proudly walked Chelsea Clinton down the aisle that October.[418]/[419]

At the wedding, a beaming Bill Clinton not only sang the new couple's praises, he also extolled the virtues of his new diet. He is a voracious reader. While contemplating Chelsea Clinton's challenge, he read *The China Study* by Colin and Thomas Campbell. *The China Study* makes a compelling, fact-based case that a plant-based diet virtually eliminates heart disease in human beings. The diet itself heals the

---

418 http://www.telegraph.co.uk/news/worldnews/northamerica/usa/8038801/Bill-Clintons-new-diet-nothing-but-beans-vegetables-and-fruit-to-combat-heart-disease.html
419 http://www.aarp.org/health/healthy-living/info-08-2013/bill-clinton-vegan.html

damaged arteries and improves blood flow. Dr. Caldwell Esselstyn, the head of Cardiac Nutrition at the Cleveland Clinic, advises Bill Clinton on his diet and health. According to Esselstyn, people like Bill Clinton who consume a plant-based diet "are heart-attack proof. They're bullet-proof from getting another heart attack. How exciting is that, particularly for somebody who has already had a heart attack!"[420]

Beyond cardiology, *The China Study* documents that a plant-based diet is effective against all chronic diseases, including diabetes, osteoporosis, Alzheimer's and most cancers. Esselstyn maintains that the different chronic diseases are manifestations of the body's reaction to unhealthy diets and lifestyle choices. In this sense, chronic diseases are really just one disease, which is susceptible to epigenetic-based treatments. For example, a plant-based diet's anti-inflammatory and biochemical properties enhance the body's natural healing mechanisms and prevent disease-causing genes from activating.

This epigenetic explanation for heart disease was not apparent to Bill Clinton's cardiac surgeon. In a press conference immediately after Clinton's in February 2010, Dr. Alan Schwartz at New York Presbyterian Hospital observed that Clinton's need for the two new stents "was not a result of his lifestyle or diet." Schwartz further noted that heart disease "is a chronic condition. We don't have a cure for this condition, but we have excellent treatments." Schwartz is hardly alone in his thinking. Dr. Clyde Yancy, then president of the American Heart Association and a cardiologist at Baylor University Medical Center made the following observation after Clinton's surgery: "Coronary artery disease is a progressive process. We like to think of it as an event, but it is a disease. There aren't any cures. We have to have constant surveillance."[421]/[422]

According to the CDC, heart disease kills 610,000 Americans each year, accounting for one in four U.S. deaths.[423] Despite significant surgical and pharmacological innovation, heart disease has remained America's leading killer for over 50 years. These grim cardiac death statistics frustrate Esselstyn, "All our cardiac interventions address

---

420   https://www.youtube.com/watch?v=J6pLRdawBw0, 20:00-20:30 in the video

421   http://usatoday30.usatoday.com/news/health/2010-02-12-clinton-heart_N.htm

422   http://www.wsj.com/articles/SB10001424052748704337004575059882438150018

423   http://www.cdc.gov/heartdisease/facts.htm

symptoms, not the root causes of the disease." He further observes, "Patients aren't afraid of pain. They aren't afraid of death. They're afraid of being abandoned."[424] Esselstyn has helped hundreds of patients overcome cardiac disease. His hands-on approach involves working with people to change negative lifestyle habits. He's on their side. He's as much coach as doctor. In this respect, his approach mirrors that of traditional healers and practitioners of integrative medicine. Human connection and relationships are fundamental to healing. With high-tech interventions and increased specialization, American medicine often loses sight of this truth. When people believe they can heal, they often do.

Mind Matters: Placebo and Nocebo Effects

The placebo and nocebo effects (Latin for "I please" and "I shall harm" respectively) illustrate how mind-body linkage influences health outcomes in positive and negative ways. A seminal article by Dr. Henry Beecher in 1955, "The Powerful Placebo," elevated the recognition of the placebo effect within modern medicine.[425] In clinical trials, placebos are benign interventions given without foreknowledge to patients who believe they are receiving actual treatments. Placebos work about a third of the time. Beecher and his team were the first to call for double-blind placebo-controlled clinical trials to account for mind-driven outcomes.

The placebo effect influences surgeries, drugs, pain-relief devices, and even acupuncture. Researchers have found several unexplainable manifestations of the placebo effect: the larger the pill the greater the effect; two sugar pills produce a stronger effect than one; injections trump pills, certain colors are even more effective in relieving specific complaints such as pain, sleeplessness or anxiety than others.[426]

Walter Kennedy coined the term "nocebo response" in 1961.[427] He had observed that negative expectations of a drug or treatment can

424   https://www.youtube.com/watch?v=J6pLRdawBw0

425   http://jama.jamanetwork.com/article.aspx?articleid=303530

426   http://www.newyorker.com/magazine/2011/12/12/the-power-of-nothing

427   *Ibid.*

generate negative outcomes independent of the therapy's intervention. Patients who believe they will experience side effects do, even when given sugar pills. The nocebo effect is less documented than the placebo effect because of ethical concerns related to conducting studies that can induce harm.

The power of suggestion and the mind-body connectivity are powerful forces in health and wellness. Behavioral science expands our understanding of how emotions, beliefs and biases influence decision-making. The pictures in our heads, the stories we tell ourselves and how we feel actually influence how we interact with one another and the world. The brain's infrastructure influences all human decision-making, but it is particularly potent in medicine.

Iora Health founder and CEO Rushika Fernandopulle tells the story of his maternal grandfather, Emanuel Muttukumaru, a highly educated professional from Sri Lanka who became a senior leader in food and agriculture at the United Nations. Muttukumaru's father died four days before his 60th birthday. Many years later, Muttukumaru's older brother Hugo died four days before his 60th birthday. Muttukumaru predicted that this would be his fate as well. Two years later, he died four days before his 60th birthday. As biologist Bruce Lipton observes, "The brain perceives and the mind interprets." Muttukumaru died four days before his 60th birthday because his mind believed he would.

A similar effect occurs when doctors deliver bad news. A firm diagnosis of terminal illness, incapacitation or the need for lifelong medications or treatments, sets in motion a string of self-fulfilling prophecies. Dr. Lissa Rankin, an OB/GYN, and author of "Mind Over Medicine: Scientific Proof You Can Heal Yourself,"[428] calls this "medical hexing." "Doctors think they're telling it to you straight," she says, "that you deserve to know, that you should be realistic and make arrangements, if necessary. But when they say such things, they instill in your conscious and subconscious mind a belief that you won't get well. This negative belief becomes a self-fulfilling prophecy. If you believe you'll never recover, you won't."[429]

428 *Mind Over Medicine: Scientific Proof You Can Heal Yourself,* Hay House, 2013
429 https://www.psychologytoday.com/blog/owning-pink/201308/the-nocebo-effect-negative-thoughts-can-harm-your-health

Words Matter

All diseases have physiologies that exhibit expected outcomes with positive and negative variation. Stress and relaxation influence individual responses to disease. They contribute to and detract from successful outcomes. As Stamatis Maraitis' and Muttukumaru's stories illustrate, the mind-body connection can even trigger spontaneous remission and death.

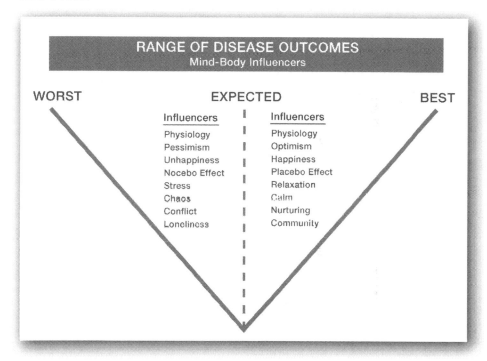

Medical conversations can be scary and dispiriting. Without being Pollyannaish, medical conversations also can be nurturing and encouraging. Positive mind-body connectivity translates into less disease and better outcomes. Happy, optimistic, engaged patients with strong support networks and nurturing care providers have more resources to fight illnesses than scared, lonely, pessimistic, disengaged patients with limited support and ambivalent care providers.

Medicine has always had great healers—doctors, nurses and other care providers who nurture disproportionate numbers of sick people back to health. Natural healers connect with patients and unleash the body's restorative capabilities. They augment modern medicine's powerful technology with empathy, compassion and kindness.

Modern medicine finds this line of reasoning fuzzy, or lacking scientific basis. Quite the contrary. Behavioral science provides deep insight into brain function, mind-body connection and the benefits of optimism. It provides proven strategies for enhancing medical communications. Medicine is much more than surgical and pharmacological intervention. Deep healing requires addressing the root causes of disease, particularly chronic diseases. This requires strong relationships and human connection. More emphasis on medical communication in medical training would improve outcomes and aid healing.

American healthcare cannot advance without exploiting the incredible powers of self-healing and human connection. In 2013, Dignity Health launched a national Hello Human kindness campaign[430] to bring humanity back into healthcare. Where medicine's technological imperative ends, human kindness continues and sustains.

Quantum Medicine

My friend Sam Pitroda is a big thinker. As a technology advisor to India's Prime Minister Rajiv Gandhi in the 1980s, Pitroda was at the forefront of India's telecom revolution. He led the movement to put phones in villages and convinced G.E.'s Jack Welch to invest in business process outsourcing (BPO) in India. He founded and was chairman of India's first Telecom Commission. More recently, Pitroda chaired India's Knowledge Commission. His company, C-Sam, developed and owned the patents for mobile wallets. Pitroda sold the company to MasterCard in 2015 and uses some of the proceeds to invest in technology projects.

On a 2014 Paris trip, Pitroda met Russian scientist Nadia Volf, who had a big idea. Volf characterizes the heart as the equivalent of an atomic plant transmitting energy to other parts of the body. She believes many cancers result from a breakdown in the energy transmission at the molecular level. Her therapy has cured a small number

---

430 http://finance.yahoo.com/news/dignity-health-says-hello-humankind-ness-133000534.html

of Stage IV cancer patients by amplifying the heart's energy to the afflicted parts of the body. Pitroda decided to fund clinical trials of Volk's methodology. His reasoning: "If it fails, I'm out $100,000. If it works, Dr. Volk will win a Nobel Prize and I'll become a billionaire."

Pitroda's foray into energy-driven therapies raises an intriguing question regarding the future direction of medical research. Today, we poison and cut people to cure cancer. We may look back in 25 years and marvel at our medical barbarism. Current biology limits the body's control functions to enzymes and hormones. It excludes emotions, consciousness and energy fields.[431] A narrow Newtonian approach to biological function may blind us to other forces that influence healing. Those forces could explain the roles belief (placebo/nocebo) and human connection (through mutual energy exchange) exhibit in the healing process.

Eighty years ago quantum mechanics revolutionized the physics world and brought understanding to previously unexplained molecular phenomenon. Is light a wave or a particle? Quantum physics reveals the answer is both. Newtonian biology postulates that chemical reactions, the source of all human activity, occur through random molecular collisions within cells.[432] Relative to cells, molecules are very tiny. It's hard to believe that the body's instantaneous and voluminous chemical reactions occur without organizing principles. Perhaps quantum mechanics apply at the molecular level in biological systems as they do in physics.

Another friend Dr. Ogan Gurel is an Ivy-League-trained neurosurgeon with expertise in biochemistry and molecular biophysics. As a Harvard undergraduate, he conducted molecular dynamics research with Martin Karplus, the 2013 winner of the Nobel Prize in Chemistry. Professor Karplus' research examines "the electronic structure, geometry, and dynamics of molecules of chemical and biological interest."[433] Gurel's research examines the electromagnetic characteristics of proteins and their potential modulation for disease diagnosis and therapy.

---

431 https://www.youtube.com/watch?v=62la_URbPCI
432 *Ibid.*
433 http://faculty.chemistry.harvard.edu/martin-karplus/home

More potential evidence that human energy systems contribute to sickness and healing.

Connecting Eastern and Western Medicine

In many respects, quantum medicine with its emphasis on energy exchange connects modern medicine to traditional medical practices. In traditional Hindu medicine (i.e. Ayurveda), "chakras" are energy wheels that align nerves, organs and fluids. Chakras must remain open and flowing for human beings to flourish. Healers employ meditation, massage and yoga to bring mind, body and spirit into balance. These Eastern healing therapies now flourish worldwide. The Chinese Medicine Meridian System incorporates an energy distribution network with 12 pathways (meridians) through which energy (chee) flows within the body.[434] Understanding of the body's energy-distribution system forms the basis for successful acupuncture treatments, now used in many U.S. hospitals for treating pain. West meets East. Yin and Yang balance.

Human language hints at an energy-infused existence. We sense a spark. Get charged up. Feel amped. Describe a room as "electric." Become drained. Happy people live longer. Isolation and a lack of social connection diminish resilience. Lonely people are prone to disease and die sooner. In traditional societies, shunning becomes a death sentence. Modern living breeds isolation. Connecting isolated individuals to their communities is vital to societal health and wellness.

Much as quantum mechanics expanded physics beyond its Newtonian boundaries, discoveries in brain plasticity, behavioral science, mind-body connectivity and biochemistry are expanding medicine beyond Newtonian (cause-effect) treatment models. Evidence abounds that human connection supports healing and well-being. The irony of modern medicine is how it diminishes human connection and ignores its healing power in pursuit of disease specialization and technical mastery. It may well be true that modern medicine can only advance as it recaptures its human spirit.

---

434 http://www.acos.org/articles/the-chinese-medicine-meridian-system/

CHAPTER 14

NUDGING TOWARD WELLNESS

The greatest wealth is health.
VIRGIL

*In order to change, we must be sick and
tired of being sick and tired.*
ANONYMOUS

W atching hockey in June is unnatural, but that's what I found myself doing in 2015 as the Chicago Blackhawks captured its third Stanley Cup in six years. Given hockey's continuous play, networks cram loads of commercials into limited commercial breaks. The following two commercials played incessantly and capture America's opposing mindsets regarding wellness:

- Hardee's 4th of July launch for its Great American Thickburger, a half-pound hamburger topped with a sliced hot dog, kettle chips and condiments bound together by a load of American cheese. The commercial featured a bikini-clad supermodel chomping on the burger in a hot tub on the flatbed of a pickup truck driving along an aircraft carrier cruising the Hudson River as fireworks exploded before the New York City skyline. What could be more American?

- John Hancock's Life Insurance Company's promotion of its Vitality program, lower-cost life insurance for healthy individuals who share their biometric data—prove you're healthy and the company will lower your life insurance. The ad featured a trim professional woman in a suit climbing office steps while checking her FitBit.

These commercials capture the dichotomy embedded within American culture regarding health, lifestyles and values. Americans enjoy their God-given right to eat fattening food while bearing individual responsibility for their health. Powerful commercial forces challenge the better angels of our nature and create a widening lifestyle divide between the healthy and unhealthy to the detriment of American society. Maintaining the status quo is not acceptable. How can we make it easier for people to choose more John Hancock and less Hardee's?

The Way Home: Toward Connection and Wholeness

Awareness of healthy behaviors, diet, and lifestyle is growing. Increasing numbers of films, books and commentaries reveal the magnitude of

America's personal, community and institutional lifestyle challenges. Documentaries such as *Food Inc., Fast Food Nation, Supersize Me, Fed Up, Forks Over Knives* and *That Sugar Film* expose how Big Food, government and Madison Avenue have contributed to American obesity, chronic illness and diminished life quality and economic productivity. Similarly-themed books include *The End of Overeating* by David Kessler; *The Omnivore's Dilemma* and *In Defense of Food* by Michael Pollen; *Salt, Sugar, Fat* by Michael Moss; *Fast Food Nation* by Eric Schlosser and *The China Study* and *Whole* by T. Colin Campbell. Even television shows like *The Biggest Loser* increase cultural and public awareness of obesity and negative behaviors while teaching healthier habits.

Despite greater awareness, obesity continues to rise. Since 2008, Gallup-Healthways has issued a State of American Well-Being Report that calculates obesity rates (BMI score of 30 or higher) based on self-reported information from millions of survey respondents. The 2014 report[435] pegged national obesity at 27.7 percent, up from 27.1 percent in 2013 and significantly higher than the 2008 level of 25.5 percent. Importantly, the Gallup-Healthways analysis links higher obesity with lower well-being scores. The following paragraph summarizes this connection:

> *The Well-Being Index includes 2.2 million surveys, captures how people feel about and experience their daily lives, and measures well-being across five elements: purpose, social, financial, community and physical. Previous Gallup and Healthways research shows that high well-being closely relates to key health outcomes such as lower rates of healthcare utilization, lower workplace absenteeism and better workplace performance.[436]*

It's not a new finding that health, community and well-being are interconnected. The 1998 McArthur Foundation study on successful aging found that lifestyle choices have more impact on health status than heredity.[437] Employing 10 years of longitudinal data, McArthur research-

---

435   http://www.well-beingindex.com/2014-obesity-report
436   *Ibid.*
437   http://www.barnesandnoble.com/w/successful-aging-john-wallis-rowe-md/1112272374#productInfoTabs

ers John Wallis Rowe and Robert L. Kahn found that the four keys to successful aging are challenging the mind; challenging the body; a strong community and spirituality. Their conclusions challenged conventional wisdom on aging. Much as Dan Buettner observed with Blue Zone residents, active engagement improves health and vigor in old age. The overall living goal is "compressed mortality"—to live long, and die fast rather than linger through an extended, diminishing, and costly decline. Too many Americans live long lives diminished by chronic disease.

While America's obesity growth trend has not reversed, there's positive evidence regarding food consumption patterns. Meat consumption, for example, is decreasing while vegan products are moving from niche to the mainstream. Soda consumption is also declining[438] while bottled water sales are on track to surpass soda sales by 2017.[439] Milk consumption is also declining. Milk is a major source of dietary fat and unhealthy animal protein. The U.S Department of Agriculture tallied milk sales in 2012 at 6 billion gallons, the lowest amount since 1984.[440] Consumption of milk substitutes (almond milk, soy milk, coconut milk) is growing modestly. In the United Kingdom, sales of milk alternatives increased by 40 percent between 2011 and 2014.[441]

Even America's per capita sugar consumption is declining. After peaking in 2004 (at 388 calories for children and 341 for adults), consumption has declined slowly since (329 calories for children and 300 for adults in 2010.)[442] Despite that positive trend, American consumption of added sugars, particularly fructose, remains too high and poses our largest public health challenge. Even at the lower level, American sugar consumption remains more than double the levels recommended by the American Heart Association. Announced in January 2016, the U.S. government for the first time will suggest dietary guidelines

---

438 http://www.wsj.com/articles/water-water-everywherein-bottles-1440581400

439 http://www.wsj.com/articles/water-water-everywherein-bottles-1440581400

440 http://business.time.com/2012/09/07/got-milk-increasingly-the-answer-is-no/

441 http://www.theguardian.com/lifeandstyle/wordofmouth/2014/mar/10/quinoa-cappuccino-soy-almond-oat-milk-dairy-alternatives

442 http://www.obesity.org/news/press-releases/us-adult

for added sugar consumption. This represents a major public health victory. Sugar is ubiquitous and addictive. Reining in sugar consumption will require a comprehensive program that engages individuals, families, communities, employers and government. For decades, food companies have employed behavioral science to encourage sugar consumption. It's time to take a page from their playbook.

Behavioral Science: Explaining the Irrational

Traditional economics assumes market participants have perfect information and act rationally. Prices alone determine purchasing behavior. Traditional economists ignore externalities when developing elegant models to explain market behavior. In the real world, people are not rational. Emotions and circumstances influence financial decision-making. Overconfident and fearful investors hold on to losing stocks too long and exit markets at the wrong time.

The same brain infrastructure that influences financial decision-making influences lifestyle choices. Human being's penchant for over-valuing immediate gratification overwhelms long-term health goals. We eat the glazed doughnut even though we know it's unhealthy. Alternatively, we won't want the glazed doughnut if we don't see it. That's the logic underlying cafeteria placement of healthier foods in more prominent locations. It becomes easier for people to make healthier choices.

Behavioral economics emerged to explain why human behavior often deviates from expected behaviors. Beginning in the 1970s, path-breaking research by Nobel Laureate Daniel Kahneman and his partner Amos Tversky established behavioral economics' power to explain irrational choices. In *Thinking Fast and Thinking Slow*, Kahneman described two types of thinking. System 2 thinking is cognitive and requires the brain to process variables, data and situational cues to make informed decisions. It is slow and resource-intensive. By contrast, System 1 thinking is instinctive and fast. If human beings used System 2 thinking to flee saber-tooth tigers, they'd be dead before making the decision to run. System 1 thinking relies on flash reactions and ingrained biases, known as heuristics, to form instant opinions and make quick choices. System 1 thinking is generally right (thank goodness) but not always.

Heuristics can lead to suboptimal choices and behaviors. Complicating matters, the human brain does not easily recognize when it is employing instinctive reactions over cognitive reasoning. Individuals assume they are employing rational decision-making when instincts are actually driving their decision-making. One school of thought maintains human beings make all decisions with System 1 thinking and employ System 2 thinking to justify chosen behaviors. Habits are a form of System 1 thinking. Individuals create habits over time by carving new neural pathways in the brain. Once established, habits become efficient, instinctive behaviors. Like instincts, most habits are good, but they aren't always.

In their 2008 best-selling book, *Nudge: Improving Decisions about Health, Wellness and Happiness,* Richard Thaler and Cass Sustein applied behavioral science to "nudge" individuals into making beneficial healthcare choices. The authors describe this approach as "libertarian paternalism." It incorporates three basic human traits: bounded rationality; bounded willpower; and bounded selflessness. Behavioral science employs the adjective "bounded" to emphasize that System 2's rationality, willpower and selflessness have limits and operate within boundaries. Outside the boundaries, System 1's instinctive and habitual behaviors dominate.

Bounded Rationality describes how the amount of available information informs decision-making quality. Less available information translates into inferior decision-making. People take mental shortcuts that encourage poor lifestyle choices. To exploit bounded rationality, Thaler and Sustein recommend that cafeterias array food choices to encourage healthier choices. Most people engage in mindless eating. Paternalistic libertarians can tame this impulsive behavior by adjusting environmental factors such as plate size (smaller), glass shape (thinner) and food placement. Altering these factors encourages smaller portions and healthier food choices.

Changing "default options" can also improve behaviors. Researchers Dan Goldstein and Eric Johnson found that simply changing the default option from "not a donor" to "donor" significantly increased the number of organ donors.[443] Similarly, making apples available for snacks instead of cookies leads people to accept apples as their default choice. It's too much effort to obtain less-healthy options. Out of sight. Out of mouth.

The principle of "loss aversion" explains why it is more effective to tax unhealthy products than subsidize healthier alternatives.[444] High taxes on unhealthy items (like Mayor Bloomberg's repealed tax on sugary beverages in New York City) generate more health-conscious purchases (think water) than discounting those items. Avoiding the penalty (tax) and related loss aversion gets better results than simple discounts on healthy foods. Economists observe that taxing unhealthy products always reduces their consumption. Accordingly, cigarette taxes have reduced cigarette purchases significantly. It's why the beverage industry fought NYC's proposed sugar tax so fiercely. It would have worked.

Bounded Willpower recognizes that willpower is a limited resource. Once used, it requires time to replenish. As willpower diminishes, decision-making suffers. People have less capacity to override instinctive behaviors. Automatic rather than rational responses predominate. A short-term benefit ("that donut looks tasty") trumps longer-term goals ("must reduce sugar intake"). Diminished willpower also contributes to decision-making fatigue, reduced self-control and impulsive default-option behaviors.

To enhance bounded willpower's influence, stores like Walgreens employ reward programs to encourage healthier choices. Rewards trigger positive biochemical release and make people feel better about smarter choices. Health clubs use commitment contracts to reinforce willpower. People contract to make a charitable donation if they fail to reach a fitness goal. Loss aversion kicks in and provides added motivation to accomplish the goal. "Channel factors" (minor environmental adjustments) encourage desired behaviors. Colleges gives students maps to guide them toward free vaccinations. Using positive language to frame choices engenders more compliance. More people will use

---

443 https://www.thersa.org/discover/publications-and-articles/rsa-blogs/2013/02/increasing-organ-donation—but-not the way-you-think/
444 http://www.sciencedaily.com/releases/2010/02/100224142046.htm

condoms when described as 95 percent effective than when described as 5 percent defective. Like any muscle, willpower grows when exercised. Behavioral strategies that enhance willpower make it even stronger.

Finally, **Bounded Selfishness** recognizes that fairness governs most behavior. In repeated experiments, people from all countries and cultures punish unfair individuals even if the punishment comes at their own expense. A classic example is the two-person exercise where one person divides $10 and the other decides whether to accept the proposed split. Most people propose 50-50 or 60-40 splits and most counterparts accept that offer. Greedier participants offer 90-10 or 80-20 splits. In overwhelming numbers, counterparties reject those unfair offers, even though they forgo a small payment themselves. Bounded selfishness provides behavioral limits to acceptable actions.

Exploiting bounded selfishness enables paternalistic libertarians to design programs that reward altruism and encourage reciprocal behaviors. In 2007, Banner's Chief Administrative Officer Ron Bunnell and his wife, Barb Bunnell, participated in America's first altruistic kidney exchange program.[445] An altruistic volunteer, Matt Jones, whom they'd never met, donated his kidney to Barb Bunnell. Ron Bunnell then donated his kidney to Angela Heckman. The altruistic chain resulted in more than 20 kidney transplants. Fairness and reciprocity nudged individuals to honor their commitment even after their loved one had received a transplanted kidney. Establishing health-driven societal norms (e.g. smoking only outside) also reinforces desired behaviors. Human beings have large brains to navigate complex social environments. Fairness, altruism, reciprocity and societal norms are powerful conduits to encourage communal harmony. Behavioral science can use these deeply-held human instincts to nudge healthier behaviors.

Make It Fun. Make It Easy.
Americans know they need to eat smarter, smoke less and move more. Getting Americans to actually do these things requires reorienting

445 http://www.people.com/people/archive/article/0,,20325493,00.html

home, work and play environments. Emotional connection is essential. That's why it's easier to quit smoking with a friend. Convergence media is among a wave of disruptive, accessible technologies (kiosks, activity trackers, home monitors, decision aids) that gives consumers new tools to manage their health. Hip, user-friendly smartphones with powerful apps make behavioral changes fun while connecting participants to like-minded friends. Wellness-friendly work environments also encourage healthy living.

Psychologist B.J. Fogg runs the Persuasive Tech Lab at Stanford and is expert at designing strategies to alter behavior. Fogg believes the following three elements are essential for behavioral change: Motivation (high to low); Ability (easy to hard) and Triggers (natural and designed). When a desired behavior does not occur, one of these elements is missing. Fogg has assembled these elements in his Fogg Behavior Model (FBM) that incorporates three core motivators, six simplicity factors and three types of triggers. Behavior change requires Libertarian Paternalists to get specific (identify desired behaviors and outcomes), make it easy (simplicity changes behavior) and use the right triggers (no behavior change happens without a trigger). FBM provides a powerful framework for stimulating behavior change.[440] Within that context, here are several proven tactics for promoting healthier behaviors:

Make it Easy: Set achievable goals, take baby steps, make it cheap, make it fast and understandable;

Measure: Track food consumption and activity. Make healthy choices top of mind. Find ways to transmit data automatically to personal health records;

Celebrate Success: Applaud achievements in public and virtual ways. People have unlimited capacity for positive feedback. People will walk several flights of stairs to win virtual merit badges;

---

440 http://behaviormodel.org

Eliminate Negative Cues: Get the cookies out of the house; take a walk to beat the afternoon blahs;

Encourage Team Activities: Bind people in wellness activities, such as competitions, mutual commitments and coaching. Behavior change is always easier with a buddy; and

Calibrate Incentives: Offer positive and negative rewards. Make it fun, edgy and entertaining to complete a health assessment. Make it painful and expensive not to.

Making Wellness Cool

Thirty years ago, "tree hugger" was the derisive term applied to environmentalists. Today it's cool to be green. Markets love cool. Companies respond with products and services for cool customers. Hybrid cars, LEED-certified hotels, reusable water bottles and all manner of environmentally friendly products and services populate American commerce. The environmental movement changed attitudes and behaviors. A similar wellness movement is now underway. Americans are waking up to our national lifestyle challenge and the market is following with healthier foods, activity trackers, lifestyle management tools, entertainment and media attention.

Targeted and cool messaging works. Ask Texas. In 1985, the Texas Department of Transportation was spending $20 million a year to pick up beer bottles and other trash from the state's highways.[447] The biggest litterbugs were young men and traditional appeals weren't reaching them. Ad men Mike Blair and Tim McClure of GSD&M came up the slogan "Don't Mess with Texas" to persuade "bubbas in pickup trucks"[448] to stop littering. The slogan appeared on road signs along major highways, in television and radio commercials and in print advertisements. It worked. Between 1986 and 1990, litter on Texas highways decreased 72 percent.[449]

447 https://en.wikipedia.org/wiki/Don't_Mess_with_Texas
448 http://priceonomics.com/the-surprising-origins-of-dont-mess-with-texas/
449 Tim McClure and Roy Spence, *Don't Mess with Texas: The Story Behind the Legend*, Idea City Press, 2006,

Through similar messaging strategies, health advocates found that the yuck factor was more effective at encouraging hand washing among rural women in West Africa than education campaigns. Likewise, premature wrinkle warnings reduced tanning-bed usage among teenage girls substantially more than skin cancer education.

Human connection, the cool factor, heuristics, triggers and technology are smart tools that Libertarian Paternalists can employ to make it easier for people to make better lifestyle choices. It's best when people think that the behavior change is their idea. In many ways, using these strategies levels the playing field and gives wellness a fighting chance against sophisticated messaging from commercial enterprises. It needs to be as cool to eat a veggie burger as it is the Great American Thickburger. American health and wellness depend on it.

Wellness Heroes: Rebels with a Cause

Lost in macro-sector analysis are the personalities of individuals that change society—the people that really make a difference. Most healthcare professionals strive to make their products and services a little better. They pursue incremental improvements on existing systems, lowering costs and enhancing efficiency. They don't tilt at windmills. In contrast, "Wellness Heroes" want more than better products and services. A passion for fixing healthcare infuses their personal identities and daily activities. They're committed, often charismatic, change agents doing whatever it takes to make healthcare better.

These unique individuals are Rebels with a Cause, and they're at the vanguard of market-driven healthcare reform. Their visions, rhetoric and business models align with customer and societal demands for better, more affordable and convenient healthcare services. Above all, they want Americans to lead healthier, more productive lives. Ignore these rebels at your own peril. They're intent on tearing down America's underperforming, sickness-focused, activity-based, consumer-resistant healthcare system. They intend to replace it with products and services that provide real value to everyday people. They are transforming lives and reinventing how Americans think about health and wellness. They embody America's best hope for healthier, more productive and more humane communities.

Dan Buettner and The Blue Zones

Working with *National Geographic* scientists, author Dan Buettner began investigating the secrets of longevity. His work began as an interactive school program and morphed into a quest to discover and research the communities where people lived the longest. The team settled on the five places: Sardinia; Okinawa; the Adventist community in Loma Linda, California; the Nicoya Peninsula in Costa Rica; and the Greek island of Ikaria (Stamatis Maraitis' home). Buettner's observational research centered on finding common characteristics that enable people to live long, happy and healthy lives.

The preface to Buettner's first book, *The Blue Zones: 9 Lessons for Living Longer from the People Who've Lived the Longest*, tells the story of Sayoko Ogata. When Buettner met Ogata in 2000, she was a hard-charging Japanese executive working with Buettner's team in Okinawa. An interview in a tiny fishing village with a 99-year old woman named Ushi Ogimi changed Ogata's life. Ogimi was an energetic big-hearted woman who made everyone around her happy. For the rest of the trip, Ogata thought about Ogimi. In the following passage, she captures the power of Ogimi's lifestyle:

> *the simplicity of her life, how she made people around her feel good, how she was not worried about getting something in the future or sad that she had missed something in the past. Gradually I was starting to think, I want this to be my goal.*

Ogata realized she wanted to be like Ogimi, so she quit her Tokyo job, moved to a rural community got married, had a couple kids and now leads a simple, reflective life. She's not "chasing the carrot anymore." She follows Buettner's 9 centenarian lessons:

1. Move Naturally
2. Eat 20 percent Less

3. Eat Plants
4. Drink Red Wine
5. Live with Purpose
6. Take Time to Relax
7. Belong to a Spiritual Community
8. Put Family First
9. Emphasize Social Connection[450]

Buettner has established Blue Zone communities in more than 20 cities and has dramatically improved the health of over 5 million Americans to date. The goal is to optimize local environments for health and wellness. Strategies include better walkability, healthier foods, increased social connectivity and lifestyle coaching.[451] Go Dan!

Colin Campbell and The China Study

One of America's best selling nutrition books, *The China Study*,[452] underscores the numerous health benefits of plant-based diets and the dangers associated with animal protein consumption.[453] Author T. Colin Campbell, the Jacob Gould Schurman Professor Emeritus of Nutritional Biochemistry at Cornell University, is a world-renowned advocate for plant-based diets. His son, Thomas M. Campbell III, with whom he co-authored the book, is a practicing physician. The Campbells are empiricists. They apply science to reach conclusions on a controversial topic: the relationship between animal-based diets and chronic disease.

Their book is based on the most comprehensive epidemiologic study of nutrition and health undertaken to date.[454] The China-Cornell-Oxford Study, conducted in association with the Chinese Academy of

---

450 *The Blue Zones*, Dan Buettner

451 https://www.bluezones.com/speaking/dan-buettner/

452 T. Colin Campbell, Ph.D. and Thomas M. Campbell II, *The China Study*, 2004, First BenBella Books.

453 http://wellandgood.com/2011/09/23/china-study-cheat-sheet-10-things-you-need-to-know/

454 *Ibid.*

Preventative Medicine,[455] involved 6,500 adults in 65 rural counties in China. It also analyzed mortality rates of 50 families chosen at random in each county. Colin Campbell was a lead scientist on the study. Cornell University, the University of Oxford and the government of China funded the project. Their research reported 8,000 statistically significant associations between lifestyle, animal-protein consumption and disease variables.[456] Their findings are well-documented, sobering and controversial.

The China Study also narrates Colin Campbell's personal journey toward a healthier lifestyle. Growing up on a dairy farm in upstate New York, Campbell was a strong initial believer in the benefits of the traditional American diet. He studied veterinary medicine and ultimately earned his Ph.D. at Cornell University in nutrition, biochemistry and microbiology. Campbell's research led him to the conclusion that animal-protein consumption is a leading cause of cancer and heart disease. The vituperative negative reaction by many to his scientific findings on nutrition surprised Campbell but shouldn't have. His research challenges fundamental tenets of the dairy, meat and processed food industries. As chronicled in the last chapter, Bill Clinton and millions like him are following Campbell's nutritional advice and leading remarkably healthy lives.

Campbell has consumed a plant-based diet since the early 1990s. Well into his 80s, Campbell is the epitome of good health, writes prolifically and travels the country tirelessly speaking on diet, nutrition and health. Go Colin!

Esther Dyson and The Way to Wellville

Esther Dyson is a Swiss-born, Harvard-educated journalist, philanthropist, investor and commentator. *Time Magazine* named her one of 10 most influential women in technology.[457] She is a highly successful angel investor and is using her investment knowledge to spearhead an inno-

455 https://en.wikipedia.org/wiki/China%E2%80%93Cornell%E2%80%93Oxford_Project

456 *Ibid.*

457 https://www.google.com/search?q=esther+dyson&ie=utf-8&oe=utf-8

vative program, The Way to Wellville, to build healthier communities. Its tag line is "five places. five metrics. five years." HICCup, the non-profit organization Dyson founded to manage the initiative, invited applications from mid-sized cities nationwide to spend five years immersed in health and wellness activities while sharing experiences, results and insights. Dyson and her team will measure success based on specific communitywide and individual health metrics.[458] Forty-two communities from 26 states applied and in August 2014, HICCup selected the following five communities to participate: Clatsop County, Oregon; Lake County, California; Muskegon, Michigan; Niagara Falls, New York and Spartanburg, South Carolina. The program launched in 2015 and now generates regular reports and loads of data. They're still developing the five key metrics.[459]

Dyson's approach updates traditional place-based efforts to improve local health through community movements.[460] Instead, HICCup runs like a venture fund and uses similar terminology. Dyson's team is using a portfolio approach to test multiple strategies and tactics. It employs accelerators to turbocharge results and share learning. The team describes Wellville as an "open source, evidence-generating" project with a "central data repository." HiCCup employs a sophisticated media strategy to raise awareness and attract partners/investors. Like all angel investors, Dyson knows there will be failures but expects successes.

Dyson hopes that American health, and not just the healthcare system, will improve as Wellville chronicles and operationalizes winning strategies. She wants the Wellville project to inspire participants, generate useful data and share "lessons learned" broadly.[461] The Way to Wellville is a bottom-up, evidenced-based, self-learning, market-oriented initiative that may redefine and transform urban living. Go Esther!

---

458 http://www.forbes.com/sites/robwaters/2014/07/25/finding-the-way-to-wellville-small-cities-compete-to-get-healthier-in-esther-dysons-latest-venture/

459 http://www.hiccup.co/challenge/

460 http://www.forbes.com/sites/robwaters/2014/07/25/finding-the-way-to-wellville-small-cities-compete-to-get-healthier-in-esther-dysons-latest-venture

461 Ibid.

Rushika Fernandopulle and Iora Health

With undergraduate, medical and public policy degrees from Harvard, Dr. Rushika Fernandopulle initially believed flaws in American healthcare resulted from system failures. He sought to fix these system problems as a practitioner, consultant and investor before concluding American healthcare needed a new, built-from-scratch operating model.

Fernandopulle launched Iora Health in 2011 to reinvent and disrupt primary care delivery in the same way Southwest reinvented and disrupted the airline industry. Iora's model focuses on the whole person, treats root causes of disease and emphasizes wellness. The company's tag line says it all, "We're Restoring Humanity to Healthcare." Fernandopulle believes strong personal relationships between care providers and members will engender trust, promote wellness and facilitate coordinated care delivery. Everything is different at Iora: no fee-for-service payment; doctors tailoring services to patients and communities; a self-built electronic medical record; and care teams consisting of doctors, nurses and health coaches.

Iora's product is elegant in its simplicity. Members have access to salaried physicians, coaches and behavioral health professionals who coordinate any required specialty care. Co-insurance disappears. Full coverage of health insurance expenses begins after customers pay their program deductible. Only prescription drugs require member co-pays. All Iora members receive the following benefits:

- Unlimited, no-charge primary care visits at Iora Health Centers;

- A dedicated, personal care team available by phone, e-mail, text or video chat;

- 24/7 access to Iora Health doctors;

- Access to a national network of 850,000 physicians, medical professionals and hospitals;

- Prescription drug coverage, online ordering and optional home delivery; and

- Complimentary wellness classes including nutrition, yoga, cooking and overall fitness.

Five years and $50-plus million in raised capital later, Iora operates in 11 markets and is expanding rapidly. Customers love the service. Care providers love the operating model. Providers, payers, employers and unions want Iora as their primary care partner. Offering holistic health and wellness services to engaged members who trust their care teams may be the way America overcomes its ineffective, high-cost sickcare system. By providing services everyone wants, Iora is truly reinventing primary care services. Fernandopulle has a big vision and is betting big on rela-tionship-based care delivery. Iora is value-creation in action. Go Rushika!

Suparna Ferreira and Bienestar

Suparna Ferreira left her cushy planning job at Sutter Health to form Bienestar[162] in 2013. Having made her own journey to better health, Ferreira yearned to create a company that did the same for others, par-ticularly low-income individuals. Under her leadership, Bienestar has developed a highly effective, experiential, community-based, scalable program that changes lives. Despite not speaking Spanish Ferreira moved to Guadalajara, Mexico to launch Bienestar's programming. Guadalajara provided a low-cost site to refine the company's train-the-trainer model and would benefit enormously from Bienestar's services.

Obesity levels in Mexico are exceptionally high. Bienestar has graduated four classes and is launching more. I attended Bienestar's first graduation ceremony. There is nothing more powerful than wit-nessing regular people, most afflicted with chronic disease, gain the knowledge, tools and confidence to tackle their healthcare challenges. Bienestar plans to expand into the U.S. in 2016. Go Suparna!

---

162 http://nuestrobienestar.org/index.php?pg=Home&loc=

Dean Ornish, MD and Lifestyle Management

Roughly 90 percent of cardiac-bypass-surgery patients revert back to unhealthy behaviors within two years.[463] Nearly dying isn't enough to stimulate permanent lifestyle change. Dr. Dean Ornish does not accept this failure rate. A physician and founder of the nonprofit Preventive Medicine Research Institute in Sausalito, California, Ornish also serves as clinical professor of medicine at the University of California, San Francisco.[464] Through his writing, research and clinical programs, Ornish has helped countless individuals undertake "comprehensive lifestyle changes that improve chronic conditions and transform lives."[465]

Ornish's program incorporates diet, exercise and other lifestyle modifications undertaken within a supportive and nurturing community. Ornish believes individuals must experience the benefits of lifestyle change to make those positive changes permanent. Ornish notes, "When we become more aware of how powerfully our choices in diet and lifestyle affect us, for better and worse, then we can make different ones. When you make healthy choices, you feel better quickly. This allows us to connect the dots between what we do and how we feel. Feeling so much better, so quickly, re-frames the reason for changing from fear of dying to joy of living."[466] The Ornish program has been proven to turn on genes that enhance health while turning off genes that promote heart disease and several cancers.[467] Recognizing the Ornish program's therapeutic benefits, Medicare began covering its cost in 2011 through a new Intensive Cardiac Rehabilitation reimbursement category. Go Dean!

Mike Roizen and the Cleveland Clinic

In November 2007, Cleveland Clinic CEO Delos "Toby" Cosgrove hired best-selling author (*Real Age*) and wellness expert Dr. Michael Roizen

---

463   http://www.fastcompany.com/52717/change-or-die
464   http://deanornish.com
465   http://deanornish.com/about/
466   http://ornishspectrum.com/proven-program/
467   *Ibid.*

to become the nation's first chief wellness officer. Roizen's appointment confirmed the Cleveland Clinic's commitment to the health business as well as the sickness business. Under Roizen's leadership, the clinic inaugurated its Wellness Institute in January 2008 and began an expansive campaign to engage employees, patients and communities in healthy lifestyle choices. The Wellness Institute's programs focus on stress reduction, smoking cessation, movement and nutrition.

Job 1 was improving the health of the Cleveland Clinic's employees. Roizen used multiple, comprehensive strategies to build a sustainable wellness culture that improves health, strengthens communities and reduces hospital admissions. They changed vending machines to healthier options, revised menus, went smoke-free on campus, offered free health club memberships and yoga classes, invested in stress reduction and constructed walking paths. It took years, but the Clinic grabbed headlines in early 2015 when it finally kicked McDonald's out of its food court.[468]

The wellness-oriented changes Roizen has instituted are paying dividends. As of 2013, clinic employees had collectively lost over 330,000 pounds and the clinic had saved $15 million in employee health costs. The institute collects biometric data on 97 percent of the clinic's workforce. Clinic employees who achieve key health benchmarks (the five normal: blood pressure, cholesterol, blood glucose, body mass index and tobacco residue in urine) receive a $2,000 health insurance rebate. Benefits of the clinic's wellness initiatives have spread to the larger community. For example, Cleveland has one of the nation's lowest smoking rates. The institute demonstrates that when companies embrace wellness, better employee health follows. Go Mike!

Tryggvi Thorgeirsson and Sidekick Health

As a medical doctor and graduate student at the Harvard School of Public Health, Tryggvi Thorgeirsson became fascinated with behavioral economics and its potential applications in health and wellness. To

---

468 http://money.cnn.com/2015/08/19/news/companies/cleveland-clinic-mcdonalds/
http://www.cleveland.com/healthfit/index.ssf/2015/08/cleveland_clinic_closing_mcdonalds_in_its_food_court.html

deepen his understanding, Thorgeirsson co-wrote a scholarly article[469] on behavioral economics and lifestyle interventions for a March 2013 issue of the *American Journal of Preventive Medicine*. Daniel Kahneman's research on System 1 (intuitive) and System 2 (deliberative) cognition has been particularly relevant in Thorgeirsson's research.

Upon returning to his native Iceland, Thorgeirsson realized that most wellness applications rely on System 2 thinking while System 1 thinking governs most behavior. Building on this insight, Thorgeirsson launched the company GoodlLifeMe featuring Sidekick,[470] a playful mobile app that employs sophisticated System 1 motivational techniques to engage users in "fun, friendly and personalized" wellness activities.

Sidekick is catching on in Europe and Asia while undergoing rigorous testing. Sweden's largest occupational health organization is employing Sidekick with promising early results. A large U.S. retailer is evaluating the product for an expected trial. GoodLifeMe plans to launch Sidekick in the U.S. during 2016. Wellness may never be the same. Go Tryggvi!

Take a moment to celebrate these eight Wellness Heroes and those like them. Respect their commitment. Learn their stories. Spread the word. These "rebels with a cause" will nudge America toward becoming a better, fairer, more productive and healthier place to live, work and play.

Demand-Driven Change Generates Super-Hero Results

As American society strives to build healthier communities, it confronts nature's cruel trick (human beings aren't build for modern life) and an unholy trinity of processed food, industrialized agriculture and a healthcare system that treats symptoms of chronic disease instead of its root causes. These realities are mutually reinforcing and diminish America's overall health status. They're making Americans sicker, more isolated and less productive.

---

469 http://www.ajpmonline.org/article/S0749-3797%2812%2900757-X/abstract
470 http://www.sidekickhealth.com/

Lifestyle transformation is the only way to reverse these negative trends. Consumers influence market dynamics with every purchase they make, every meal they eat and every activity they pursue. Demand-driven reform generates super-hero results. The good news for Americans is that better lifestyle decisions (and purchases that support them) will make us happier, help us feel better, give us more energy and lead to more productivity. As more Americans embrace healthier lifestyle decisions, the market will respond with better and more available products and services for health-oriented buyers.

Improving the health and wellness of America's communities is this generation's greatest challenge. Since chronic disease disproportionately afflicts low-income communities, failure to reverse negative lifestyle trends threatens America's quality of life, prosperity and sense of fair play. Innovation and rising to big challenges are American hallmarks. Epigenetics, behavioral psychology, cool technology and social connection are powerful tools for improving individual and community wellness. We should use them all. It's time to NUDGE America and Americans toward wellness. It will make our country better, our communities more prosperous and, most importantly, our people healthier.

CONCLUSION

NOT "TOO BIG TO FAIL"

*When the music stops, in terms of liquidity, things will
be complicated. But as long as the music is playing,
you've got to get up and dance. We're still dancing.*[471]
CHUCK PRINCE, CITIGROUP CEO, JULY 9, 2007

*The difficulty lies not so much in developing
new ideas as in escaping from old ones.*
JOHN MAYNARD KEYNES

*It ain't what you don't know that gets you into trouble.
It's what you know for sure that just ain't so.*
MARK TWAIN

---

471 http://www.ft.com/cms/s/0/80e2987a-2e50-11dc-821c-0000779fd2ac.html. Said to
a *Financial Times* reporter in response to a question regarding concerns about a potential
downturn in the leveraged finance market for sub-prime mortgages. Prince and Citigroup
eventually "danced" right off a cliff.

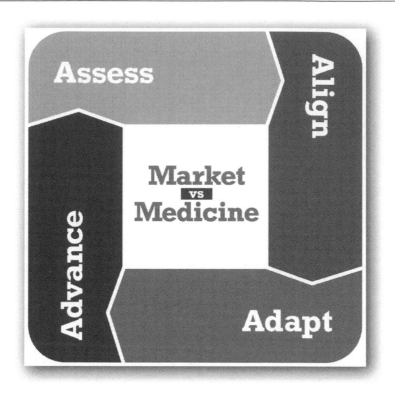

In mid-January 2016, the Academy of Motion Picture Arts and Sciences released its 2015 Academy Award nominees. Among the nominees for Best Picture was *The Big Short*, the film version of Michael Lewis' best-selling book on the financial instruments that turbocharged America's housing bubble and led to the 2008 financial crisis. The book's full title is *The Big Short: Inside the Doomsday Machine.* The doomsday machine refers to Wall Street's creation and massive application of highly profitable collateralized debt obligations (CDOs). The most-traded CDOs packaged individual mortagages into tiered-debt instruments.

Financial engineering does not create value, it redistributes risk. With mortage-backed CDOs, the underlying mortgages were oftern so bad that they pushed AAA-rated debt instruments into default. In one movie scene, an investor looking to short (e.g. bet against) the housing market interviews a Miami stripper who owns five houses with five mortgages. The mortgage companies never checked her income. When Wall Street ran out of real mortgages to package together, they created synthetic CDOs to keep the doomsday machine rolling.

In the mid-2000s almost everyone believed America's inflated housing market would continue rising in value. No one imagined it could collapse. Mania set in. Greed proliferated. The stakes and risk spiraled upward. *The Big Short* profiles a handful of people who saw through the mirage. This group included a few powerful insiders like research analyst Meredith Whitney. More often than not, these contrarians were marginal players like Scion Capital founder Michael Bury, a former neurologist with Asperger's Syndrome.

There are eerie parallels between the behavior of the big banks leading up to the financial crisis and the current behavior of incumbent health companies wrestling with healthcare transformation. Wall Street's biggest failings resulted from hubris, denial and limited imagination. The banks thought they had conquered financial risk and placed too much trust in their analytic models. Wall Street professionals simply could not imagine catastrophic market failure and willfully ignored signals of profound weakness in the housing sector.

Hubris, denial and limited imagination infect many health company executives today. They overestimate their ability to control market forces and simply cannot imagine massive restructuring of healthcare's supply and demand relationships.

The most disturbing element of the financial crisis was the extent to which mainstream participants, who should have known better, participated in CDOs' creation, validation and massive distribution. This included not only the Wall Street banks, but also the rating agencies, law firms, accounting firms, bond insurers, credit providers, regulators and financial advisors. Their collective support amplified the housing bubble's magnitude. Their professional conduct was technically legal but morally irresponsible. Even as mortgage default rates increased, Wall Street banks kept peddling CDOs to investors and to themselves—right up to the point they went off the cliff, taking the global economy with them. In healthcare's transforming marketplace, many health companies are exhibiting similar lemming-like behavior.

Failure of Imagination: Health Companies and U.S. Healthcare System Transformation

Like 2005 was for the housing industry, 2015 was a great year for health companies. Healthcare accounted for 18 percent (almost 500,000) of the country's 2.6 million new jobs. New hospital employment exploded to 172,200 from 42,400 in 2014.[472] Health systems are building again.[473]/[474] After several years of below 3 percent annual growth, U.S. healthcare spending is now growing at more than 5 percent per year and total U.S. healthcare expenditure exceeds $3 trillion.[475] Thunder follows lightning. As providers add new labor and facility costs, they raise prices. As provider costs increase, so do insurance premiums. Not surprisingly, health insurance plans pursued 20 to 40-plus percent rate increases for 2016.[476]

---

472 http://healthleadersmedia.com/page-1/HR-324438/Healthcare-Job-Growth-Set-Records-in-2015

473 http://www.modernhealthcare.com/article/20150721/NEWS/150729959

474 *Ibid.*

475 http://healthleadersmedia.com/page-1/FIN-323375/US-Healthcare-Spending-Hits-3-Trillion-Mark

476 http://www.nytimes.com/2015/07/04/us/health-insurance-companies-seek-big-rate-increases-for-2016.html

While commentators often characterize payer-provider negotiations as zero sum (i.e. one wins at the other's expense), both payers and providers prosper when health insurance premiums increase. Significant payer income originates from self-insured employers as a percentage of administered claims. More claims translate into more income. The Affordable Care Act's 15 percent limitation on profits further incentivizes health insurance companies to increase top-line revenues. Fifteen percent of a bigger number translates into bigger profits.

Providers exhibit reciprocal behavior. Activity-based payments shape treatment patterns. More is better. Higher payment is better. Providers distribute facilities and services to maximize reimbursement payments. Health system revenues and income increase with higher treatment volume and greater commercial insurance payment. The result is more money flowing into the healthcare sector without meaningful improvement in health status or treatment outcomes. Healthcare wins. America loses.

As revenue flows back into healthcare, there's an audible sigh of relief coming from health companies. Their old playbooks still work. Far too many are doubling down on activity-based payment while giving lip service to value-based delivery. Their financial success, however, relies upon a rickety and artificial economic model (supply-driven demand) that pays for volume, not value. Like Wall Street with CDOs, healthcare's over-reliance on fee-for-service payment reflects greedy, short-term thinking. Fee-for-service medicine is healthcare's doomsday machine. It's a cancer destroying the integrity of American healthcare.

Fee-for-service medicine encourages overtreatment, distorts medical records (to maximize reimbursement payment), underfunds behavioral health, discourages preventive care and disengages patients from medical decision-making. It's excessively expensive, fragments care delivery and delivers suboptimal outcomes. It erodes trust between patients and care providers. Fee-for-service medicine is inflating an acute-care bubble just like CDOs inflated America's housing bubble. The healthcare market is overdue for correction.

Healthcare's metaphor about the dock and boat is overused and increasingly irrelevant. With one foot on the fee-for-service dock and one foot in the value-based-care boat, healthcare executives wait for the right time to jump toward value as the boat pulls away from the dock. Continuing to straddle the volume-value divide, however, is an implicit admission that health companies tolerate suboptimal treatment outcomes to generate incremental revenues. Somewhat tongue-in-cheek, MultiScale CEO Jim Harding says there's a secret room in every health company with a flashing OPTIMIZE REVENUE neon sign. Metaphorically, that room dictates too many care-management decisions in American healthcare.

Here's the rub: America is pushing back. The American people want, deserve and are demanding better, more convenient and compassionate healthcare at lower prices. Thousands of companies are pursuing business models that give American consumers better healthcare services. The old playbook still has force, but its magic is evaporating. Following the old playbook also carries embedded danger. The wider the gap between artificial supply-driven prices and competitive prices, the greater the opportunity for competitors to steal away customers with higher-value services.

Value-based competitors are fighting for market share the American way—by delivering better services to customers at lower prices. Incumbent health companies have a choice. They can continue to use the old playbook, milk the system for ever-higher payments and risk losing market relevance. Alternatively, they can leap toward value, embrace customers and help fix America's broken healthcare system. Here's my advice to health company executives: Don't act like Wall Street bankers. Put customers first. Make quality Job 1. Focus on value. Resist easy short-term gains. Strive for long-term value. It's the right thing to do. It's also the smart business strategy. Everybody wins when health companies deliver better care at lower prices in customer-friendly venues.

Not "Too Big to Fail"

There is a major difference between the Wall Street banks and healthcare industry incumbents. With the people's money, the U.S. government rescued the big banks to keep the economy moving and stimulate recovery. It tasted bad, but the country had to do it. Despite consuming almost 20 percent of the U.S. economy, healthcare is a fragmented industry with no essential companies. There will be no government bailouts. Instead, there will be greater transparency and accountability. Consequently, no healthcare company is immune from market forces. Healthcare companies delivering value will differentiate, gain market share and earn the trust of American consumers. Those that don't will fade away.

In his autobiography, German physicist and Nobel laureate Max Plank made this depressing observation about advancing science:

A new scientific truth does not triumph by convincing its opponents and making them see the light, but rather because its opponents eventually die, and a new generation grows up that is familiar with it.[477]

Entrenched beliefs don't relinquish their prominence easily. After all, the Catholic Church put Galileo on trial for asserting the Earth revolved around the sun. Exhibiting the same fierce resistence, many traditional health companies fight against value-based healthcare services. They may as well be fighting against gravity. As disruption roils U.S. healthcare and value-driven companies proliferate, entrenched incumbents will disappear one funeral at a time.

Restructuring healthcare is good for America. Shifting resources out of acute care services into better primary and preventive care will improve health, wellness and productivity. While fixing the country's broken healthcare system is essential, America's greatest challenge is reversing negative lifestyle behaviors and enabling individual Americans to make smarter lifestyle choices. Healthcare companies must be a big part of the solution. This requires them to shift emphasis from treating chronic disease's symptoms to treating its root causes. They must exhibit a greater willingness to consider alternative therapies and partner with others to advance community wellness.

John Maynard Keynes observed, "The difficulty lies not so much in developing new ideas as in escaping from old ones." This is certainly

---

477 Max Plank, *Scientific Autobiography and Other Papers*, pages 33-34, 1949

true in healthcare. Old thinking and revenue-first business models stymy progress. There are, however, timeless business truths that progressive healthcare companies are embracing: Businesses exist to serve customers; Customers shape industries through their purchasing decisions; Business must align operations with marketing to win customers' trust; and, most importantly, Value Rules!

Acknowledgments

After making the decision to leave investment banking, I hired professional coach Cam Anderson from Toronto to help me sort through post-banking professional opportunities. Or so I thought. Instead, Cam forced me to think through what I really wanted to do and identify what obstacles were obstructing me. Tough work. The most important exercise required my constructing a 2-by-2 matrix to evaluate specific opportunities. The challenge was to pick the "x" and "y" axes. After much introspection, my axes became "impact" and "enjoyment." I use that matrix regularly to make professional decisions. At our last session, Cam insisted I should write a book. He was certain I needed to share my perspective on healthcare reform. I wasn't so sure. He persisted and I ultimately agreed. Four hundred-plus pages later, Cam was clearly right. There would be no *Market vs. Medicine (MvM)* without Cam Anderson.

During my Peace Corps service in Liberia, I often heard the African proverb that it takes a village to raise a child. In the almost two years since I began writing *MvM*, it's become very clear that it requires a team and a robust professional network to do justice to this book's core theme – that market-driven activity by companies striving to deliver better healthcare outcomes at lower prices more conveniently will transform and elevate America's broken healthcare system.

Let's start with the *MvM* team. We have a great one. Another Canadian, Keith Hollihan, served as the *MvM* project manager. Keith is a free-spirited, intellectually curious, gifted writer and ridiculous hockey fan. His greatest moment was shaking hands in a gym shower at age 17 with Wayne Gretzky. Keith brought discipline, dogged determination, inspiring insights and good humor to our creative process. Despite holding down a full-time day job, Jessica Elin spent countless hours researching, conducting interviews and writing. Although not a healthcare expert, Jessica embraced our cause and unearthed nugget after nugget of valuable insights and examples. Growing up in South Bend, Jessica became a ridiculous Notre Dame fan. Except for time carved out to watch their football and basketball games, she seemed to dedicate all her enormous energies and talents to bringing *MvM* to fruition. Lalitha Ramachandran is the glue that binds our collective efforts together, particularly since team members all live and work in different cities. She managed to do all this while getting married, earning a work visa, moving to New York and then moving to Boston. Lalitha is always in high spirits, eager for new challenges and dedicated to building our small company, 4sight Health.

Lalitha has also been the bridge to the professional service companies we engaged to produce, market and distribute *MvM*. This includes Spry Digital (incredible branding and design work including the book cover), Global IP Law Group (securing trademarks and dealing with the Indian company that copied our website address) and most importantly Gini Dietrich and her team at Arment-Dietrich, our remarkably creative PR team that designed and helped execute our *MvM* brand ambassador program, social media engagement strategies and website optimization efforts. Nobody does it better.

Our final team member was copy editor Linda Wilson. Great copy editors are a rare commodity, particularly ones with healthcare expertise. Copy editors have the granular focus to catch every single misspelling, punctuation discrepancy and out-of-place font while keeping a book's big-picture flow at top of mind. Linda caught every mistake and multiple repeated paragraphs. She also offered numerous suggestions to improve *MvM's* narrative. I have no idea how she does this, but our error-prone *MvM* team is enormously grateful for Linda's skillful copy editing. She's made *MvM* clearer and better. I actually thought I'd found one phrasing error she'd missed. It gave me a momentary pleasure. No one is perfect. Turned out I was wrong. Former *Modern Healthcare* editor Dave Burda introduced both Linda and Keith Hollihan to me. For this great service, I owe Dave multiple beers. We thank Clive Pyne from Clive Pyne Book Indexing for his great job in putting the book index together.

The *Market vs. Medicine* team enjoys life, thinks out-of-the-box, focuses on what's important and gets the job done. We all embrace *MvM's* larger mission to make American healthcare better. This gets us up in the morning and keeps us going through long days and nights. I couldn't be more thankful for their support, effort, professionalism and friendship.

Now the network. Cautionary warning: it's big.

Let's start with the Health Management Academy. I've been a member and participant in Gary Bisbee's and Sherrie Jones' visionary industry forum almost from its inception in the late 1990s. The Academy regularly assembles marquee health system leaders and industry representatives for in-depth exploration of events, innovations and strategies shaping U.S. healthcare. Through the years, I've gained countless insights, developed great friendships and witnessed tangible improvement in health company operations. It's been exciting to contribute to the collective wisdom that emerges from committed professional engagement. As I was leaving investment banking two years ago, the Academy welcomed me as their first "Author-in-Residence" and eased my transition out of banking into thought leadership, strategy and venture investing. For this and so many other reasons, *Market vs. Medicine* caries the Health Management Academy Press label. Thank you Gary and Sherrie.

Next, I'd like to recognize several enlightened health systems and health system leaders. Top of the list are Banner Health and Fairview Health Services. I was present at Banner's creation as its investment banker in 1999 and have witnessed its emergence into one of the nation's great health companies. *MvM's* chapter 11 chronicles Banner's rise to greatness. Banner's senior team and board, including John Hensing, Dennis Dahlen, Dave Bixby, Wil Carden and Ron Creasman, were remarkable in helping us understand and narrate their story. In particular, I want to single out Banner's CEO Peter Fine and Chief Administrative Officer Ron Bunnell. They were extremely generous with their time, candid with their observations and insightful on their company's evolution.

It's hard to be a native Minnesotan and not be a fan of Fairview and the University of Minnesota. I led Fairview's investment banking team for almost a decade, but didn't truly comprehend the company's operating complexity until serving as an advisor during Fairview's 2012-2013 merger discussions with Sanford Health. Blending academic and community-based operations is a heroic undertaking. Operating in the advanced Twin Cities marketplace, Fairview's leaders embrace the challenge of moving to value-based care and have the scars to show for it. Many current and former Fairview leaders are great friends and dedicated change agents. These include Dan Anderson, Mark Dixon, Kim Faust, Jim Fox, Patrick Herson, Dave Leach, Chuck Mooty, Dave Murphy and Gordy Alexander. I want to single out three younger, gifted and fearless leaders: Dan Fromm; Mark Hansberry and Brent Asplin. Like many in their generation, they understand the current system is not sustainable, fear it could collapse on their watch and are pro-actively working to transform it from the inside. Dan, Mark and Brent repeatedly take professional risks to advance value-based care. I admire their courage and the courage of their like-minded peers. American healthcare can't advance without dedicated professionals, like them, committed to better outcomes at lower costs.

Without going into extensive detail, I'd like to recognize the following current and former health company executives for their accomplishment, friendship and inspiration: Lars Houman, Don Jernigan and Terry Shaw from Adventist Health System; Dominic Nakis, Scott Powder, Lee Sacks and Bill Santulli from Advocate Health Care; Duncan Gallagher from Allina; Tony Speranzo and Kathy Arbuckle from Ascension Health; Gail Hanson and Nick Turkel from Aurora Health Care; Denny Herrick and Nick Vitale from Beaumont Health; Kevin Roberts from BJC Healthcare; Paula Noble from Children's Memorial; Tom Corrigan from Christiana Care; Jay Herron, Peter Maddox and Tom Royer from CHRISTUS Health; David Brown, Steve Glass, Tony Helton, Mike Harrington, Ann Huston, George Mateyo, Mike Roizen and Peter Volas from the Cleveland Clinic; Dave Eager (former Peace Corps Volunteer) from Dallas Children's; Michael Blaszyk and Lisa Zuckerman from Dignity Health; David Okabe and Ray Vara from Hawaii Pacific Health; Jonathan Perlin from HCA, Jamie Caillouette, Bob Gorab and Dereesa Reid from Hoag Orthopedic Institute; Ann Carr, Mike Cottrell and Stephanie McCutcheon from Hospital Sisters Health System; Clay Ashdown, David Dirks, Brent James and Bert Zimmerli from Intermountain Healthcare; Trent Green and Linda Hoff from Legacy Health System; Lynn Britton and Shannon Sock from Mercy; Pete McCanna and Omer Sultan from Northwestern Medicine; Lynn Eickholt Peter Markell and Debra Sloan from Partners HealthCare; David Brown, Mike Butler, Rod Hochman and Amy Compton-Phillips from Providence Health and Services; Peter Butler and Larry Goodman from Rush University Medical Center; Kelby Krabbenhoft and Dave Link from Sanford Health; Dan Gross, Rick LeMoine, Mike Murphy and Ann Pumpian from Sharp Healthcare; Rick Afable from St. Joseph Hoag Health; Bill Thompson and Kris Zimmer from SSM Health Care; Keith Pitts from Tenet Healthcare; Mark Johnson, Bill Leaver, Matthew Kirschner and Kevin Vermeer from Unity Point Health; and Brad Bond, Fred Rothstein, Paul Tait and Tom Zenty from University Hospitals Health System.

Several academic colleagues, most notably Nancy Kane and Zeke Emanuel, merit special recognition. Nancy and I first met in the late 1980s when she was an under-appreciated faculty member at the Harvard School of Public Health and I was a very green investment banker. We wrote a case study, became great friends and have collaborated on numerous speaking and writing projects. Now an eminent Associate Dean at HSPH, Nancy is a passionate, knowledgeable and insightful advocate for healthcare reform. We don't always agree, but the conversations are always energetic, high-spirited and interesting. Zeke and I met a few years ago, became quick friends and have travelled the country together visiting health companies Zeke describes as "practicing 2020 medicine today." His deep regulatory and practice expertise and my market and business knowledge complement one another. Sparks fly when we discuss healthcare. It's great fun. David Meltzer is an accomplished academic, skilled physician and great friend who juggles more than any human should at the University of Chicago School of Medicine. I tested out many of *MvM's* core concepts at the Dartmouth Institute in 2014. If it could play there, it could play anywhere. Elliott Fisher, Bob Hanson, Ellen Meara, Jonathan Skinner and the legendary Jack Wennberg listened, provided constructive feedback and encouraged my literary journey. Let's see if they invite me back. My great friend, frequent author, sometime collaborator and erratic golf partner, Charlie Wheelan, bridges Dartmouth and UChicago. Charlie keeps plugging away and his example is a constant reminder of the tenacity required to be an accomplished writer.

I work closely with two organizations, Cain Brothers and Leavitt Partners, that have deep healthcare expertise, powerful analytics and high-performance service platforms. Cain Brothers CEO Rob Fraiman and I attended Colgate together. Rob is the best healthcare investment banker I know. Rob and his partners (Carsten Beith, Dan Cain, Jim Cain, Bart Plank and Rhett Thurman among many others) have built an expansive practice across the spectrum of non-profit healthcare, corporate finance, funding and strategic advisory services. The 4sight Health team learns something new from Cain Brothers every time we undertake thought leadership projects together.

Under the expert guidance of former Health and Human Services Secretary Michael Leavitt and CEO Rich McKeown along with their firm's leadership team (Andrew Croshaw, Brett Graham, David Smith,

Susan Winckler and Vince Ventimiglia among others), Leavitt Partners provides unique perspectives on the evolving healthcare marketplace through focused roundtables, cutting-edge research and unique analytics. I'm particularly impressed by the breadth of expertise and multiple perspectives Leavitt Partners can convene to explore topical healthcare issues. Participating in their forums has expanded my understanding of the insurance marketplace, governmental regulation, public and private exchanges and organizational governance.

Nathan Bays, Gaurov Dayal, Suparna Ferreira, John Koster, Dan Kruger, Matt Wilson and Brett Wysel have collaborated with me on thought leadership commentaries which have found their way into *MVM*. Several colleagues and friends have offered invaluable insights throughout my writing journey. These include my Harvard Kennedy School "kitchen cabinet" of Deb Oyer and Tom Weeks (my inspiration for the boxer doctor on *MvM's* cover – I really did have that strange recurring dream) along with Jim Borovsky, Fred Gaines, Karen Handmaker, Gordon McLeod, Bart Mitchell and Jay Walder.

Other very helpful friends and colleagues include Mark Achler, Chuck Addair, John Adractas, Hal Andrews, Martin Arrick, Dave Atchison, Tim Barry, Bryan Becker, Bruce Bendix, Dave Berten, Jacob Best, Gerry Biala, Anjali Bissell, William Bissell, Jim Blake, Dennis Brimhall, Jeff Bohnson, Marshall Bouton, Richard Braemer, Irene Brown, Peter Bulgarelli, David Burik, Pat Cahill, Penny Caldecott, Brion Carroll, Paul Alexander Clark, Bill Claus, Dave Chase, Lew Collens, Steve Collens, Lisa Conley, Jake Crampton, David Crane, Hal Dasekind, Daniel Diermeier, Marilyn Diamond, Stuart Diamond, Terry Diamond, Eric d'Indy, Doug Doestch, Doug Doolittle, Jim Elrod, Rushika Fernandopulle, Michael Fertik, Clive Field, Joe Fifer, Mike Froy, Lisa Goldstein, Allan Golston, Merrill Goozner, Lyric Hale, Michael Hammond, Bill Hanlon, Jim Harding, Linda Havlin, Andrew Hayek, Per Huge-Jensen, Scott Humphreys, Jeff Jones, Raja Kamal, Bonnie Kaplan, John Kenney, Rick Kimball, Caroline Kirk, Liz Kirk, Allan Kittner, Tim Knowles, Raja Krishnamoorthi, Bill Lammers, Jim LeBuhn, Chuck Lewis, Jarrett Lewis, Mike Lincoln, Isaac Majerowicz, Dave

Mason, Lisa Martin, Paul Martino, Dave McConnell, Terry McDougal, Dan Michelson, Jim Mitchell, Bharat Mitra, Mark Montgomery, Lloyd Morgan, Ben Moulton, Gail Nelson, John Nelson, Constanza Nieto, John Noonan, Vince Panozzo, Chris Payne, Pamela Peele, Sam Pitroda, Victoria Poindexter, Peter Preziosi, Neil Pritz, Margo Pritzker, Imad Qasim, Jullia Quazi, Naveen Rao, Sandy Rasmussen, Ron Redd, Larry Reichlin, Ashutosh Rhaguvanshi, Dustchin Rock, Kerry Rudy, Matthew Russell, Dave Sabey, Pankaj Sahni, Sunil Sanghvi, Sanjay Saxena, Sydney Scarborough, Frank Schell, Jordan Schlain, Dave Schoolcraft, Penny Sebring, Richard Sheer, Genie Shields, Jordan Shields, Mark Shields, Brian Sils, Adele Simmons, John Simmons, Phil Solomon, Brett Spencer, Jason Sussman, Marie-Claude Tanny, Frank Taylor, Sam Thong, Mary Tolan, Naresh Trehan, Don Trigg, Owen Tripp, Kurt Waltenbough, Terri Wareham, Chuck Watts, John Weeks, Allison Weil, Jonathan Weiss, Rick Weissinger, Randy Williams, Don Wilson, Linda Wolf, Roni Zeiger, Connie Zhai and Ying Zhan.

I apologize to those I've missed (seriously). Let me know and we'll get you into the next edition.

Three remarkable people and close friends died during the writing of *Market vs. Medicine*. I've dedicated this book to their memories. Each receives prominent mention within *MvM's* covers.

Coleman Brown was a scholar, teacher, pastor and the wisest individual I've known. An hour conversation with Coleman contained as much insight as a graduate-level course. Coleman married Terri and me, provided life-long guidance and shared his remarkable understanding of human nature, culture, politics and the American experiment. What a wonderful gift. Good and evil weren't abstract concepts for Coleman. He often quoted Reinhold Niebuhr's observation that *"man's capacity for justice makes democracy possible, but man's inclination toward injustice makes democracy necessary."* Coleman and his wife Irene helped shape the character of countless young Colgate graduates including me. We all walk this earth. Few leave deeper footprints than Coleman Brown.

Barb Bunnell and her husband Ron, Banner's Chief Administrative Officer, shared a remarkable life together that included Barb's hereditary kidney disease. Barb and Ron initiated the nation's first kidney transplant chain in 2007. Barb received a kidney from Matt Jones in Phoenix and Ron donated a kidney to Angela Heckman in Toledo. They all got tattoos together before the procedures. Ultimately, this life-giving chain stretched for over two years and generated more than 20 transplants. After her transplant, Barb shut down their kitchen even though she was a phenomenal cook. She and Ron dined out thereafter. I was part of several lively, memorable dinners before and after the surgeries. Barb was a life-force, skilled quilt-maker, passionate hockey fan and incredibly fun. Her kidney disease returned with vengeance and took her life earlier this year. The world is a sadder place without Barb's sparkling presence.

Jeff Shields and I first met in the mid-1990s. As a former Peace Corps Volunteer, I was still adjusting to Wall Street's "show me the money" culture. Jeff and his wife Genie became great friends and important role models. They were accomplished, highly principled and flat-out cool. In 2004, Jeff shifted careers and became Vermont Law School's new dean and he was great at it. Cancer cut his tenure short. After a long battle, Jeff died at their Vermont farm in August 2014. As related in chapter 7, a film crew followed Jeff the last few months of his life. He became a subject for a *Frontline* documentary on palliative care. As Jeff's body weakened, his generous spirit grew and touched all who came near. His example of dying well is inspirational. Genie describes it as "a gift." It's one we all should receive.

I dedicate this book to Terri Brady, my wife and life partner for over thirty wonderful years. On the inside of Terri's wedding band is the phrase "And the two ..." Inside of my wedding band is the phrase "... shall be as one." So it is and so it shall be.

INDEX

Made in the USA
Columbia, SC
07 December 2018